OLD LOUISIANA

Old Louisiana

By
LYLE SAXON

Illustrated by
E. H. Suydam

PELICAN PUBLISHING COMPANY
GRETNA 1988

First published by The Century Co. 1929
Published by arrangement with The Century Co.
  by Robert L. Crager & Co. 1950
Published by arrangement with Robert L. Crager & Co.
  by Pelican Publishing Company, Inc. 1988

Pelican paperback edition
  First printing, December 1988

Library of Congress Cataloging-in-Publication Data

Saxon, Lyle, 1891-1946.
  Old Louisiana / by Lyle Saxon; illustrated by E.H. Suydam --
Pelican pbk. ed.
      p. cm.
  Reprint. Originally published: New Orleans: R. L. Crager, 1950.
  Bibliography: p.
  Includes index.
  ISBN 0-88289-705-5 (pbk.)
  1. Louisiana--Social life and customs. 2. Louisiana--Description
and travel. 3. Plantation life--Louisiana. I. Title.
F374.S32 1988
976.3--dc19   88-27401
                                                    CIP

Manufactured in the United States of America
Published by Pelican Publishing Company, Inc.
1101 Monroe Street, Gretna, Louisiana 70053

TO

MRS. CAMMIE GARRETT HENRY

OF MELROSE PLANTATION

INTRODUCTION

This is the chronicle of two centuries of Louisiana plantation life, a book of footnotes to history. It is a life which began when Louisiana was a colony of France, continued through the Spanish domination and emerged in the early nineteenth century as a development peculiarly American. Louisiana plantation life and Mississippi River steamboating are closely allied, developing, succeeding, and declining together.

It has been harder to get at the truth than one might suppose, despite the many books of reminiscences which have been published. Most of these books have a tendency to cloud the picture rather than to illuminate it. They are unsatisfactory in the same way that family portraits are unsatisfactory. Our ancestors posed for their portraits dressed in their best, and they were careful to see that the artist eliminated their defects. Nowadays the paintings hang upon our walls, as remote and as magnificent as the gods on Olympus. If we had snapshots of our great-grandfathers they might not inspire us with so much awe and reverence, but we might love them more. The same quality of pretense and evasion of truth is present in much of the writing of the period; only when the writers are off-guard do they become human beings; usually they are busy being gods.

This book has been in preparation for five years and

nearly all of the material is taken from letters and diaries hitherto unpublished. In many instances I have let the men and women speak for themselves. The record presented here forms a series of interlocking stories, from the beginnings of plantation life to the Civil War, when slavery was abolished, when railroads destroyed Mississippi River commerce, and the economic structure of Louisiana life fell to pieces.

By way of introduction, I have told something of the breaking up of plantation life as I remember it, twenty-five years ago. At the end, the reader is taken on a tour through the State to visit the plantations which remain.

The illustrations are an important part of the record. Mr. Suydam went with me through the State—a journey which, with twistings and turnings, stretched out for a thousand miles—making drawings of the old houses. He has caught the spirit of these places in a remarkable way, and I consider myself fortunate in having his aid in this attempt to present the story to you.

Many people have given me assistance. I wish to thank Mr. Henry P. Dart, editor of the "Louisiana Historical Society Quarterly," for permission to use the translations by Miss Laura Porteous of the documents in the case of Temba. I wish to thank Mrs. Cammie Garrett Henry for the use of her library and for hospitality extended at Melrose Plantation. And I am grateful to many plantation people who let me rummage in their attics, and gave permission to use letters, papers, and documents, who told me stories, and who gave me mintjuleps—all of which made my task easier.

The chapter entitled "The Gay Dangerfields" has appeared in "The Century Magazine" and I wish to thank the editor for permission to reprint it here. The chapters pertaining to Christmas and New Year have been rewritten from stories of mine which appeared in the New Orleans "Times-Picayune" a few years ago.

L. S.

Contents

PART I

PLANTATION PEOPLE

CHAPTER   PAGE

I   TWILIGHT 3

II   THE GAY DANGERFIELDS 7

III   GOING TO PIECES 20

IV   FAMILY PORTRAIT 31

PART II

MASTERS AND SLAVES

V   BEGINNINGS 51

VI   AN EIGHTEENTH-CENTURY PLANTER . . 57

VII   POOR BABY! 77

VIII   TEMBA MURDERS HIS MASTER . . . 85

IX   CHANGING FORTUNES 95

X   AMERICANS IN CREOLE LOUISIANA . . 102

XI   "THE CITY OF SIN" 121

Contents

CHAPTER   PAGE
XII   A NEW ERA BEGINS   132
XIII THE PROSPEROUS YEARS 140
XIV   THE STRANGE STORY OF PAULINE   .   .   . 151

PART III

LEISURELY TIMES

XV   A YOUNG MAN OF FASHION IN 1850   .   . 165
XVI   THE YOUNG MAN'S DIARY   170
XVII LES BELLES DE LA CÔTE JOYEUSE   .   .   . 230
XVIII THE NEWS OF THE DAY 245
XIX   SIMON LEGREE 253
XX   HOW TO GET A RICH WIFE   267
XXI   AN OLD LADY'S LETTERS 271

PART IV

SPLENDOR AND RUST

XXII   A PLANTATION TOUR   293
XXIII   CHRISTMAS: THE MISTLETOE TRAIL   .   .   . 312
XXIV   ON TO NATCHEZ   322
XXV   THAT ETERNAL INDIAN GIRL   331
XXVI   WEST OF THE MISSISSIPPI 335
XXVII   SUPERSTITIONS   345
XXVIII SOME NEGRO PROVERBS   353
XXIX   BAYOU TECHE AND CANE RIVER   .   .   . 357
XXX   NEW YEAR'S EVE   367
        BIBLIOGRAPHY   383
        INDEX   385

ILLUSTRATIONS

FACING PAGE

"PARLANGE," AND A PIGEONNIER, ON FALSE RIVER, 1780........................ 16

"PRUDHOMME," NEAR NATCHITOCHES, IS

    AN EARLY LOUISIANA TYPE.. 17

THE LABATUT HOUSE ON OLD RIVER WAS BUILT IN 1790 36

THE SCOTT FAMILY HAS OCCUPIED "THE SHADES" SINCE 1808.............. 44

"ORMOND," AN EIGHTEENTH-CENTURY HOUSE NEAR

    NEW ORLEANS.. 45

"OAKLEY," WEST FELICIANA, 1808, WHERE AUDUBON TAUGHT

    SCHOOL... 80

GRANDEUR ON BAYOU ST. JOHN, ABOUT 1810 96

"MARCO," THE TRUE LOUISIANA TYPE, CANE RIVER, 1820......................112

"HICKORY HILL," ELEGANCE, 1810..113

"MELROSE," THIS IS CANE RIVER, 1833 144

"BELMONT" DROWSES ON BAYOU MARINGOUIN....................................148

"ASPHODEL," EAST FELICIANA, BUILT IN 1835 156

"THE SHADOWS" REFLECTS ITSELF IN BAYOU TECHE, 1830....................157

"ROSEDOWN" LIES DEEP IN A GARDEN, 1835 192

ILLUSTRATIONS

FACING PAGE

NEW ORLEANS CLOSES IN UPON THE SARPY HOUSE 196

A PLANTATION DINING-ROOM, WITH OVERHEAD FAN 204

"GREENWOOD," THE CLASSIC REVIVAL, IN WEST FELICIANA,
    1840 205

"OAK ALLEY" ON THE MISSISSIPPI, ABOVE NEW ORLEANS 240

"WOODLAWN" ON BAYOU LAFOURCHE, 1840 256

LOADING STEAMBOATS AT THE LEVEE 272

LUXURY ON BAYOU LAFOURCHE, "BELLE ALLIANCE," 1845 273

"MONMOUTH" AT NATCHEZ IS STURDY AND HONEST--1846 284

THE PAYNE HOUSE NEAR WASHINGTON, BUILT PRIOR TO 1849 304

L'EXQUISE--CHASE HOUSE, CLINTON 305

AN OLD HOUSE ON WALL STREET, NATCHEZ 324

"ARLINGTON" AT NATCHEZ IS GRACEFUL IN DETAIL 325

STAIRWAY AT "ARLINGTON" 332

A BEDROOM AT "ARLINGTON" 336

"SHADY GROVE," THE ERWIN HOUSE ON BAYOU GROSSE TÊTE
    --1857 348

"BELLE GROVE"--1857--IS DESERTED NOW 349

ALL PLANTATION NEGROES GO TO CHURCH 356

THE DRAWING-ROOM AT "BELLE GROVE"--AS IT WAS 357

Chapter Headings

	PAGE
PIGEONNIERES FLANK THE OLD HOUSES	3
"OAK ALLEY" PLANTATION	7
"ANGELINA" IS FALLING TO PIECES	20
A PIGEONNIERE AT "UNCLE SAM"	31
A NEGRO CABIN	51
A CABIN AT "MELROSE"	57
COTTON PICKERS	77
"D'ESTREHAN," NEAR NEW ORLEANS	85
THE DELORD-SARPY HOUSE, NEW ORLEANS	95
OLD INN AT ST. MARTINSVILLE	102
STEAMBOATS AT THE LEVEE	121
"ELLERSLIE," NEAR ST. FRANCISVILLE	132
"MADEWOOD" ON BAYOU LAFOURCHE	140
"UNCLE SAM," QUARTERS AND SUGAR-HOUSE	151
"BURNSIDE" PLANTATION	165
AT THE COTTON GIN	170
A PLANTATION-STORE	230

	PAGE
SAILBOATS IN BAYOU ST. JOHN	245
NEGROES SLEEPING ON COTTON BALES	253
BESIDE THE BAYOU	267
STEAMBOATS RIDE ABOVE THE TOWN	271
A STREET IN CLINTON	293
THE KITCHEN AT "THE SHADES"	312
THE DEVALL SUGAR-HOUSE	322
"COLOMB," NEAR CONVENT	331
CADOVILLE, A VILLAGE BESIDE THE LEVEE	335
A NEGRO BAPTIZING	345
NEGRO QUARTERS	353
A HOUSE AT NATCHEZ	357
NEGRO CHURCHES HAVE ODD SPIRES	367
A PLANTATION CEMETERY	380

Old Louisiana

Part I

PLANTATION PEOPLE

Chapter One

TWILIGHT

On the steps of an old plantation-house a boy sits waiting for the moon to rise. He leans against one of the columns which is still warm from the sunlight which has shone upon it all day. Before him the avenue of moss-draped trees stretches out to the levee and the river beyond. Fireflies make streaks of light in the darkness, and the far-off stars are blue and bright. From the garden comes the scent of summer, a blending of perfumes—roses, cape-jasmine, and magnolia.

Behind him, in the shadow of the vine on the veranda, two old gentlemen sit. The boy hears ice tinkling in their glasses as they talk on and on in their eternal condemnation of modern life. The phrase "the good old times" is repeated over and over like a refrain. The boy listens idly as his grandfather speaks:

"... We are getting old and the younger generation

cares nothing for us or for our traditions. They don't care for anything. The poetry has gone out of their lives. They don't even know how to have a good time. Who can mix a good drink nowadays? It's a lost art. Hand me the bottle, I want to sweeten my julep."

The other old gentleman answers: "Yes, we're living in the decadence. Our sons go away. There isn't any more young life left in this country. The old houses and the old families are going to pieces, and nobody cares."

"It is true, nobody cares."

"I care," the boy announces.

"Good Lord, are you still there? I thought you had gone to bed. What did you say?"

"I said I cared."

"Cared about what?"

"About what you said."

"And what did I say?"

"You said that nobody cared about anything any more."

"Oh. . . . Well, that's good. I'm glad somebody does. Hand me the bottle, Horatio, I need a little more."

"What did the boy say?" asks the other old man.

"He said that he was sorry the country is going to the dogs. He's too young to understand it, of course. I forgot he was here."

Mr. Horatio is amused. He drinks deep from his glass, then puts it down and says, "Come here, sonny."

The boy gets up from the steps and walks into the darkness. He feels a pair of hands upon his shoulders and he smells the fragrance of mint and whiskey. A voice speaks to him: "So, you care that this country is going to pieces, do you? Well, what are you going to do about it?"

"What must I do?"

"Ha! That's the question. What can any of us do?"

"We can fiddle while Rome burns," says the grandfather, chuckling. "Hand me the bottle."

The boy knows, now, that they are laughing at him, so he takes no further part in the conversation. The sky is growing lighter between the trees and from far off comes the chittering of a screech owl. The old men go on with their talk:

"Look at our friends and neighbors. Once they had everything; now they have nothing. Think of your own family, and of mine. I had everything once, but the War ended all that. Yes sir! The War ended my good times." The boy knows that Mr. Horatio is patting an empty sleeve; he has seen him do it many times before.

"That's it, the War. But it is something else, too, a sort of blight on us. I had nine children. They are all grown up now, and some of them are getting old. Only one is married, and the boy there is the only grandchild I have. Something is the matter with us."

The other laughs. "A big family is no help. Look at our friends. Look at the Dangerfields or the Blakes. Look at 'Wild Tim' Meadows. Something wrong with all of them, somewhere. Hand the bottle back again."

The boy is uncomfortable. What do the old men mean? What is wrong with the Dangerfields? He knows them well. Or the Blakes? What does his grandfather mean when he says that these families are going to pieces?

He begins thinking of them, and of himself, feeling somehow guilty that he is all that his grandfather can point to as a "result." Maybe his family is going to pieces, too.

And as he sits there, the moon rises round and red above the levee, shining full upon the white columns of the house, shining through the leaves upon his grandfather's white beard, and upon the face of the old gentleman beside him. Still the boy ponders, chin on hand. What *could* they mean?

Remembering this conversation, thirty years later, I have decided to tell you of those three families: Dangerfield, Meadows, and Blake, who the old gentlemen thought were typical of the time in which they lived, and typical of the life in Louisiana which was crumbling to pieces. None of the stories is important in itself, except in significance. The men and women in the stories are figures at the end of a pageant stretching back for two centuries. I shall tell you of them first, then go back to the pageant's beginning.

Chapter Two

THE GAY DANGERFIELDS

THE Dangerfields lived on Acacia Plantation in Louisiana, not far from the town of Baton Rouge. The house was a charming but dilapidated structure at the end of a long avenue of cedar trees, each tree shrouded with trailing Spanish moss. Beyond the cedars, on each side of the avenue, were crêpe-myrtle and acacia trees, and in summer the myrtles were rose-colored bouquets and the acacias were feathery green and gold. It was a romantic and beautiful place—rose and gold and green massed against black cedars and gray moss—and at the end of the avenue, seen through an arch of dark branches, were the white columns of the plantation-house.

The house was very old. Once white, it was now a creamy gray and the window-blinds had faded to a bluish green. There were eight large white columns across the façade, and a wide veranda upstairs and down. In fancy I can see it

7

yet—and always I see, there between the columns, a red-haired woman in a long black riding-habit, surrounded by black-and-white spotted dogs. This was Kate Dangerfield, the mother of the children that I came to see.

They were all artists, the Dangerfields were. All the children had talent for drawing. The mother had received some training as a girl, and she believed that she had missed a great career by marrying and settling down. "Settling down" is hardly the phrase, for she was far from settled. She was nearly six feet tall, and she was very handsome. In her girlhood she had been known as a dashing young lady, and, even as the mother of six children, she still dashed. She wore always a black riding-habit with trailing skirts which she would gather up and pin at her waist. In consequence, her skirt would be knee-high on one side and would trail behind her as she walked. She was dramatic; her gestures were wide and free. Her hair, now streaked with gray, she dyed bright-red in front; the back she disregarded entirely. Her oldest daughter, who was just my age, would always draw me aside and ask, "What do you think of Mama's hair, this time?"

Kate Dangerfield would stride about the house, a riding crop in her hand, a cigarette between her lips—a magnificent figure.

In those days ladies did not smoke except behind closed doors, and there was always an air of mystery about her smoking. When I first arrived there would be a pretense of hiding the cigarette; but soon I would come upon her puffing behind doors or in corners; later in my visit caution was abandoned, and the cigarette was always in her hand as she talked and gesticulated.

She was an artist, as I have said, or rather she painted pictures. She gloried in her artistic temperament. She called herself "a bohemian." It was the first time that I had ever heard the phrase. One of her eccentricities was that she never finished anything. She would take my arm and draw me along the hall of the plantation-house, pointing out a picture with her riding crop. "Now that," she would say, "is Paul and Virginia fleeing from the storm, but it isn't finished. It needs much more work on it. I have so little time, you know."

Or perhaps she would pause before a picture of three horses' heads. "Pharaoh's Horses," she would say. "How I love to paint animals! But it is unfinished. You can see that for yourself."

It was characteristic of her that she should do everything in the grand manner. I never saw her at work upon a painting, but I am sure that she painted with the same large magnificence with which she spoke and acted. In fact, the pictures looked like that. They had a startled expression—horses and men, as though surprised when confronted by the masterful woman who had created them.

Once, I remember, she paused before the portrait of a recumbent cow. "Now that," she said, "is what *I* call painting. But of course, it is not finished. Just a little old sketch that I made one day." Then she sighed and we went on to the next picture.

The daughters were like their mother, good-looking and erratic. Ada was the eldest. She was dark-eyed and olive-skinned and she was pretty in a gypsy sort of way. Magda was next, a girl of twelve, tall for her age, pale-skinned and with dark eyes and red hair. The youngest daughter was Dorothy (named for Dorothy Vernon of Haddon Hall!), a charming, dreamy child who was only eight years old, but who was already erratic about coming to meals or learning lessons or getting dressed in the morning. It was no unusual sight to see Dorothy on her calico pony, wearing her nightgown, racing down the avenue just as the breakfast bell was ringing. There were other children, twin red-haired boys, nicknamed Judge and Jury. I never knew their real names. And there was a baby in the arms of a negro nurse.

The younger children were kept in the background, but the three girls would have long arguments with their mother about horsemanship, in which they would squabble exactly as though they were all of the same age. There was constant warfare between Ada and her mother as to which of them was the better horsewoman. The mother was noted for miles around as an excellent and fearless rider, but at home the daughters disputed this. They would urge her on to bolder and more extravagant feats; they would wager that she could not ride this or that unbroken horse. And they would shriek with glee when she was thrown off—which happened frequently. Instead of spanking them all, as one would imagine, she would cringe before their criticism, and would accept their wildest dares in order to retain her supremacy. I don't know when she found time to paint, but paint she did, as scores of pictures in the house testified.

The family owned two plantations on opposite sides of the Mississippi, and Mr. Dangerfield was nearly always "over at the other place." He seldom appeared, but when he did it was always in the same way. He would ride slowly up the cedar avenue on a huge white horse, dismount, throw the reins to a waiting negro, kiss his wife and children if they were within range—and then disappear. He always shook hands with me gravely, and inquired as to my grand-father's health and my own, but he did not listen to my answers. He had a remote "office" in a wing of the house where he remained aloof; even his meals were carried there on a tray. I remember him as a shadowy figure, tall, distin-guished-looking, and absent-minded, a man with a black beard and a soft drawl. But to me he was a minor actor in the drama enacted by the female members of the family. I remember only this unsolicited statement from him: "My wife is a magnificent horsewoman, by God!"

He had good reason to be proud of her, for she was noted throughout that section of the State. She used to come galloping through the streets of Baton Rouge on a black stallion, and the shopkeepers would run to their doors to see her go by. News would spread through the streets— "Mrs. Dangerfield is in town. Watch out for the fun!"

She was the heroine of a score of mishaps. Once a horse that she was driving with a light buggy became restive on Main Street; it reared and snorted and ended by kicking the dashboard to pieces, while Kate Dangerfield, with feet firmly braced and with the reins wrapped around her wrists, gave shriek after shriek of wild laughter, and called out to those brave young men, who attempted to rescue her, that she needed no help; and she begged them to keep away until she got the horse under control. She did it, too, but not until the carriage was practically demolished.

On another day a frightened horse managed to pull the harness loose from the shafts of her carriage. She held the reins and was dragged over the dashboard into the road.

But she held on through sheer stubbornness and it was not until the horse had dashed her against a tree that she let go.

She lay there in the dust while the horse went running down the street. Men and women came out to pick her up. Every one thought that she was dead, but she sat up and laughed.

"Why that's nothing," she said. "Just a little old wild colt that I'm breaking in!"

As she was casual about risking her life, so was she casual about the affairs of the plantation household; and while she was the most hospitable woman in the world, her guests sometimes suffered severe trials.

At Acacia Plantation there were nine hunting dogs—pointers and setters—that slept in the hall. All day long there would be growls and yelps as their tails were stepped upon by some of the Dangerfields, for it was nearly impossible to go from room to room without stepping on some sleeping animal. But the dogs must have been strangely good-natured, for no one was ever bitten. There was an army of cats, too, which no one ever remembered to feed, and they were always ravenous. Going to the dinner table was like going to war. We were surrounded on all sides by cats and dogs—animals ready to snatch the food out of our mouths.

As half of the family never came to meals anyway, there were always empty chairs at the table. Mrs. Dangerfield would sit at one end and I would sit beside her; then there would be, perhaps, four empty chairs, and, down at the opposite end of the table, Dorothy would be lolling, lost in a day-dream. The others would trail in at ten-minute intervals, as the spirit moved them.

One day the cat situation became acute.

Mrs. Dangerfield, Dorothy, and I were at table, and a servant had just placed a large silver platter of roast beef in the center of the board, beyond the reach of any of us. Scarcely had the servant left the room when a black cat sprang up and began eating from the dish. Kate Dangerfield regarded it languidly and said: "This is too much. Dorothy, knock that cat off the table."

The little girl came out of her day-dream with an effort, looked narrowly at the cat, and said: "I won't touch it. That's Ada's cat. Make her come and drive it away."

And the cat continued to eat.

"Oh well . . ." said Kate Dangerfield, and reaching behind her she took a buggy whip from a rack, and came crashing down among the plates and glasses. It is true that this drove the cat away, but it also scattered gravy in every direction, inundating us in grease. Two goblets and a plate were broken, and dinner proceeded as usual.

One soon fell into the spirit of the occasion, or at least I did.

Although the house was overrun with servants, everything was left undone. Meals were always late, and sometimes forgotten altogether. One night at ten o'clock, Kate Dangerfield, who had been walking up and down the hall reciting poetry aloud, stopped suddenly, clutched her red hair, and cried out: "Good Lord! I forgot to have supper!" And to our surprise, we found that it was perfectly true. We went to the kitchen and to the ice-box; we foraged for the remains of dinner. Jars of preserved fruits were opened, cold biscuits appeared. At half past ten, instead of going prosaically to bed, we were sitting around the dining-room table in the midst of a meal.

Mrs. Dangerfield was a great teller of stories and many of them dealt with the sensational and romantic episodes of her girlhood. Her daughters scoffed openly and stifled exaggerated yawns, but they would listen for hours on end, and to their interruptions she paid not the least attention. She talked for the pleasure of talking; she "entertained us" for the sheer joy of entertaining.

One evening after dinner she walked up and down the floor of the drawing-room and recited Kipling's poems until long past midnight. She was like a woman in a dream. The poems seemed thrilling as she recited them, and though I heard midnight strike, I was far from sleepy. The candles burned low in their sconces and went guttering out, one by one, as she strode back and forth in the long room under the family portraits, her head up, her red hair coming down, her black riding-habit trailing after her, a cigarette in her hand.

> "This is the sorrowful story
> Told when the twilight fails,
> And the monkeys walk together,
> Holding each others' tails!"

It was after one o'clock when she ended. Then she got out a decanter and gave each of us a glass of Benedictine for a nightcap.

Once there was a guest in the house, a pale, aristocratic-looking woman from New Orleans. She was a distant relative who had come to spend a week at the plantation. She was totally unprepared for such a family as the Dangerfields, and her visit was not quite a success.

She had been given a room upstairs at the front of the house, a large room with a four-post bed, a sofa, two or three arm-chairs, and the other usual bedroom furniture. She appeared at breakfast the next morning looking wan and worn, and in answer to the question as to how she had slept, she answered somewhat hesitantly that she had been bothered by fleas. She said, in fact, that she had been forced to leave her bed and spend the night upon the sofa; and, as the sofa was covered with black horsehair and was very slippery, she had not slept at all.

Instead of being horrified, as the guest expected, Kate Dangerfield laughed.

"My poor Virginia! You, of all people in the world, to be bitten by fleas in my house. You, a Randolph of Roanoke!" And she was gone again in a gale of laughter.

The guest mustered a wry smile. "It was pretty bad, just the same," she said.

Mrs. Dangerfield sobered. "My dear, I *am* sorry. You have no idea how sorry I am. Really. Why didn't you come to me? There are other rooms empty here. Although," and here she laughed again, "there may be fleas in every one, for all I know."

Then she went on to explain: "You see, I haven't been in that room for months. I supposed that the servants looked after it, but instead they've left the door open and the dogs got in. It's highly probable that a dozen dogs have been sleeping on that bed all summer. It's odd about negroes and doors. Why, do you know, I've made a discovery about negroes: it is absolutely impossible to teach them to close doors after them, even in cold weather. They won't. It's some racial trait, I suppose." And she went blithely on.

"But what will you do to get rid of the fleas?" the guest asked at last.

All through breakfast we talked of possible flea remedies. Some one suggested that a young lamb be put upon the bed, the theory being that the fleas would leave the bed and take refuge in the lamb's wool. This idea delighted Mrs. Dangerfield, as it promised immediate action. She ordered one of the negro men-servants to catch a lamb and bring it to her. But the negro demurred.

"Now you know, Miz Kate, dat dey ain't a single l'il lamb in de pasture, dis time a-yeah!"

"Well then, catch me a sheep," ordered our undaunted hostess. "If a lamb is good, a sheep will be better. It's bigger, you know. More room for fleas."

A few minutes later two negro men appeared at the dining-room door; they carried a large, dirty, and very angry ram between them. The old ram's dignity was upset and he struggled to get down.

"Carry him upstairs!" ordered Kate Dangerfield.

But this was not as easy as it sounded. We all tried to help. We tugged, we pushed, we shoved, and the ram cried *"Baa-aa-aa!"* and set his hind legs. All of us took part in assisting the ram upstairs. All, that is, except the guest. She stood in the parlor door watching us, and she seemed annoyed and amused and miserable, all at once.

Finally the ram was brought into the bedroom and deposited upon the bed, and he lay there, panting and exhausted. We retired and closed the door, but we had scarcely reached the drawing-room, directly below, when there came

"PARLANGE," AND A PIGEONNIER,
ON FALSE RIVER, 1780

"PRUDHOMME," NEAR NATCHITOCHES, IS AN
EARLY LOUISIANA TYPE

a crash which set the crystals tinkling in the chandelier. Mrs. Dangerfield, who had collapsed on a sofa, and who was smoking a cigarette in order to regain her composure, cried out, "He's jumped off the bed!"

We all ran upstairs again, dogs, children, white folks, and negroes. This time the ram gave battle. He charged us, knocking one of the children down. Chairs were overturned, children screamed, dogs barked. But in the end we were triumphant. This time the servants tied the ram's legs together and put him back in bed again.

"Cover him up!" Mrs. Dangerfield ordered.

Accordingly the blankets were drawn up over the ram, and he lay there, furious, his horns on the pillow, and looking for all the world like Red Riding Hood's grandmother.

However, it was not more than ten minutes later that the second crash came and the ram was free again. The struggle lasted all day. The room was a wreck, chairs and sofa overturned, a mirror broken and the disorder unbelievable. It was not odd that the guest remembered an important engagement in New Orleans and left suddenly in the afternoon.

Oh, charming people, the Dangerfields were, galloping about the country on horseback, a gay cavalcade, hunting, shooting clay pigeons, or riding to hounds. Looking back upon them now, across twenty years, I can think of no more delightful times than those I spent with the gay and eccentric family at Acacia Plantation.

When I grew older, I lost sight of them. I went away to school, then work took me out of Louisiana. Years passed before I returned. When I inquired for them I found that the girls had married, the father had died, and like so many other country families, they had lost their plantations. Kate Dangerfield, they told me, had moved to another plantation in the northern part of the State. I wrote to her, but the letter was returned unclaimed.

But it was only last year that I saw her again. It came about like this: I sat in the lobby of a New Orleans hotel, waiting for a man who had invited me to luncheon. Nearby sat two sunburned men who wore broad-brimmed Panama hats. So near they were that I could hear what they were saying, and suddenly my attention was caught by a bit of talk:

". . . a most remarkable woman, I tell you. Why, just the other night she heard a noise in her hen-house, and she went out to see what was after the chickens. It was a wild-cat. You'd think that any woman would be afraid, but not that one! Why, man, would you believe it, she put her foot on that wildcat's head and held it there until her son came with a pistol and shot it, right under her foot!"

"What did you say her name was?" asked the other.

"Mrs. Kate Dangerfield," he answered.

I sprang up. "Where is she?" I demanded. "I must see her. I knew her years ago."

"If you hurry, you can catch her at the station," the planter said. "She's in town for a day's shopping. I left her a few minutes ago. She's headed for the Union Station to catch the one-fifteen train."

I ran from the hotel, caught a taxi and reached the station with only two minutes to spare. The gateman let me through to the platform and I ran along beside the train, looking in at the windows. But just as I was about to give up the search, I saw her walking along the platform. She was strangely unchanged; still red-haired, still straight, and she wore a long black dress, cut like a riding-habit. A negro girl followed her, her arms full of parcels. I caught Kate Dangerfield's hand as she put her foot on the step of the coach.

She greeted me as though we had parted the day before. "How in the world did you know that I was in town to-day?" she asked.

"I overheard a conversation in a hotel," I answered. "It was about a remarkable woman who put her foot on a wildcat's head and held it until her son came with a pistol."

She laughed and made the sweeping gesture that I remembered so well.

"Why, that was nothing," she said. "It's just talk. It was a little bit of an old wildcat. I thought it was an owl."

Chapter Three

GOING TO PIECES

In Louisiana one often hears the remark that such and such a family has "gone to pieces." As a child I used to picture that dire calamity in my mind. Did the men and women explode, I wondered—heads going in one direction, arms and legs in another? Or did they drop to pieces languidly, leaving a finger here and a toe there? Both pictures were depressing enough.

Later, I learned what people meant when they said such things, but for some unexplained reason the phrase still brings to my mind the idea of bodily disintegration. In the thirty years that my memory covers, I can remember several families which went that way. And of all such families, our old friends the Meadowses were most characteristic. I shall tell you their story, not because it is important, but because it is typical. They began with everything and ended with nothing. It was all pathetic and, at the same time, ridiculous—a humorous tragedy without even death to give it dignity.

The family came from Virginia, or rather the family of Tim Meadows lived there. "Wild Tim," as he was called, married his first cousin, a girl from a Louisiana plantation. She was the last of her family and was very poor, and her marriage was considered an excellent thing for her. Every one spoke of it, thirty-five years ago when the ceremony took place, and they were still talking of it six or seven years later, when I first remember them. People said what a lucky girl Fanny had been, to marry into a family so outrageously rich. For the Meadows family had an estate at Saratoga Springs, a town house in Richmond, and a yacht and a cottage at Norfolk. There was a small plantation in Louisiana that Wild Tim had inherited from a great uncle. The Louisiana property was hardly worth mentioning when compared to the grandeur of the other places. Nevertheless it was something. In addition to all this, Tim's father had nearly two million dollars in stocks and bonds.

The wedding must have been grand enough to satisfy even the envious ones, and everybody congratulated Fanny and talked about her as though she were Cinderella. She went away with Tim and letters came back telling of her good times on the yacht and at Saratoga, and of how they rode to hounds in Virginia. This went on for fifteen years.

Then Tim's father died and the property was divided equally between him and his sister. The sister lost no time in marrying an Italian nobleman and going to live in Rome. She turned all of her inheritance into cash and brought it with her to Italy, where her count invested it. Unlike many

international marriages, hers was happy. The Count was a
good business man and her investments prospered.

But Wild Tim, now possessed of nearly a million dollars
in cash and much valuable property, determined to become
a financier. Or, at least, that is probably the way he thought
about it. Heretofore he had been a jolly, good-natured,
hospitable, hard-drinking young man, who entertained in
Virginia and who came to Louisiana to his wife's old home
at Christmas time, driving in a magnificent carriage with
his wife and small daughter, just so every one could see
what a lucky girl Fanny was. That is the way I remember
him, driving about, making calls on New Year's Day. The
little girl was just my age.

Every one said that Wild Tim was the best company in
the world; they said he was amusing, he was entertaining,
and so on. All in all, a good fellow. I suppose that he really
was amusing and entertaining, although great wealth has a
tendency to make men appear cleverer than they are, and in
our part of the world there were few indeed who were so
rich. At any rate, Tim was an excellent host. Everybody
conceded that. His Christmas parties were famous in
Louisiana. He always served champagne. I was too young to
have any, unfortunately, and when I grew old enough to
indulge in it, Wild Tim had stopped giving parties.

Since he had everything he wanted out of life, it was
impossible for him to believe that he should not always
have everything. His was one of those sanguine tempera-
ments; he believed in himself implicitly. One Christmas,
shortly after the fortune had been divided, he left his wife
in Louisiana and went to New York to take a little look at
Wall Street. In six months he was back in Louisiana again,

without a penny. He was never able to account for the money he lost, and I do not remember that he even tried to account for it. It was gone, but there was no need to worry. That was what he told his wife, at least, and she repeated it about the neighborhood, although she did seem a little vexed, as I remember. They would sell their property, and the yacht, she said, and another fortune would be theirs. So Tim sold the Richmond house and the yacht and the house at Saratoga Springs. To his surprise the forced sale did not bring anything like the amount that he anticipated. When fees were paid and the money was in hand, it was a mere fifty thousand dollars. A bagatelle. A man couldn't live on that, he said, not Wild Tim Meadows, anyway. So he went back to Wall Street again, and the fifty thousand dollars followed after the million.

His wife, being an old-fashioned lady of the old-fashioned South, left the entire business management to her husband, but she was shocked and surprised to hear of the second misadventure. It dawned upon her, probably, that her days of luxury were numbered. There was still a piece of property in Florida or somewhere, and she prevailed upon him to sell that and to invest the money—it was ten or fifteen thousand dollars—in the small Louisiana plantation. He had retained the Louisiana property only because he could not sell it for any price, and it was his wife's idea that the plantation, with careful management, would support them. Then, too, she would be among her old friends and it would not matter if the family lived simply. She had done it before and she could do it again.

So Wild Tim settled among us and gave his attention to the few hundred acres of rolling land suitable for growing cotton. He knew nothing whatever about farming, but with characteristic assurance he said that the life of a planter was just the life for him, and he began to discuss his ancestral acres as though the planting of cotton was a thing in which he excelled. But the money disappeared so rapidly that he found himself with only a huge red barn to show for his efforts, and there was no money to build a dwelling or buy even a few mules and farming implements. A pretty mess indeed.

There was only one thing to do, so he did it. He wrote to the countess and asked her for a loan. She was surprised, but she was willing to help a little. The count objected, or so she wrote, but she did send five thousand dollars, intimating, I am afraid, that it was all that she would lend, and advising Wild Tim to make the best of it. But the five thousand dollars disappeared before the house was half completed. And it was never completed. It was unfinished inside, with rough walls and floors, but it would do until he arranged for something better, he said. Into this cabin they moved the fine furniture from the Richmond house, or as much as the dwelling would hold. There were fine rugs on the floors, and the rough board walls were covered with old sporting prints and engravings. The hall was hung solidly with family portraits—magnificent old paintings of dead and gone aristocrats, who stared before them with cold eyes, as though they thought they had come down in the world, which they had indeed.

Mrs. Meadows was expecting another baby. In fact, it was born shortly after they moved into the new house. Wild Tim, feeling that it was necessary to make at least one grand gesture in his wife's community, went into town and ordered all of the champagne that was to be had from the local dealer in wines and liquors. He invited the whole country-side to attend the christening and to drink champagne. All the plantation people from the surrounding country, as well as many families from town, went to the Meadows house that night to drink champagne in honor of the new-born son. The fact that Tim never had enough money to pay for the champagne destroyed his credit, and to this day the family must pay cash for all they buy—which isn't much.

The daughter was about fifteen years old when the second child, a boy, was born, and she had received the rudiments of education. Her governess had taught her to chatter in French, she could play badly upon the piano, and she had the other usual accomplishments considered necessary to a young lady of fortune. But, alas and alack, her schooling stopped now, for Wild Tim was reduced to real poverty. He was not able to get straight with the world again. This was twenty years ago, and he has never been able to get straight. He did try various schemes, and a second loan from the reluctant countess gave him enough money to start a chicken farm. But instead of beginning in a small way, he bought elaborate incubators and brooders which he could never learn to manipulate. In six months the money was all gone, and the chickens too. Another time he borrowed enough from some old friends to start a career as a florist. Florists made lots of money, he said; I remember hearing him tell my grandfather all about it. But he never had enough money to begin properly, and the only year that the flowers were doing well, a sudden frost killed them all.

His daughter spent her time in visiting former friends who were rich enough to entertain a young lady of her station in a proper manner. They welcomed this charming girl into their homes, but she was like her father—impractical, stubborn, and incapable of economy. When she had visited every one that it was possible to visit and when all of her fine clothes were worn out, she was forced to come home again. Her one chance of escape was disappearing, for she was now nineteen and there was no suitor in sight. The fine matches which would have been possible for her in former years were out of the question now, and there could be no thought of the fashionable Miss Meadows marrying one of the town boys, the son of some ordinary merchant or small farmer. And so Fannye—she was named for her mother, but she had added another letter to her name— became twenty-one, and then twenty-two. In the meantime the son was growing up without any education at all. The house was remote; they had no horses or carriages, and in those days the sons of plantation-owners did not attend the public schools in Louisiana. There were good private schools, but the Meadows family could never afford one. His mother seemed incapable of teaching him anything, his father was now too irascible, and Fannye went about bathed in tears. It was odd, but in losing his money Wild Tim lost his happy, good-natured disposition. Life for the Meadows family became cruel. The time came when they were without the necessities of life. And always their blind senselessness kept them from getting anywhere. Everything that Tim Meadows touched seemed to fail, and he became crabbed and quarreled with every one. He would spend his entire time in talking of the good old days and of fox-hunting in Virginia, while his wife sewed for neighbors and did the odd jobs that she could get.

When Fannye was twenty-five she left home and went to look for work in New Orleans, but she was too much like her father to be a success at anything. She was untrained, and she had never been able to add or subtract. Her jobs were always of the type in which money was handled—either clerking in a store or working as cashier—and she managed to lose each job before a week was out. She was easily confused and would cry if accused of making a mistake, and her carelessness got her into endless scrapes.

She was rather pretty, with soft yellow hair and large, limpid blue eyes, and if a man accosted her in the street and said, "Haven't I met you before somewhere?" she would think that perhaps he really had met her, and would stop and argue about it, trying to remember who he was. The man usually convinced her that he was an old friend. It seemed incredible to her that any man she met in the street should treat her otherwise than as a perfect gentleman should treat a lady. Her life in New Orleans consisted of getting jobs and losing them, of meeting men and making engagements with them. Later she sprang screaming from taxi-cabs, when they attempted liberties. She never learned anything at all from experience. She was like her father in that, too.

Her trips to New Orleans always ended in the same way. She would return crushed and broken to the country, where she remained in misery, and made her family miserable, too. Like her father, she was always inventing magnificent schemes to make money, schemes which always came to nothing. One month she determined to study interior decorating, and the next she decided to give up interior decorating for the life of a book agent. The month after that she was sure that fame and fortune awaited her on the stage. But as she could never secure a job with an interior decorator, nor an interview with a theatrical manager, and as she found it impossible to memorize the sales talk for selling books, all these plans came to nothing in the end. And so it went on, from year to year.

Each season the Meadows family was a little poorer, if possible. The diamonds had been sold long since; an antique dealer had bought the old furniture. The sporting prints had disappeared from the walls. At last, even the family portraits went.

I used to go and see the family sometimes, for I was one of the few people who *were* still willing to listen to tales of fox-hunting in Virginia. And Fannye's frank confessions amused me. I would listen by the hour while she told of the pitfalls which awaited good girls in the wicked city, and I would urge her to try her luck again, not that I thought she had even a remote chance for success, but because I thought starvation in the city was preferable to suicide at home. And she was always threatening suicide, which made her brother laugh, her mother cry, and her father curse.

The last time I went to their house I witnessed a tragedy. Old Tim Meadows—he is truly old now—had read an advertisement in a magazine. The advertisement pertained to a miraculous knitting machine. "BUY OUR MARVELOUS KNITTING MACHINE FOR $75 AND BECOME INDEPENDENT FOR LIFE. WE FURNISH YARN AND BUY ALL THE SOCKS THAT YOU KNIT, AT $3 A PAIR. A SKILFUL KNITTER CAN EARN $9 A DAY AT HOME IN HIS SPARE TIME. WHY NOT YOU?" It was something like that. It is characteristic of the Meadows family that they believe any-

thing that they see in print. Old Mr. Meadows wrote to a
friend that he had not seen in thirty years, and asked for
the loan of seventy-five dollars, sending his personal note
for sixty days, and writing somewhat mysteriously that he
was going into a lucrative business.

His wife and daughter begged and pleaded with him
not to throw the money away, but he was quite sure of his
future. His fortune would be built up again by means of the
knitting machine. In his mind he saw himself making money,
buying other machines, hiring negro labor for a dollar a day
to operate hundreds of similar machines. There was no end
to it. He explained it all, carefully, and then explained it
over again, asking for my support and agreement.

As I have said, I was at the Meadowses' house the day
the knitting machine arrived. It was a complicated device
with shuttles and spools and many clicking wheels. I saw
the old man take it out of the crate, while his wife and
daughter wept in each other's arms by the back door. He
chuckled and cursed by turns as he assembled the machine,
but an hour later the chuckles and curses had ceased and he
came, rather shamefacedly, to say that he was unable to
manipulate the damned thing, and would his wife please
come and see what she could do?

She came, and she succeeded in knitting one very curious looking sock; it was all out of shape, and the heel was
really no heel at all; but old Tim Meadows was jubilant.
He began one of his own, amid many expletives. But the
thread broke, the shuttles caught, and the wheels refused
to turn. In another hour the machine was a twisted mass of
torn worsted and broken wheels. It ended when the old
man flew into a rage and kicked the machine down the front

steps to complete destruction on the brick-paved walk, while wife and daughter wailed afresh over the money it represented.

The last thing that I heard about the Meadows family was that a lawyer had entered suit against the old gentleman for a seventy-five dollar promissory note.

Chapter Four

FAMILY PORTRAIT

TENNIS BLAKE and I were in the same class at school. He was a red-haired, freckle-faced boy of fourteen, and I liked him because we always laughed at the same things. His family and mine had been neighbors and friends in Louisiana for sixty years, so our friendship was encouraged; frequently he came to meals at my grandfather's house, and sometimes I went home with him over Sunday. He lived with his sister and two maiden aunts at Dublin Plantation, on the Mississippi River, opposite the town of Baton Rouge. The dilapidated old house stood in a curve of the levee, very near the river, and was buried in a thicket of trees and Cherokee-rose hedges. The Blakes were aristocratic, romantic, and poverty-stricken.

The fields were rented out to a tenant farmer, but the ladies of Dublin retained the plantation-house for their residence, and derived a dubious income from the rental; for

when taxes and interest on the mortgage were paid, there
was little enough left. However, what the Blake ladies
lacked in purse they made up in pride. As girls they had attended "finishing-schools" in the North. Miss Seena, the
elder, who was probably sixty years old but who seemed
an aged woman to me, played gaily upon an old square piano
and frequently lifted her voice in song. Miss Nelly had
studied elocution and sometimes recited dramatic pieces,
such as "The Maniac" or "The Old Violin." She wore her
dark hair in ringlets in the style of her girlhood, and wore
in summer a billowing gown of white and green sprigged
muslin.

Tennis had been named in honor of Alfred Lord Tennyson, but only his aunts dared call him that; if I did, he
hit me. His sister Elaine (probably called so for the Lily
Maid of Astolat) was a fat little girl with red hair, cowlike
eyes, and a string of freckles across her upturned nose. She
was considered delicate, and was taught at home. At eleven
she developed poetic tendencies, and I remember her best as
a tawny-haired girl both puny and fat, who sat hunched up
in a big chair, a pencil clenched in a chubby hand, scribbling
like mad. When she concentrated on a difficult line, she
squinted her eyes and put out her tongue; and her aunts
whispered, "Sh! Sh. . . !"

Tennis confided to me that his sister's poetry was "vile"
but her aunts discussed it by the hour and read obscure
meanings into it. "She's gifted," Miss Seena would say;
and Miss Nelly would sigh—as though Elaine were suffering from disease—and would repeat, "Yes, truly gifted."

Only occasionally Elaine played with us, and when she
did she demanded that we play games of knights and ladies.

But Tennis and I preferred scouring the swamps for wild grapes and muscadines, riding our ponies through the brush, or swimming in the river. Sometimes we smoked corn-silk cigarettes behind the barn and discussed our somewhat garbled ideas of obstetrics.

The house—it has vanished into the Mississippi these twenty years—was unpretentious but very old. It was a single-storied structure of cypress painted white, four rooms wide and two rooms deep; a broad veranda extended entirely around it; squat, white columns of masonry supported the overhanging roof. There were no windows, but double doors in every room which opened upon the porch—double glass doors swinging in and double wooden doors swinging out. Wide sliding doors connected all of the rooms, and the whole house could be thrown open like a pavilion in summer. Birds flew in and out at will.

At a distance of perhaps fifty feet from the ends of the house stood twin octagonal towers of whitewashed brick. Each tower contained two rooms, one above the other, and each tower was surmounted by a high, octagonal roof with a weather-vane. These were the *garçonnières,* or boys' houses, built for the sons of the old plantation-owner as his family had multiplied. Beyond each *garçonnière* and slightly behind it, was a smaller, similar tower—the dove-cotes.

The group of five buildings was set in a grove of live-oak trees and had once been surrounded by a flower garden. When the plantation was in its prime, the aspect must have been charming—the low central house and the twin towers flanked in turn by pigeon-houses, all as carefully placed as ornaments on an old-fashioned mantelpiece. But when I knew it, hedges had overgrown the house, and festoons of

vines draped themselves from tree to tree; the garden had
disappeared in undergrowth; only a few pale roses peered
out of the thickets and an occasional pomegranate tree scattered its crimson blossoms. The doors of the house stood
always open, and birds and butterflies flew in and out. At
night owls hooted and there was an incessant booming of
bullfrogs.

After supper we would gather in the parlor, where candles burned under hurricane shades on the mantel and at
either end of the square piano. Miss Seena, wearing a rippling black gown, would seat herself at the keyboard and
after a few tinkling chords would sing "Twickenham Ferry"
in a strong, though cracked voice. If we applauded—or even
if we didn't—she would oblige us with the *Shadow Song*
from "Dinorah," ending with such a shower of vocal fireworks that Tennis and I would choke with suppressed
laughter. When the song was ended she would remain motionless, her face upturned, her gray hair silver in the
candleshine, her wrinkled hands lying on the yellowed keys.
In her arm-chair, Miss Nelly would sigh and wipe her eyes.
"Beautiful, sister . . . beautiful. . . ." But Elaine, whose
poetic tendencies did not preclude a debased taste in music,
would speak pettishly from her corner: "Play 'The Frolic
of the Frogs,' Aunt Seena."

When the music was over, Miss Nelly would recite for
us. There were dreadful times when she would attempt to
teach Tennis and me to deliver some poem "suitable to
young gentlemen" of our age. At these times she would
elucidate to us the secrets of elocution. It seemed simple
enough as she explained it, for only five positions were necessary to portray the whole gamut of human emotions—or at

least those emotions suitable for the drawing-room. I shall never forget those positions, nor shall I forget the names of them.

"This," she said, "is the first position." She stood erect, peering at us with her black, short-sighted eyes, and holding up her long sprigged muslin gown so that we could observe her feet.

"You see, it is very simple. Right foot forward, left foot back, with left toe turned out. The weight rests upon the left foot. You must lean back in repose." She suited the words with the proper gesture. "The hands must hang at the sides or be folded loosely before you. This is the first position, and it is called *The Lady, the Gentleman, or the Speaker.*"

Tennis and I agreed that perhaps we could do that much, and she went on with the lesson.

"Now," she continued, "suppose that some one opened a red velvet box and showed you a beautiful string of pearls. What would you do?"

Tennis and I said that we didn't know what we would do.

"Why, you would lean forward, throwing the weight of the body upon the right foot, and raise both hands level with your elbows, palms turned out, indicating surprise and pleasure." She assumed the posture and announced, "This is *Gentle Animation.*"

"Must you always do that when you are surprised?" Tennis wanted to know.

"Yes, always," said his aunt.

"I'd rather clap my hands," Elaine announced.

"That would be very unladylike," said Aunt Seena. "But you mustn't interrupt your Aunt Nelly any more. She is teaching you a valuable lesson—something that you can use all of your life, when speaking in public. Go on, Nelly."

"The next position is a very dramatic one. You'll like this, Tennis. Now tell me, if you saw a child run over by a carriage (or a street-car, if you happened to be in New Orleans at the time), what would you do?"

"Scream," said Elaine, but her aunts ignored her.

"I'd pull it out from under the wheels," Tennis boasted.

"Exactly!" said Miss Nelly, "or failing that, you would make a gesture of appeal, like this!" And she fell upon one knee, with both arms extended before her, simulating horrified abandon.

"Explosion!" she cried.

"I thought you said it was a child under a street-car," said Tennis.

"Explosion is the technical name for the gesture," said his aunt, still on her knees. "And the one that follows is called *Prostration."* She sprang erect and held her clasped hands toward heaven, her head was thrown back, her eyes closed. "The child has been run over, you see, and you are powerless to help it. Your gesture signifies despair, and at the same time it is an appeal to the Almighty."

She stopped; the child under the street-car was abandoned to its fate.

"And is that all?" asked Tennis.

"No, there is another necessary gesture, but it has no part in tragic recitation. It is called *Vulgar Ease.* Like this!"

She stood with feet wide apart and her hands on her hips. Tennis and I could not restrain our laughter, the gesture was so unlike her. We expected to be reproved for levity, but she seemed gratified.

THE LABATUT HOUSE ON OLD RIVER WAS BUILT
IN 1790

"You're right," she said. "This is a comic gesture. It is used to denote a person in one of the lower walks of life. Rustic amazement, you might say."

"I know," said Elaine. "You'd use that if you wanted to pretend that you were that bad old woman in 'The Tale of Two Cities.' You know who I mean. She sat under the gallows and knitted all the time when the French aristocrats were having their heads chopped off."

"That was the guillotine, not the gallows," said Tennis grandly. "Trust you to get it wrong."

His aunts reproved him for teasing his little sister, Elaine put out her tongue at him, and Miss Nelly continued to talk of elocution.

"Suppose we have Elaine recite Tennyson's 'Lady Clare,'" she said. Tennis groaned as Elaine got heavily upon her feet, pleased to show her airs and graces. She began in a singsong voice, and Miss Nelly prompted from her arm-chair:

> "It was the time when lilies blow,
>   And clouds are highest up in air,
>   Lord Ronald brought a lily-white doe
>   To give his cousin, Lady Clare."

"That's right, Elaine, *The Lady, the Gentleman, or the Speaker.*"

> "I trow they did not part in scorn:
>   Lovers long betroth'd, were they.
>   They two will wed the morrow morn:
>   God's blessing on the day!"

"*Gentle Animation,* Elaine, on the last line."

"All right, Aunt Nelly," and Elaine tilted forward dan-

gerously and held up her hands, palms outward, as though
she were saying, "Do tell!"

> "God's blessing on the day!
> 'He does not love me for my birth,
> Nor for my lands so broad . . .' "

"Gesture, Elaine!"
"Yes'm."

> " 'Nor for my lands so broad and fair;
> He loves me for my own true worth,
> And that is well,' said Lady Clare."

"No! No!" cried Miss Nelly, "No *Explosion* yet!"
Undaunted, Elaine rose from her knees and continued to
recite. When she came to the entrance of "old Alice, the
nurse," Miss Nelly ordered *Vulgar Ease,* and each remark
of Alice's that followed was treated in the same way. Lady
Clare, as befitting her station, went forth and back between
The Lady, the Gentleman, or The Speaker and *Gentle Animation,* with occasional departures into *Explosion* and *Prostration.* Poor Elaine was taxed hard when the dialogue
became dramatic, and bounced heavily from character to
character and from gesture to gesture:

> " 'Are ye out of your mind, my nurse, my nurse?'
> Said Lady Clare, 'that ye speak so wild?' "

"*Explosion!*"

> " 'As God's above . . .' "

"*Vulgar Ease!*"

> ". . . said Alice, the nurse,
> 'I speak the truth: you are my child.' "

Elaine struggled on, but when she came to the verse about tearing off the brooch of gold and flinging away the diamond necklace, Miss Nelly kept crying out: *"Explosion! Prostration! Explosion! Prostration!"* until the poor girl was so mixed up that she forgot the lines completely. However, with a little prompting and encouragement, she finished triumphantly on *Gentle Animation* (a sad anti-climax, I thought) and stood waiting for our applause. Then she acknowledged our plaudits with a curtsy (also learned from Aunt Nelly), and retired to her chair, bathed in happiness and perspiration.

Strange nights those were in the parlor of Dublin Plantation, while poesy reigned or the piano tinkled, as bats sailed in and out of the open doors. I remember it all as a series of disconnected pictures. Now an evening—now morning sunlight in the garden . . .

Late one afternoon when Miss Seena, Miss Nelly, Tennis, and I were sitting on the gallery, Elaine burst upon us with a poem which she had composed on the spur of the moment. She stood with hands clasped behind her and recited doggedly:

> "Over the meadows, the wild girl ran;
> She ran so fast, she dropped her fan.
> 'Where are you going in such haste?'
> 'To get some water, to make some paste!' "

Tennis and I laughed, but the aunts entered into a discussion that lasted until supper time. Miss Seena said that Elaine had been strangely quiet that day, and this poem was no surprise. She added that she thought the poem needed

some explaining, and Tennis and I agreed with her. But as
no explanation was proffered by the eleven-year-old poetess,
the two ladies began to expound their theories. They agreed
that the setting was rural, the word "meadows" in the first
line indicated it clearly. But they were not at all sure about
the status of the heroine—the "wild girl."

"Do you suppose," asked Miss Nelly, "that the girl is
actually insane? Or is she only full of girlish glee and high
spirits?"

"I wondered about that, too," said Miss Seena. "I am
inclined to believe that the girl is only wild as a bird is
wild; free, a creature of the great outdoors."

"Then what did she want with paste?" asked Tennis.

"We will come to that in good time," said Miss Seena
curtly.

"It seems obvious to me," said Miss Nelly, "that our
heroine is the child of well-to-do parents, and it seems that
they are strongly attached to her. They are worried, ob-
viously, by her haste . . ."

"And the fan denotes a certain fastidiousness of costume . . ."

"Or perhaps it was a hot day . . ." said Miss Nelly.

"That may be, but even so. . . . The fan indicates that
her costume was in keeping. . . ." said Miss Seena.

"In keeping with what?" asked Tennis.

"Don't use that tone to your aunt, Tennis, it is ill-bred."

"I'm sure that he did not intend to be impertinent, sister,
and I think I ought to answer his question. You see, Tennis,
there is much more to this poem than you think. Elaine had
something very definite in mind when she wrote it."

"Yes'm," said Tennis, winking broadly at me.

"Where were we, Seena? Oh yes, the girl had thrown away her fan. The fact that she dropped it, or threw it away, might be taken to mean that she was really insane, or at least very flighty."

"I attribute the loss of the fan to mere girlish heedlessness," said Miss Seena firmly, "but at any rate, she ran fast and the fan was lost. That much is certain, for there is no mention of retrieving it."

"That brings us to the third line," said Miss Nelly, "the question as to her destination: 'Where are you going in such haste?'"

"That seems to bear out my point," said Miss Seena. "Her parents, friends, or guardians—or whoever asked the question—are gently-bred people. The phrase 'in such haste' proves that. They modify their question. They show interest and real concern as to the speed with which she was running. If they had merely said, 'Where are you going?' the reader would have been left in doubt. As it stands, the line is complete."

They both nodded and sighed as they prepared to grapple with the last and most difficult line of the verse. They could not agree on the punctuation. If it were divided by a comma: "To get some water, to make some paste," it was clear enough; but if it were *two* sentences, the line was open to lengthy discussion. "To get some water," might indicate thirst—"it was a hot day, you know"—and the water might have no connection whatever with the paste. In the end they decided that only a comma was used, and that the little girl was running to get water to make paste, and in that case it was probable that she wanted to make a scrapbook and was not really wild at all—except in a nice way—

but was a studious little girl who probably picked up her fan on the way home.

For the sake of argument, Tennis disagreed violently with the decision, and his aunts—fair in all things—called Elaine and asked her. But the youthful poetess replied rudely that she had forgotten what she *did* mean. So we never knew.

There was another time, too, when Elaine was the center of the picture for a brief time, but on this occasion her aunts were not so pleased.

In the parlor were three swords which were family relics. One was from some ancestor who had been an officer in the American Revolution, and the others dated from the Civil War. All had been carried by Blakes who were now dead and gone, and often we listened to the stories of those departed gentlemen; sometimes, for a treat, we were allowed to examine the swords.

One Sunday afternoon, while Tennis and I were sorting out fishing tackle and the aunts were taking a nap, Elaine reached the high point of whimsy. She appeared between the columns of the veranda draped in a damask table-cloth and waving a sword in her hand. "I'm Joan of Arc, and I've been hearing voices from on high!" she announced.

We were interested to hear that.

"What did they say?" asked Tennis.

"They told me to lead the force to victory," she answered.

Nothing loath, Tennis and I went into the parlor, armed ourselves with the remaining weapons, and Joan of Arc led us out to fight. Unfortunately, there was no enemy in sight

but one old white rooster which was pecking at a yellow
rose-bush, and with one indignant squawk he disappeared
into a hedge and could not be dislodged. So Elaine looked
about for armies which might be lurking among the shrubbery. Tennis and I followed after, feeling rather bored;
but just as we had decided to fight a duel, Elaine cried out:
"The foe! The foe!"

We had reached the edge of the flower garden, and
beyond the hedge lay a corn-field. The young corn was shoulder high and waved in the breeze. Elaine swung her sword
and a corn-stalk fell to the ground. Emboldened, she attacked another, and a third. Tennis and I sprang into the
fray and we all began slashing in every direction, screaming
as we slashed: "Take that! and that! and that!"

Yelling like wild Indians, rather than like followers of
the blessed Maid of Orleans, we went down the field, de-
stroying the corn as we went. At any sign of weakening,
Joan of Arc would cry: "Fie, for shame, to leave a woman
undefended!" and we would begin afresh, slashing right
and left.

Nearly half an acre of corn lay flat on the ground, when
an angry voice cried out: "You damned little devils! I'll
beat the life out of all of you!"

Joan of Arc stood with sword uplifted, as though petri-
fied. Suddenly she yelled "Oh! Oh!" and began to run.
Tennis and I retreated in her wake. Swords were thrown
aside and Joan's damask table-cloth lay forgotten among the
broken cornstalks. No longer were we knights of old pursu-
ing the foe, but three scared children pursued by an angry
farmer.

The aunts, hearing our wails of anguish, came running

out to meet us. They gave us succor, and listened to the complaint of the furious man. They were quite calm as they promised to reimburse their tenant for his loss, and our hopes of escaping punishment flamed high. But we were not to escape. Miss Seena explained that we had behaved foolishly, had destroyed property and had taken the swords without permission. In addition, the best Sunday table-cloth was a ragged ruin. We must be punished, and'punished we were. Supperless we were sent to bed in the middle of a glowing summer afternoon—and we went without a murmur of protest. However, at twilight the aunts weakened and by eight o'clock we were forgiven and fed. We ended the evening as usual with music and poetry in the parlor.

Although there were five bedrooms in the house, Tennis and I preferred to sleep in one of the *garçonnières,* and when I was a visitor there, this was allowed. When the evening's conversation was at an end, Tennis and I would take a lantern and go out into the tangle of bushes which lay between the house and the outbuildings. The lower floor of the *garçonnière,* set flush with the ground and paved with brick, was musty and damp, and once a black snake went sliding across the floor as we entered; but the room above was both charming and comfortable. It was the first octagonal room I had ever seen, and the fact that it was in a tower made it romantic. There were four windows— north, south, east, and west—and the stairs rose between the north and west windows. A large four-post bed with a canopy and curtains nearly filled the room; it stood with its headboard between the south and east windows, and there was just room to walk between the foot of the bed and the stair-rail. In the other two wall spaces stood an *armoire,* or

E.H.Suydam

THE SCOTT FAMILY HAS OCCUPIED
"THE SHADES" SINCE 1808

"ORMOND," AN EIGHTEENTH-CENTURY HOUSE
NEAR NEW ORLEANS

wardrobe, and a chest of drawers surmounted by a small
mirror. There were two straight chairs wedged in somehow; that was all. But how strange and delightful it seemed
to lie there in bed, watching the shimmering fireflies in the
topmost branches of the trees—or looking out on one side
beyond the trees to the fields of sugar-cane billowing in the
moonlight, or on the other side toward the levee and the
Mississippi River, a very short distance away. We would
lie there talking together for hours, while the rusty weather-
vane turned protestingly overhead, and the bullfrogs and
crickets sang their eternal song.

One night in the spring, when the river was high against
the levee, we saw a steamboat pass, higher than our heads.
The river beyond the levee was invisible and the huge, il-
luminated steamboat passed by like a monster in a dream.
It was so near that we could hear the negro roustabouts
singing on the decks, and the puffing of the exhaust pipes.
It seemed to come out of nowhere, gliding above the tops of
the trees, and it disappeared toward some inevitable and
unimagined destination.

The proximity of the river was one of the chief charms
of Dublin Plantation, but in the end it brought disaster.
Year by year the river had eaten into the bank. Long before
my time, the avenue of oaks before the house had been swallowed up, and the public road ran some distance behind the
dwelling. As I remember it, the group of buildings lay in a
curve of the levee, snugly, as though a protecting arm
had been thrown around them. But one year the Blakes
were notified that the caving bank necessitated moving the
levee back even further, and when this was accomplished,
the house was left outside on the batture, at the very edge

of the river itself. The Blake ladies were forced to go; they moved into the town of Baton Rouge, taking with them their furniture—or that part of it which a cottage could accommodate.

Tennis and I went back once, after the house was left to its fate. The shrubs in the garden were half covered with rippling water. We went in through the back door and walked into one empty room after another. There were long lines of dust where the matting had been ripped up; a dusty picture frame with a broken glass leaned against the wall. We went upon the veranda in front, where water covered the lower steps. For the last time we read our names written on one of the white columns; we had measured ourselves against it when we were both eight years old. The measuring of children against that column had been a custom in the family; for near our names were others—that of Tennis's father, long dead, and of Miss Seena and Miss Nelly as little girls. Names of friends were there, too. Among them I found the childish signature of one of my uncles; I had never noticed it before. There was a date beside it—1879.

And then, suddenly—as though I had heard a bell tolling—the feeling of doom was upon me; it was part fear of the rushing river which moved so pitilessly against the old house, and part sorrow for the destruction of a place in which I had been so happy. I shivered.

Tennis stood with his back turned toward me. His shoulders twitched. When he spoke, his voice was hoarse. "Let's go," he said.

The rising river destroyed the house that spring. The

trees in the garden were washed away, and the roof floated downstream. For a few years after that, the white columns and one *garçonnière* remained, but now they too are gone. Yes, gone as completely from the earth as the two old ladies who once lived there.

Elaine, surprisingly enough, married a rancher and went to live in west Texas; and Tennis, old freckle-faced Tennis, fell with a burning airplane in France in 1917. And now there is not one of that family left in Louisiana.

Part II

MASTERS AND SLAVES

Chapter Five

BEGINNINGS

LET us consider beginnings in Louisiana for a moment.
De Soto discovered the Mississippi in 1541, but it was
not until one hundred and twenty years later that La Salle
explored the river to its mouth. The French were entrenched
in Canada and believed that with fortifications at various
strategic points along the Mississippi, they would be able
to hold forever the lands along its banks as a vast empire
for France. A stronghold near the river's mouth was necessary. In 1697 Iberville was sent over from France to colo-
nize Louisiana. He founded Biloxi on the Mexican Gulf
coast and visited the site of the city of New Orleans. He
died in 1702 and his brother, Bienville, was appointed to
succeed him. Bienville founded New Orleans in 1718.
Natchitoches, on Red River, was founded a few years
earlier. Colonists settled along the Mississippi at the hills
of Baton Rouge, the bluffs of Natchez and in that rich

delta called Pointe Coupée, near the junction of the Mississippi, the Red River, and the Atchafalaya. Southern Louisiana was but a wilderness divided by a network of waterways, bays, rivers, creeks, lakes, and bayous. (A bayou is a stream which flows out of a river into another body of water—a natural spillway. It is not fed by springs, and, unlike a creek, it does not run dry. These slow-flowing streams preserve a balance between river and lake or river and bay, or between two rivers.) All civilization in early Louisiana was along the waterways. Water was the only means of transportation.

One of the most important names in early Louisiana history is that of John Law. Born in Scotland, he first gained notoriety as an extravagant gambler. Exiled from England he went to live in Holland where he evolved a system of state control of banking which France, under the Regent, adopted at a time of great financial stress, due to the extravagances of Louis XIV. His next exploit was the establishment of the "Company of the West" sometimes called the "Company of the Indies." The result was the "Mississippi Bubble" in which tremendous fortunes were made and lost. Louisiana was exploited as a fabulous land of gold. Hundreds of Frenchmen sold everything and set out for the new Eden. There were well-to-do Frenchmen, Swiss soldiers, and thrifty German farmers. The riffraff of the Paris streets came as laborers; shiploads of women from French jails were sent out as wives for colonists; ships loaded with brute negro slaves arrived from the Guinea coast. Only a wilderness awaited them, there was no food, no shelter, and no escape. The strong lived and the weak died. Out of such extravagant beginnings came Louisiana.

Bienville notes in his diary that he planted indigo and "a few sugar-canes from Martinique" in 1718. The first census shows a score of planters in the immediate vicinity of New Orleans. These men arrived from France with enough money to buy land and negro slaves. They grew a staple crop of indigo. They raised also enough produce to furnish themselves and their slaves with food, but this was incidental. The Jesuit priests had a large land grant beginning from what is now Gravier Street in New Orleans and ending far uptown. They introduced sugar-cane into the colony. From it they made molasses, and an alcoholic beverage called *taffia,* a sort of rum. Sugar was not granulated until 1795 when Étienne de Boré made his famous crop which brought twelve thousand dollars, a large sum for that time. The planters then turned their attention to sugar. Later still, cotton became an important crop. At the height of the plantation prosperity, both cotton and sugar were planted; rice as a staple came later still.

The era of plantation life in Louisiana is ended. It had its beginnings when the French colony was founded. Creole prosperity reached its height at the end of the Spanish régime in New Orleans. In 1803 the Creoles were at their zenith. They suffered in competition with the Americans who came flocking to the rich delta of the Mississippi after the Louisiana Purchase. The Creoles, for all their luxury, were essentially simple in their tastes. They liked good food and comfort. Their houses were strong and austere. Even that magnificent figure which typifies Creole magnificence—Bernard Marigny, the man who entertained princes—lived in a simple house. It was large but not elegant; it was richly furnished, but it was built for ease rather than

display. Ornate elegance came into fashion oniy twenty
years before the Civil War. Oddly enough, nearly three
fourths of the fine plantation-houses standing in Louisiana
to-day were built by Americans. This is easily explained
when one remembers that the period of large fortunes came
to Louisiana in the thirty years between 1830 and 1860.

Many intelligent persons believe that the plantation era
—the "good old times" in Louisiana—lasted for more than
a century. Roughly speaking, the prosperous plantation era
corresponds with the steamboat era—a scant sixty years.
Steamboats appeared on the Mississippi in 1811, and steamboating reached its zenith thirty years later; in another
thirty years its glory had departed, for the railroad had
supplanted it.

Prosperity on the plantation covers almost the same
period. It had its beginning in the eighteenth century. In
1803 and in the three decades following, thousands of
Americans flocked to the fertile shores of the Mississippi,
bringing money and slaves with them. Huge fortunes were
made, and the Americans built fine houses on their
plantations.

The Civil War freed the slaves. The railroads destroyed
steamboating. The economic scheme of Louisiana fell to
pieces in 1861. Prosperity on the plantation had brought
prosperity to the city; the wealth accrued by slave labor was
distributed in New Orleans. The Civil War ended all that.
And Louisiana, from having been one of the richest States,
became the poorest. There was a second blooming in the
ten years between 1880 and 1890. In 1885 a Cotton Exposition was held in New Orleans, and the South determined to
rebuild along its old lines. Then came the boll-weevil and

the slow migration of negroes northward. Hard times came back again. Still the Louisiana planter was rooted in his tradition. He had always done things in a large way, and he continued to try to do so.

I remember perhaps fifty plantations which were in operation in my childhood. There was a time when the names of as many moderately prosperous planters were known to me. Now, thirty years later, I do not know more than five of these families that are still living on their plantations. The old people have died, the young people have realized that it is a losing fight and have abandoned it. The magnificent houses are falling into ruin. Many of them are deserted. They are built in the grand manner, they stand in isolated spots, and it is impossible to live in one without many servants. Planters cannot afford many servants nowadays.

And yet, Louisiana is commercially prosperous to-day. Until a few years ago there were few manufacturing enterprises in the State, although there was abundant raw material. Nowadays there are many such enterprises. New Orleans appears to be flourishing; Baton Rouge, Shreveport, and Alexandria—small towns thirty years ago—are prosperous cities to-day. Once Louisiana towns were picturesque, full of eccentric old people and crumbling old houses; to-day they are modern. They are filled with automobiles, radios, five-and-ten-cent stores, and all the other hall-marks of prosperous urban life in America. But the old charm has departed; the romantic quality has gone.

Louisiana was essentially an agricultural country; this is still true in a measure, but plantations no longer boast vast acreage and hundreds of laborers.

This is the rough outline of plantation life in Louisiana, and now I shall let the plantation people speak for themselves.

Chapter Six

AN EIGHTEENTH-CENTURY PLANTER

LE PAGE DU PRATZ, one of the first Louisiana planters, has left a complete record of his travels and adventures in the lower Mississippi Valley. It forms a part of his "History of Louisiana" which was published in France in 1750 or thereabouts; the only copy which I have been able to find is an English translation, published in London in 1774. The volume is rare nowadays and is little known.

Le Page du Pratz was the contemporary and friend of Bienville and came to Louisiana at the time of the founding of New Orleans in 1718. He sailed from Rochelle and arrived at Massacre Island in the Mexican Gulf after an uneventful voyage of five months' duration. He describes the island and tells of finding human bones scattered on the beach. These were the bones of those Frenchmen and Germans who came to Louisiana under the auspices of John Law's Company of the West. They had been abandoned at Massacre Island with no food and no shelter; and unable to escape, they died there in great numbers. In order to rid the island of its evil reputation, Bienville changed its name to Dauphin Island in the year that du Pratz arrived.

According to the account by du Pratz, he set sail from the island accompanied by his hired servants and effects "and a letter to M. Paillou, major-general at New Orleans." He stopped to observe the Pascagoulas, an Indian tribe on the coast of what is now the State of Mississippi. He approved of the Pascagoulas, or "The Nation of Bread," and after a short visit, he continued to explore the islands east of the Mississippi. He did not ascend the river, however, but took the safer route through Lake Borgne and Lake Pontchartrain, then through Bayou St. John—called "Tchoupic" by the Indians because the water was muddy —and arrived in New Orleans sometime in February 1719. Here he bought an Indian slave, a woman to cook for him, and he also acquired "several strong black fellows" to take along with him to his grant of land. Near New Orleans he built a rude palmetto-covered house on the banks of Bayou St. John. And it was here that his Indian slave woman introduced him to his first alligator.

It was almost night [he writes] when my slave perceived, within two yards of the fire, a young alligator, five feet long, which beheld the fire without moving. I was in the garden hard by, when she made me repeated signs to come to her; I ran with speed, and upon my arrival she shewed me the crocodile, without speaking to me; the little time that I examined it, I could see its eyes were so fixed on the fire that all our motions could not take them off. I ran to my cabin to look for my gun (as I am a pretty good marksman) but what was my surprise, when I came out, and saw

the girl with a great stick in her hand attacking the monster. Seeing me arrive, she began to smile and say many things which I
did not comprehend, as she belaboured the reptile. But she made
me understand, by signs, that there was no occasion for a gun to
kill such a beast; for the stick she shewed me was sufficient for the
purpose.

Later, another Frenchman told him that the daring of
the Indian slave girl was nothing unusual, and explained that
she was of an Indian nation which lived on the lake shore;
and that he "need not be surprised by what the girl had
done, for the whole country was full of such creatures, and
that Indians pursue them, kill them, and eat part of their
tails, making good cheer on them."

The land along the bayou was fertile and du Pratz made
a garden and planted peach stones, which "immediately began to sprout and by autumn had made trees four feet high
with branches in proportion." He joined in the work of
building a levee before the village of New Orleans to prevent another overflow by the Mississippi; and he took active part in the affairs of the town. But, hearing much praise
of the country of the Natchez, two hundred miles up the
river, he determined to move there.

His Indian slave girl was highly pleased when he told
her of his decision, and sang the praises of the country,
which had once been her home. The skies, she assured him,
were finer, and the hunting good, and her relations, who had
retired there after their war with the French, would "bring
everything that we want." She ended her discourse by announcing that every one in that country lived to reach a ripe
old age. So Le Page du Pratz and his friend, M. Hubert,
with their slaves and effects, moved first into the town of

New Orleans for a brief time, and after buying more negro slaves, both men and women, set out on a voyage up the river. The party traveled in canoes and *pirogues,* the latter a sort of canoe made from a cypress log, the ends pointed, the central portion scooped out.

The two Frenchmen went ahead of the party, paddling in a large canoe.

I had been told that I had only to take powder and ball with me in order to provide my whole company with sufficient game to maintain us; for which purpose it was necessary to make use of a paddle, instead of oars, which make too much noise for the game. I had a barrel of powder, with fifteen pounds of shot, which I thought would be sufficient for the voyage; but I found by experience that this was not sufficient for the vast plenty of game that is to be met with upon that river, without ever going out of your way. I had not gone above twenty-eight leagues, to the grant of M. Paris du Vernai, when I was obliged to borrow of him fifteen pounds of shot more. Upon this I took care of my ammunition, and shot nothing but what was fit for our provision, such as wild ducks, summer ducks, teal, and saw-bills. Among the rest I killed a carancro [carrion crow or buzzard], wild geese, cranes, and flamingoes. I likewise often killed young alligators, the tails of which was a feast for the slaves, as well as for the French and Canadian rowers.

But though du Pratz meant to be careful, he could not resist shooting many times for sport. There are accounts of "monstrous crocodiles" which he destroyed, some of them twenty feet long.

At a small settlement on the Mississippi, he met a French missionary priest who told him how difficult it was to convert the Indians to Christianity.

I asked him if his great zeal for the salvation of the savages met with any success; and he answered me that notwithstanding the profound respect the people shewed him, it was with the greatest difficulty he could get leave to baptise a few children at the point of death; that those of an advanced age excused themselves from embracing our holy religion because they were too old, say they, to accustom themselves to its rules; that the chief who had killed a physician that attended his son for a distemper of which he died had taken a resolution to fast every Friday while he lived, in remorse for his inhumanity with which he had been so sharply reproached by him. This grand chief attended both morning and evening prayers; the women and children likewise assisted at them sometimes, but the men, who did not come very often, took more pleasure in ringing the bell.

At last the voyagers reached a bluff two hundred feet high, where the French had built Fort Rosalie. This was the site of the present city of Natchez. Here he was entertained at the fort and found the place to his liking. After a few days' search, he found land suitable to his needs, and bought it from the Indians who lived there. It was several hundred acres, but he does not mention the price. His plantation was situated on the Natchez Trace—an old Indian road which de Soto had described two hundred years before as "worn deep in the earth"—and there was a spring of fresh water near an Indian hut. Here he put his slaves to work at clearing the ground and they "immediately cleared six acres of the white walnut (or hiccorie) trees" which had been growing there. He repaired the Indian hut for his own use and his slaves built another cabin for their quarters. Here du Pratz lived "pretty much like our woodcutters in France."

M. Hubert and his family—not mentioned before in du

Pratz's account—arrived and took up land adjoining that of du Pratz. All went well for a time until du Pratz was stricken with a strange disease which caused his thigh to swell. He suffered great pain and walked with difficulty.

"I consulted our surgeon about it, who caused me to be bleeded; on which the humour fell on the other thigh, and fixed there with such violence that I could not walk without extreme pain." He then went to New Orleans—no easy undertaking—and consulted physicians there, but they told him they could do nothing; they talked of mineral waters and of French resorts, and urged him to go back to France. But du Pratz refused to do this and returned to his cabin on the bluff at Natchez. Two of his negro slaves ran away, and du Pratz, confined to his bed, was miserable.

"I decided to resort to one of the Indian conjurers, who are both surgeons, divines, and sorcerers; and who told me he would cure me by sucking the place where I felt pain." Accordingly, the Indian medicine man began operations. He made incisions in the hips of the Frenchman with a piece of flint, and proceeded to suck the wounds "with such energy that I cried out in pain for half an hour while the treatment continued." Oddly enough, du Pratz felt better the next day and allowed the Indian to repeat the treatment. On the third day a poultice was put upon his wounds and in eight days he was "perfectly cured."

One of his slaves sickened and died "of a defluxion on the breast, which he catched by running away into the woods, where his youth and want of experience made him believe he might live without the toils of slavery." But the other slaves worked in the fields, clearing the ground and planting tobacco. A neighbor came to call, M. de Montplaisir, and assisted du Pratz in planting his crop. Produce was sold to "passing pedlars" who took their goods down the river to New Orleans. Two years passed by.

In 1722 du Pratz decided to visit New Orleans and Biloxi again, for he was not satisfied with the way his affairs were going. The goods which he shipped down the river brought little in return, and his letters from France were intercepted in New Orleans. In making the trip he visited nearly every settlement in Louisiana, and his account tells us that there were six thousand people in it. But these six thousand were scattered from Biloxi, on the coast of the Gulf of Mexico, up the Mississippi to Illinois.

New Orleans, at this time, he describes as "much improved" and goes on to say that at the time of his first arrival there it was unworthy of the name of a town; now all is different. There is a church, a convent of Capuchins. The streets are regularly laid out. There is a prison or guard-house, and two rows of barracks. There is a broad levee planted with trees, and in the evening the citizens of New Orleans walk abroad in the moonlight. A brick-yard is in operation. The houses are built of timber and brick, and are set within gardens. "And," he adds briefly, "some women are there."

As he ascended the Mississippi, he saw the village of Bayou Goula, which was small but neat; and beyond, one hundred and twenty miles upstream from New Orleans, he visited the settlement of Baton Rouge.

Baton Rouge is also on the east bank of the Mississippi [he writes], and it was formerly the grant of M. Artaguette d'Iron; it is there that we see the famous cypress tree of which a ship-carpenter offered to make two *pettyraugres* [pirogues], one of sixteen and the other of fourteen tons. Some of the first adventurers who landed in this quarter happened to say that the tree would make a fine walking-stick; and as cypress is red wood, it was afterwards called *le Baton Rouge*.

And just here, our historian indulges in a flight of fancy: "The height of this cypress tree could never be measured," he assures us, "as it rises out of sight!"

He tells of the grant of M. Paris du Vernai at Bayou Goula, and of the plantation of the Marquis de Mézières at Petits Ecores (Little Cliffs) where "a little rivulet falls into the Mississippi, a place which so attracts the buffaloes that they are often found in great numbers on the banks."

At Pointe Coupée was the grant of M. de Meuse, "with a fort, a garrison, and a commandant stationed there," and on Red River, some distance from the Mississippi, is the post of Natchitoches, "founded by M. St. Denis in 1715." A trail led from Natchitoches into Mexico, "and many Spaniards are seen passing back and forth." There was much talk of gold and silver mines, du Pratz tells us, but the riches were not forthcoming to those who settled in Natchitoches and the colony has "a disappointed air." He secured a horse and rode through a part of the inland country, but was disappointed to find that the land was not so rich as that lying along the water-course, and that there were "scarce any other plants than pine trees."

At home again, du Pratz writes of Louisiana's first slave insurrection, or rather the first attempt made by slaves in the colony to destroy their masters. It is an interesting account, told at first hand, and I shall give his version of it, uncolored by any comment of mine:

A female negroe receiving a violent blow from a French soldier for refusing to obey him, said in her passion that the French should not long insult negroes. Some Frenchmen overhearing these threats, brought her before the Governor, who sent her to prison. The Judge Criminal not being able to draw anything out of her, I told the Governor, who seemed to pay no great regard to her threats, that I was of the opinion that a man in liquor and a woman in passion generally speak truth. It is therefore highly probable, said I, that there is some truth in what she said; and so, there must be some conspiracy ready to break out which cannot be formed without many negroes of the King's plantation being accomplices therein; and if there are any, I take upon me, said I, to find them out, and arrest them, if necessary, without any difficulty or tumult.

The Governor and the whole Court approved of my reasons: I went that very evening to the camp of the negroes, and from hut to hut, till I saw a light. In this hut I heard them talking together of their scheme. One of them was my first commander and my confidant, which surprised me greatly; his name was Samba.

I speedily retired for fear of being discovered, and in two days after, eight negroes, who were at the head of the conspiracy, were separately arrested, unknown to each other, and clapt into irons without the least tumult.

The day after, they were put to the torture of burning matches; which, though several times repeated, could not bring them to make any confession. In the meantime, I learnt that Samba had in his own country been at the head of a revolt by which the French lost Fort Arguin; and when it was recovered again by M. Perier de Salvert, one of the principal articles of peace was, that this negroe should be condemned to slavery in America; that Samba, on his passage, had laid a scheme to murder the crew, in order to become master of the ship; but that being discovered, he was put in irons, in which he continued until landed in Louisiana.

I drew up a memorial of all this; which was read before Samba by the Judge Criminal; who, threatening him again with torture, told him he had ever been a seditious fellow: upon which Samba directly owned all circumstances of the conspiracy, and the rest

being confronted with him, confessed also; after which, the eight
negroes were condemned to be broke alive on the wheel, and the
woman to be hanged before their eyes; which was accordingly
done, and prevented the conspiracy from taking effect.

Although the French managed to put down the negro insurrection which threatened, they were less successful with
Indian wars. The situation at Fort Rosalie was growing
acute; the Natchez Indians were tired of the tyranny and
oppression of the officers at the garrison, who had made
slaves of many of them and had treated others with cruelty.
Accordingly the Indians planned to kill all of those in the
settlement and fort. They carried out their plan to the
last detail.

A group of the Natchez entered the fort, pretending
that they had come to sell fowls. They scattered through
every part of the building, and at a given signal they attacked, scalping the commander Sieur de Chepart (or
d'Etcheparre). The war whoops of the Indians gave the
signal to the others, who had remained hidden in the woods;
Indians poured into the fort, killing all they met.

This lasted until four o'clock in the afternoon, when the
massacre ended. Then the Indians had all the heads of the French
brought into the public square, with the booty they had taken.
The spoils they divided among themselves. As they had spared
as many French women as they could during the massacre, they
brought them all together and put them into two houses where
they were kept under surveillance. They took the negroes as slaves.

So much for the brief record. In all there were 144 men,
thirty-five women, and fifty-six children killed. Many of them
were mutilated or "burned and tortured" before they were

murdered. A few who managed to escape brought the news
to New Orleans.

The entire neighborhood was laid waste; nearly the entire white population was killed, and the rest driven away.
Luckily for our story, du Pratz escaped and lived to write
his book.

Later, he secured more land, planted indigo and tobacco,
and made experiments with sugar-cane and with silk-worm
culture. At his most prosperous time du Pratz had a comfortable house, several hundred acres under cultivation and
more than fifty slaves. He has left an interesting treatise
called "The Negroes of Louisiana; Of the Choice of
Negroes; of their Distempers, and the Manner of Curing
Them." As this is the first record of plantation life, I shall
quote the treatise here. For it served as a guide to many
Frenchmen and, at a later time, to Americans who settled
in Louisiana.

Having finished my account of the natives of Louisiana, I shall
conclude this treatise with some observations relating to the negroes;
who, in the lower part of the province especially, perform all the
labours of agriculture. On that account I have thought proper to
give some instructions concerning them, for the benefit of those
who are inclined to settle in that province.

The negroes must be governed differently from the Europeans;
not because they are black, nor because they are slaves; but because
they think differently from the white men.

First, they imbibe a prejudice from their infancy, that the white
men buy them for no other purpose but to drink their blood,
which is owing to this, that when the first negroes saw the Europeans drink claret, they imagined it was blood, as that wine is of
a deep red colour; so that nothing but the actual experience of the
contrary can eradicate the false opinion. But as none of those slaves

who have had that experience ever return to their own country, the same prejudice continues to subsist on the coast of Guinea where we purchased them. Some who are strangers to the manner of thinking that prevails among the negroes, may perhaps think that the above remark is of no consequence, in respect to those slaves who are already sold to the French. There have been instances however of bad consequences flowing from this prejudice; especially if the negroes found no old slave of their own country upon their first arrival in our colonies. Some of them have killed or drowned themselves, several of them have deserted (which they call making themselves Marons), and all this from an apprehension that the white men were going to drink their blood. When they desert they believe they can get back to their own country by going around the sea, and may live in the woods upon the fruits, which they imagine are as common everywhere as with them.

They are very superstitious and are much attached to their prejudices, and little toys which they call *gris-gris*. It would be improper therefore to take them from them, or even speak of them to them; for they would believe themselves undone, if they were stripped of those trinkets. The old negroes soon make them lose conceit of them.

The first thing you ought to do when you purchase negroes, is to cause them to be examined by a skilful surgeon and an honest man, to discover if they have the venereal or any other distemper. When they are viewed, both men and women are stripped naked as the hand, and are carefully examined from the crown of the head to the sole of the feet, then between the toes and between the fingers, in the mouth, in the ears, not excepting even the parts naturally concealed, though then exposed to view. You must ask your examining surgeon if he is acquainted with the distemper of the yaws, which is the virus of Guinea, and incurable by a great many French surgeons, though very skilful in the management of European distempers. Be careful not to be deceived in this point; for your surgeon may be deceived himself; therefore attend at the examination yourself, and observe carefully over all the body of the negro, whether you can discover any parts of the skin, which though black like the rest, are however smooth as a looking glass, without any tumor or rising. Such spots may be easily discovered; for the skin of a person who goes naked is usually all over wrinkles. Wherefore if you see such marks you must reject the negro, whether man or woman. There are always experienced surgeons at the sale of new negroes, who purchase them; and many of those surgeons have made fortunes by that means; but they generally keep their secrets to themselves.

Another mortal distemper with which many negroes from Guinea are attacked, is the scurvy. It discovers itself by the gums, but sometimes it is so inveterate as to appear outwardly, in which case it is generally fatal. If any of my readers shall have the misfortune to have a negro attacked with one of those distempers, I will now teach him how to save him, by putting him in a way of being radically cured by surgeons; for I have no inclination to fall out with those gentlemen. I learned this secret from a negro physician, who was upon the king's plantation, when I took the superintendance of it.

You must never put an iron instrument into the yaw; such an application would be certain death. In order to open the yaw, you take iron rust reduced to an impalpable powder, and passed through a fine search, you afterwards mix that powder with citron juice till it be of the consistence of an ointment, which you spread upon a linen cloth greased with hog's grease, or fresh lard without salt, for want of a better. You lay the plaster upon the yaw, and renew it evening and morning, which will open the yaw in a very short time without any incision.

The opening being once made, you take about the bulk of a goose's egg of hog's lard without salt, in which you incorporate about an ounce of good terebinthine; after which take a quantity of powdered verdigris, and soak it half a day in good vinegar, which you must then pour off gently with all the scum that floats at top. Drop a cloth all over with the verdigris that remains, and upon that apply your last ointment. All these operations are performed without the assistance of fire. The whole ointment being well mixed with a spatula, you dress the yaw with it; after that put your negro into a copious sweat, and he will be cured. Take special care that your surgeon uses no mercurial medicine, as I have seen; for that will occasion the death of the patient.

The scurvy is no less to be dreaded than the yaws; nevertheless you may get the better of it by adhering exactly to the following prescription: take some scurvy-grass, if you have any plants of it, some ground-ivy, called by some St. John's wort, some water-cresses from a spring or brook, and for want of that, wild cresses; take these three herbs, or the two last, if you have no scurvy-grass; pound them, and mix them with citron-juice, to make them a soft paste, which the patient must keep upon both his gums till they be clean, at all times but when he is eating. In the meantime he must be suffered to drink nothing but an infusion of the herbs above named. You pound two handfuls of them, roots and all, after washing off any earth that may be upon the roots or leaves; to these you join a fresh citron, cut into slices. Having pounded all together, you steep them in an earthen pan in a pint of pure water of the measure of Paris; after that you add about the size of a walnut of powdered and purified saltpetre, and to make it a little refreshing to the negro, you add some powdered sugar. After the water has stood one night, you squeeze out the herbs pretty strongly. The whole is performed cold, or without fire. Such is the dose for a bottle of water Paris measure; but as the patient ought to drink two pints a day, you may make several pints at a time in the above proportion.

In these two distempers the patients must be supported with good nourishment, and made to sweat copiously. It would be a mistake to think that they ought to be kept to a spare diet; you must give them nourishing food, but a little at a time. A negro can no more than any other person support remedies upon bad food, and still less upon a spare diet; but the quantity must be proportioned to the state of the patient, and the nature of the distemper. Besides, good food makes the best part of the remedy to those who in common are but poorly fed. The negro who taught me these two remedies, observing the great care I took of both negro men and negro women, taught me likewise the cure of all the distempers to which the negro women are subject; for the negro women are as liable to diseases as the white women.

When a negro man or woman comes home to you, it is proper to caress them, to give them something good to eat, with a glass of brandy. It is best to dress them the same day, to give them something to sleep on, and a covering. I suppose the others have been treated in the same manner, for those marks of humanity flatter them, and attach them to their masters. If they are fatigued or weakened by a journey, or by any, distempers, make them work little; but keep them always busy as long as they are able to do anything, never suffering them to be idle, but when they are at their meals. Take care of them when they are sick, and give attention both to their remedies and their food, which last ought then to be more nourishing than what they usually subsist upon. It is your interest so to do, both for their preservation, and to attach them more closely to you, for though many Frenchmen say that negroes are ungrateful, I have experienced that it is very easy to render them much attached to you by good treatment, and by doing them justice, as I shall mention afterwards.

If a negro woman lies-in, cause her to be taken care of in everything that her condition makes necessary, and let your wife, if you have one, not disdain to take the immediate care of her herself, or at least to have an eye over her.

A Christian ought to take care that the children be baptised and instructed, since they have an immortal soul. The mother ought then to receive half a ration more than usual, and a quart of milk a day, to assist her to nurse her child.

Prudence requires that your negroes be lodged at a proper distance, to prevent them from being troublesome or offensive; but at the same time near enough for you conveniently observing what passes among them. When I say that they ought not to be placed so near your habitation as to be offensive, I mean by that smell which is natural to some nations of negroes, such as the Congos, the Angolas, the Aradas, and others. On this account it is proper to have in their camp a bathing place formed by thick planks, buried in the earth about a foot or a foot and a half at most, and never more water in it than about that depth, for fear lest the children should drown themselves in it; it ought likewise to have an edge, that the little children may not have access to it, and there ought to be a pond without the camp to supply it with water and keep fish. The negro camp ought to be inclosed all round with palisades, and to have a door to shut with a lock and key. The huts ought to be detached from each other, for fear of fire, and to be built in direct lines, both for the sake of neatness, and in order to know easily the hut of each negro. But that you may be as little incommoded as possible with their natural smell, you must have the precaution to place the negro camp to the north or north-east of your house, as the winds that blow from these quarters are not so warm as the others, and it is only when the negroes are warm that they send forth a disagreeable smell.

The negroes that have the worst smell are those that are the least black; and what I have said of their bad smell, ought to warn you to keep always on the windward side of them when you visit them at their work; never to suffer them to come near your children, who, exclusive of the bad smell, can learn nothing good from them, either as to morals, education, or language.

From what I have said, I conclude that a French father and his wife are great enemies to their posterity when they give their children such nurses. For the milk being the purest blood of the woman, one must be a step-mother indeed to give her child to a negro nurse in such a country as Louisiana, where the mother has all conveniences of being served, of accommodating and carrying their children, who by that means may be always under their eyes. The mother then has nothing else to do but to give the breast to her child.

I have no inclination to employ my pen in censuring the over-delicacy and selfishness of the women, who thus sacrifice their children; it may, without further illustration, be easily perceived how much society is interested in this affair. I shall only say, that for any kind of service whatever about the house, I would advise no other kind of negroes, either young or old, but Senegals, called among themselves Diolauss, because of all the negroes I have known, these have the purest blood; they have more fidelity and a better understanding than the rest, and are consequently fitter for learning a trade, or for menial services. It is true they are not so strong as the others for the labours of the field, and for bearing the great heat.

The Senegals however are the blackest, and I never saw any who had a bad smell. They are very grateful; and when one knows how to attach them to him, they have been found to sacrifice their own life to save that of their master. They are good commanders over other negroes, both on account of their fidelity and gratitude, and because they seem to be born for commanding. As they are high-minded, they may be easily encouraged to learn a trade, or to serve in the house, by the distinction they will thereby acquire over the other negroes, and the neatness of dress which that condition will entitle them to.

When a settler wants to make a fortune, and manage his plantation with economy, he ought to prefer his interest to his pleasure, and only take the last by snatches. He ought to be the first up and the last abed, that he may have an eye over everything that passes in his plantation. It is certainly his interest that his negroes labour a good deal; but it ought to be an equal and moderate labour, for violent and continual labors would soon exhaust and ruin them; whereas keeping them always moderately employed, they neither exhaust their strength nor ruin their constitutions. By this they are kept in good health, and labour longer with more good will; besides, it must be allowed that the day is long enough for an assiduous labourer to deserve the repose of the evening.

To accustom them to labour in this manner I observed the following method: I took care to provide one piece of work for them before another was done, and I informed their commander or driver in their presence, that they might not lose time, some in coming to ask what they were to do, and others in waiting for an answer. Besides I went several times a day to view them, by roads which they did not expect, pretending to be going a hunting or coming from it. If I observed them idle, I reprimanded them, and if when they saw me coming, they wrought too hard, I told them that they fatigued themselves, and that they could not continue at such hard labour during the whole day without being harmed, which I did not want.

When I surprised them singing at their work and perceived that they had discovered me, I said to them cheerfully, "Courage, my boys, I love to see you merry at your work; but do not sing so loud, that you may not fatigue yourselves, and at night you shall have a cup of Taffia (or rum) to give you strength and spirits." One cannot believe the effect such a discourse would have upon their spirits, which was easily discernable from the cheerfulness upon their countenances, and their ardour at work.

If it be necessary not to pass over any essential fault in the negroes, it is no less necessary never to punish them but when they have deserved it, after a serious enquiry and examination supported by an absolute certainty, unless you happen to catch them in the fact. But when you are fully convinced of the crime, by no means pardon them upon any assurances or protestations of theirs, or upon the solicitations of others; but punish them in proportion to the fault they have done, yet always with humanity, that they may themselves be brought to confess that they have deserved the punishment they have received. A Christian is unworthy of that name when he punishes with cruelty, as is done to my knowledge in a certain colony, to such a degree that they entertain their guests with such spectacles, which have more of barbarity than humanity in them. When a negroe comes from being whipped, cause the sore parts to be washed with vinegar mixed with salt, Jamaica pepper, which grows in the gardens, and even a little gunpowder.

As we know from experience that most men of a low extraction, and without education, are subject to thieving in their necessities, it is not at all surprising to see negroes thieve, when they are in want of everything, as I have seen many badly fed, badly clothed, and having nothing to lie upon but the ground. I shall make but one reflection. If they are slaves, it is also true that they are men, and capable of becoming Christians besides, it is your intention to draw advantage from them, is it not therefore reasonable to take all the care of them that you can? We see all those who

understand the government of horses give an extraordinary attention to them, whether they be intended for the saddle or the draught.
In the cold season they are well covered and kept in warm stables.
In the summer they have a cloth thrown over them to keep them
from the dust, and at all times good litter to lie upon. Every morning their dung is carried away, and they are well curried and
combed. If you ask those masters, why they bestow so much pains
upon beasts? they will tell you, that, to make a horse serviceable to
you, you must take a good deal of care of him, and that is for
the interest of the person to whom a horse belongs so to do. After
this example, can one hope for labour from negroes, who very often
are in want of necessities? Can one expect fidelity from a man, who
is denied what he stands most in need of? When one sees a negro,
who labours hard and with much assiduity, it is common to say to
him, by way of encouragement, that they are well pleased with
him, and that he is a good negro. But when any of them, who
understand our language, are so complimented, they very properly
reply, "Masser, when negro be much fed, negro work much; when
negro had good masser, negro be good."

If I advise the planters to take care of their negroes, I at
the same time shew them that their interest is connected in that
with their humanity. But I do no less advise them always to dis-
trust them, without seeming to fear them, because it is as dangerous to shew a concealed enemy that you fear him, as to do him an
injury.

Therefore make it your constant custom to shut your doors
securely, and not to suffer any negro to sleep in the house with
you, and have it in their power to open your door. Visit your
negroes from time to time, at night and on days and hours when
they least expect you, in order to keep them always in fear of being
found absent from their huts. Endeavour to assign each of them
a wife, to keep them clear of debauchery and its bad consequences.
It is necessary that the negroes have wives, and you ought to know
that nothing attaches them so much to a plantation as children.
But above all do not suffer any of them to abandon his wife, when
he had once made choice of one in your presence. Prohibit all fight

ing under pain of the lash, otherwise the women will often raise squabbles among the men.

Do not suffer your negroes to carry their children to the field with them, when they begin to walk, as they only spoil the plants and take off the mothers from their work. If you have a few negro children, it is better to employ an old negro woman to keep them in the camp, with whom the mothers may leave something for their children to eat. This you will find to be the most profitable way. Above all do not suffer the mothers ever to carry them to the edge of the water, where there is too much to be feared.

For the better subsistence of your negroes, you ought every week to give them a small quantity of salt and of herbs of your garden, to a better relish to their *Couscou,* which is a dish made of the meal of rice or maize soaked in broth.

If you have any old negro, or one in weak health, employ him in fishing both for yourself and your negroes. His labour will be well worth his subsistence.

It is moreover for your own interest to give your negroes a small piece of waste ground to improve at the end of your own, and to engage them to cultivate it for their own profit, that they may be able to dress a little better, by selling the produce of it, which you ought to buy from them upon fair and just terms. It were better that they should employ themselves in cultivating that field on Sundays, when they are not Christians, than do worse. In a word, nothing is more to be dreaded than to see the negroes assemble together on Sundays, since, under pretence of Calinda or the dance, they sometimes get together to the number of three or four hundred, and make a kind of Sabbath, which it is always prudent to avoid; for it is in those tumultuous meetings that they sell what they have stolen to one another, and commit many crimes. In these likewise they plot their rebellions.

To conclude, one may, by attention and humanity, easily manage negroes; and, as an inducement, one has the satisfaction to draw great advantage from their labours.

Chapter Seven

POOR BABY!

THE massacre at Fort Rosalie brought terror to the people
of New Orleans and panic to those living on isolated
plantations.

As long as Bienville had been in charge of the colony,
men felt safe enough, for he was adroit in his treaties with
the Indians and managed to keep them quiet; but with
Perier's administration the Indian troubles began in earnest.
We have seen what happened at Fort Rosalie, and with this
carnage the Indians were emboldened.

Finding that the plantations offered rich spoils, they
would descend suddenly, while master and slaves were at
work in distant fields, set fire to the dwelling, and steal what
they could carry. The planter could offer but little resistance,
and the Indians grew even bolder. Groups of them went
from plantation to plantation, killing the white men and taking the women prisoners. The negroes they took away with
them, to sell as slaves.

During the entire administration of Perier there was a
series of cruel and bloody Indian wars. The old records are
full of horrors: a French planter was attacked and scalped;
his wife was seized and carried off into the woods, there to
be used by twenty Indians before she was mutilated and
killed. A German planter returned from New Orleans to find
his house in ashes, his slaves gone, and his wife's nude body,
with both breasts cut off, hanging from a tree, fixed there
by her long flaxen hair.

The French were not less cruel in their reprisals. A
group of soldiers captured four men and two women of the
Natchez nation, and Governor Perier ordered them publicly
burned on the levee at New Orleans.

For this brutality, the Indians sought revenge. It was a
bad time. An Indian approached the palisade at New Orleans carrying a naked white child in his arms—it was
thought that the little girl was one of those children taken
captive at Fort Rosalie; he offered the child to a guard, in
exchange for a blanket. Because the blanket was not forthcoming at once, the Indian dashed out the child's brains
against a tree, threw her body on the ground and made his
escape into the near-by forest.

Perier's soldiers marched against the Indians, captured
a village and brought two hundred captives in chains to New
Orleans. There the Indians were taken aboard French vessels, and sold as slaves in Santo Domingo. In the meantime,
the African leaders on the Guinea coast brought savage captives taken in battle to the seashore, where they were sold
as slaves to the French who brought them to New Orleans
to be auctioned off as laborers to the colonists.

Pirates sailed the waters of the Mexican Gulf. Sometimes a cargo of slaves was stolen before it reached New Orleans. When the Ursuline nuns sailed from France to found a convent in New Orleans, they were attacked by pirates off the Louisiana coast. Looking back upon it, the period seems fabulous. Nuns and pirates, slaves and Indians, fire and bloodshed—it forms a pageant as preposterous as one of those overly romantic operas which New Orleans was to applaud fifty years later.

Perier had been recalled to France and Bienville sent back to govern Louisiana again; but Bienville's hand had lost its cunning with the Indians, and his wars against them did little good. He was hampered by lack of money and men. In the end he returned to France, broken with grief and disappointment. The Marquis de Vaudreuil was appointed to succeed him.

Nor was de Vaudreuil an Indian-fighter. On the contrary, he was a gentleman typical of the French court of that time. He was very rich. He brought his wife to Louisiana with him. A whole shipload of furniture and rich trappings accompanied them. He established a sort of court in New Orleans. There were balls, with court dresses *de rigeur,* where gaily uniformed officers danced with bejeweled women. This was the beginning of fashionable life in the colony. It was during de Vaudreuil's administration that the first play was produced in Louisiana. It was called, ironically enough, "The Indian Father," and was presented in the governor's house in 1753. And as de Vaudreuil's régime produced the first theatrical entertainment, it also produced the first dancing master. His name was Baby.

Baby! It was a strange fate that brought the dancing

master from Paris to New Orleans, and led him to a comic death in the wilderness. Of all the incredible characters of old Louisiana, Baby comes first. He was a Parisian, born and bred, and he followed de Vaudreuil to New Orleans in order to instruct the colonial children in the art of dancing.

And here he was, a canary in a nest of jaybirds, a butterfly in an ant-hill. New Orleans was a rough village, surrounded by a wooden palisade. Within its walls was a motley crew of Frenchmen, Swiss, and Germans; a sprinkling of priests; a group of nuns; a sorry lot of abandoned aristocrats, trailing their bedraggled velvets through the muddy streets; men from jails and prisons of France; a few courtezans, now the industrious and respectable wives of colonists; and many plain bourgeois shopkeepers, wig-makers, laborers, and artisans, and their hard-working wives.

Separate from them, were the officers and their wives, and also the rich planters who had come from France with enough money to invest heavily in land and slaves. These formed the official society, and it was their children that Baby had come to teach.

But pickings were poor for dancing masters, and the children of the rich were few and far between. So Baby did what he could. He taught the rich, but he also taught the poor to dance. He became a dancer in the cafés and cabarets. He rode through the muddy streets on a little mule, with his feet touching the ground, until, as Gayarré the historian says, "it was as though both man and beast were walking together." He was tall and thin and sallow, with twinkling gray eyes. His legs were unusually long and he walked with an airy grace through mud puddles, as though he were

E H Snydam

"OAKLEY," WEST FELICIANA, 1808, WHERE
AUDUBON TAUGHT SCHOOL

ready to dance the minuet. The eccentricities of Baby's mind as well as those of his body made him a well-known figure in the colony. He was called "the Don Quixote of dancing."

Baby's fame spread to the outlying plantations of the German Coast, and the planters offered the dancing master both hospitality and monetary reward, if he would come sometimes to their plantations in order to instruct their children. So Baby sallied forth on his little mule. At first he was timorous, and went only to those plantations nearby, but in time he went further and further afield.

The savages were still giving trouble, in fact at no time since the colony's foundation had the incursions of Indians been more harassing to the planters. The attacks followed close one upon the other.

One day a party of Indians made their appearance at the plantation of a man called Cheval, on the German Coast, seized the guns of a number of Frenchmen and slaves who were working in the fields, and entered the planter's dwelling. The men in the field, finding themselves defenseless, ran for their boats and crossed the Mississippi to safety on the other side. But two white men, called Bouchereau and Rousseau, and two negroes determined to stand their ground and fight until the end. Although there were fifty or more Indians, and only four of them, they opened fire on the Indians, attempting to drive them out of the house. Both Frenchmen were soon killed and the Indians sallied out to scalp them, but the two negroes fought so stoutly for the bodies of their masters that they killed two Indians and drove the rest back into the house. Then a shot from ambush felled one of the slaves and the other was wounded. It was only then that the remaining negro turned to escape. He plunged into the Mississippi and despite the loss of blood from his wounds, managed to swim half-way across before he was picked up by a boat.

The Indians took what they wanted from the house and set it on fire. Then they went on toward the next plantation. The trail led through the wilderness. Well pleased with themselves and with their spoils, the Indians halted among thick trees to prepare for their attack on the neighboring dwelling, which was just ahead.

As they stood there, they heard a strange sound which came nearer and nearer. It was a man's voice singing, and the song was a gay *chanson* of far-away Paris. It was Baby, the dancing master, riding to the plantation to give a lesson. On he came through the checkered shade, toward the spot where the savages lay hidden.

From the thicket the Indians peered out, surprised by what they saw. Baby was dressed in his best, a suit of shiny green cloth, of fashionable cut. He wore an immense gray beaver hat, and held himself as majestically as though he were ready to bow. He was riding upon his diminutive mule, and his long legs almost touched the ground. He wore long, sharp spurs of glittering Spanish silver and carried an enormous red umbrella, open to protect himself and his mule from the sun.

The Indians, after their first surprise, ran out, with deafening whoops, determined to kill the man and steal the mule. The undertaking appeared easy.

But here they were mistaken. Baby had no weapon but a hunting knife, and it is doubtful that he had ever struck a blow before. But now, confronted by the Indians, he put up a valiant fight. His thin arm brandished the knife with astonishing rapidity, and his long legs, firm and muscled with years of ballet dancing, kicked right and left. The thorn-like spurs tore the flesh of the Indians nearest him, as he kicked at their most vulnerable parts. His voice rose to a falsetto shriek as he kicked with all his might, and the cries of the Indians became yells of pain. They took to their heels.

Baby had been wounded, but his legs were still of service to him. He ran like the wind. Ahead of him lay the house where he had intended to give a lesson, and he bounded toward it. The Indians, recovering themselves, took after him, but he managed to reach the door.

The cottage belonged to a young man named Guillaume, and he had with him ten or twelve little girls and boys—both white and black—whom he had assembled that Baby might teach them to dance. These children, and young Guillaume, had been forgotten when the rest of the population took to their boats; and as the house was remote, they had known nothing of the attack by the Indians. But now, with blood-smeared Baby on the doorstep, they realized that they were fighting for their lives. Guillaume dragged the dancing master inside and barred the door. The cabin was stoutly built and the windows were closed by heavy batten blinds. Although Guillaume and Baby had but one gun between them and little ammunition, they defended themselves so well, and killed so many of the Indians, that the savages retreated into the wilderness, carrying their dead with them.

But Baby had received his death wound. All night long the young man and the children ministered to him, and early the next day a wagon was procured, and he was taken back to New Orleans. He died before sunset, laughing in his delirium because he thought himself back in his beloved Paris. It is said that every child in New Orleans attended his funeral.

Chapter Eight

TEMBA MURDERS HIS MASTER

HERE is the story of Temba the hunter, a slave who murdered his master. It is taken from a group of antique Spanish documents belonging to the Louisiana Historical Society. These worm-eaten papers are bound together and labeled "The Criminal proceedings officially brought to find the agressor who killed Juan Baptiste Cezaire Lebreton, on the night of May 31, 1771, by the discharge of a gun, together with the prosecution of the accomplices in the assassination."

The record is doubly interesting, because it gives an idea of primitive plantation life in the latter half of the eighteenth century; and because it establishes, under the signature of the judge and the prosecuting officers, that torture was used to extract confession from two negro slaves who had fallen under suspicion. At the time of this trial, Louisiana was a colony of Spain.

The first record is written on June 1, 1771, the day after the murder. It is signed by Governor Unzaga in New Orleans. It states that Jean Baptiste Lebreton was killed at midnight by his own slaves. "A part of his house took fire, and said Lebreton, going out on the gallery of the house to put it out, was fired on by a musket by which he was killed." Governor Unzaga orders that two physicians, Jean Ruby and Francisco Lebeau, go to the plantation and examine the body in order to determine the cause of Lebreton's death. Jacinto Panis and Dionisio Braud are notified to go and make an examination of the premises and report what they find.

The next papers in the file are the reports of the doctors, who certify that they went to the Lebreton plantation, situated two leagues from the city on the right and upper side of the river. They arrived at nine o'clock in the morning and found Lebreton lying on his face on the south side of the gallery of his house, bathed in blood. His shirt was pierced with ball and bird-shot. From the wounds the doctors conclude that the man died instantly. They removed some of the bird-shot from the wounds as evidence. They sign their names to the report.

Many witnesses are called, and on the same day we have the testimony of Alexandro de Clouet, a neighboring planter. He swears that at midnight he was aroused by Congo, the negro coachman of Mr. Lebreton, who told him that his master's house was on fire and that Lebreton would be burned up in it. The witness rose to the rescue and found that only an outbuilding was burning. This building was apart from the house and the dwelling escaped destruction. Mr. de Clouet testifies that he found the body of Lebreton lying on the gallery, clad only in a shirt. The witness, declaring that he believed the murderer or murderers to be among Lebreton's slaves, took count of the negroes and found four missing. The missing negroes were Malet, Dédé, Temba, and Juan Augustin. The other negroes had assisted in putting out the fire, and were all present when the witness arrived. The four missing negroes bear a bad reputation, he states, and thereby ends his testimony.

Luis de Launay testifies next. His statement is much the same as that of the man who has testified before. He adds that he had a conversation with the overseer, who told him that three or four bad negroes were missing at the time of the fire and the murder. Some time later the missing negroes returned, saying that they had accompanied some negresses to the plantation of Mr. Wiltz. The overseer had told de Launay that the negro Temba, employed as a hunter of game for Lebreton, had been scolded only an hour before the fire, because he very often went away from the plantation to sleep.

Lorenzo Wiltz is called. His testimony repeats what de Launay has said, but he adds that the negro Temba has a bad reputation and, because of his occupation as hunter, he always carries a gun. Wiltz testifies that he ordered the negroes to bring their guns to him. He examined them and found that one was freshly loaded with bird shot. He cannot say whose gun it is, as the guns had been piled up in a heap before him.

The negroes are now called, beginning with Pedro, the negro overseer. He testifies that he was called to the fire, and that when he arrived he saw his master on the upper gallery of the house shouting to the slaves to save the chickens and to put water on the kitchen and hen-house. The witness, as overseer, was directing the slaves in their work of putting out the fire when he heard a shot. He asked who had fired, and the negroes with him said that it was probably Mr. Lebreton summoning negroes from distant cabins. But a moment later a negress called Juana, one of the house servants, began screaming. The negroes rushed to the house and found their master dead, lying in a pool of blood. The overseer did not wish to touch the body, so he called the neighbors—white men. These gentlemen arrived and assembled the negroes to question them. Four slaves were missing. The overseer names them. Temba has been scolded only an hour before the fire, for going to sleep at the cabin of a negress on an adjoining plantation. Despite the scolding, Temba had gone away as soon as Mr. Lebreton retired. Temba returned after the white men had arrived at the plantation. He carried his gun with him; it was put in the pile of guns on the gallery. This ends Pedro's testimony. He signs with a cross, as he cannot write.

Juana is called next. She is Mr. Lebreton's house slave. She testifies that she was on the lower gallery when she heard a shot fired and the sound of some one running away. She was frightened, but ran upstairs and called her master. He was lying dead. She called the others. She testifies, as the others have done, that earlier in the evening her master had scolded Temba because he was sleeping away from the plantation. Temba, she says, fell on his knees and asked his master's pardon, which was granted by Mr. Lebreton who said, "For this time only, and that he must be careful for another time or he would pay for all." Temba was not at the fire but came an hour later with Mr. de Launay. She does not sign as she cannot write. The officials sign for her and she makes a cross.

Now Temba the hunter is called. He does not speak Spanish and testifies through an interpreter. He testifies that Pedro, Mrs. de Villemont's slave, awakened him at one of the cabins on Mr. Robert's plantation, where he was sleeping, and told him that his master's house was on fire and that Mr. Lebreton had been killed. It seemed to him impossible, as he had left home only a short time before. He took his gun and ran back to the plantation. He went upon the upper gallery where Mr. de Launay questioned him. Temba is then asked why his master scolded him. He testifies that it was because he had slept in the woods for two nights. Mr. Lebreton had told him to call the overseer to whip him, but that he, Temba, had begged for pardon, and that his master had relented. Temba is now reminded that he had promised his master not to leave the plantation at night, or to sleep elsewhere. Temba says that Mr. Lebreton had only forbidden him to sleep in the woods.

Temba is asked why he carried his gun at midnight, when he came back to the plantation, and he replied that he had taken it with him when he went away, in order to have it for use early in the morning when he intended to kill some birds for his master. It was his business to hunt game for his master's table, he said. He was asked at whose house he was sleeping, and he said at the house of Marianne, a slave of Mr. Robert's. Asked again why he had carried his gun to Marianne's cabin, he said that it was because he was afraid to leave it behind for fear that it would be stolen. He was asked when he had last loaded his gun, and replied that he had loaded it the morning before the murder, shortly after he had killed two rabbits. No one saw him load it; he was alone in the woods. This ends his testimony. He signs with a cross as he cannot write.

The slaves are questioned over and over, Juana, Pedro, Dédé, Marianne, and Mirliton. Bits of suspicious evidence are brought out. Antonio, a blacksmith, testifies that he suspects Temba because Mr. Lebreton's dog "Brava" was on the gallery and did not bark, and that Brava was familiar with Temba, often following him about. He barked if the other negroes came near the house.

Another investigation is made at the Lebreton plantation. Temba's game-bag is examined. It is made of crude linen and divided into two divisions; one side is intended for game, the other for shot and powder. The bird shot found in the bag is identical with that taken from the wounds of Lebreton. However, other slaves have similar ammunition in their game-bags.

The negroes are questioned again, as to their ages, occupations, and of their previous experiences. The reason for this is not quite clear, and scores of pages produce nothing new. Temba says he is forty years old, a hunter and a bachelor. Pedro says that he is also forty years of age, and a hunter and a bachelor. Marianne says she is unmarried and works in the field. Mirliton says that his real name is Francisco, and that Mirliton (reed-pipe) is a nickname; he is forty-five, married, and a blacksmith. And so on.

On June 7, Governor Unzaga finds himself unsatisfied with the evidence and orders that Temba be brought to the Calabozo and tortured until he confesses. Unzaga signifies his intention of seeing the torture himself, and of asking questions at that time. On June 9, an order is issued that

Marianne's cabin be searched. This is done the same day, and in a trunk or box is found a small amount of ammunition and a powder-flask, said to belong to Temba. In another box are Marianne's clothes, "both white and colored, all soiled." Among them was a piece of white handkerchief freshly torn. This cloth is compared with the wads found on the gallery of the Lebreton plantation-house the morning after the murder. Both handkerchief and wads are similarly stained with rust.

Temba is taken from his cell and led to the torture chamber. The Spanish officials gather around him as he is stretched on the rack. Before the torture begins, Temba's statement is read to him and he is asked to speak. He says that he has told all that he knows. The question is put to him three times, but Temba does not change his story.

The torture begins. The wheel turns slowly and the ropes creak as they draw tight. The negro slave grits his teeth to keep from crying out. His bones crack, his joints are dislocated. He moans. Unzaga questions him again. Temba screams "Jesus! Jesus!" and again, "There is Jesus!"

Then he begs for the torturer to stop turning the wheel, crying out that it was Mirliton who killed his master. It was Mirliton who set fire to the shed. "He fired his gun at the same time I did." And he cries again, "Jesus! Jesus!"

This brings something new into the case. Only one shot was heard but Lebreton was riddled with a charge of bird shot unusually large. Temba's confession explains this: two shots were fired simultaneously.

Temba, still stretched on the rack, is asked what motive they had for killing their master, and he replies that it was

because his master was bad and would not give them time off
to go and see their women. He is questioned as to the hour
that he went to Marianne's, and says that it was directly
after the murder: "The star was very high, it was after half
past eleven." He is asked who gave him the wads for his
gun, and replies that he loaded it himself. He got the ammunition and powder himself. He is asked where he has put
the rest of the rag used in wadding his gun, and he replies,
"at Marianne's." He took it without her knowledge. The
torn handkerchief is shown to him, and he identifies it. He
is asked where he stood when he fired and he replies that he
stood in the garden while Mirliton stood on the steps. He
is asked who set fire to the shed, and he replies that Mirliton
brought red hot embers from his cabin. Unzaga holds up
his hand in signal to the torturer; the rack is released and
Temba sags to the floor. All present sign the statement
which has been written down as Temba speaks.

At this moment news is brought to the torture chamber
that Mirliton has hanged himself with his girdle from the
bars of his cell. It is evident that he heard the cries of
Temba under torture. The officials rush to the other part of
the prison and have the negro cut down. He revives and is
dragged immediately to the torture room. Temba's confession is read to him, and he denies everything. He is asked,
then, why he attempted to kill himself. He replies that he
did not intend to do so, that he was playing with his girdle.

The document is so worm-eaten at this point that it is
difficult to decipher the rest of it, but the next paper refers
to the "confrontation" of Mirliton by Temba; it is also
indecipherable. The next document is Unzaga's order to
put Mirliton on the rack.

Mirliton is fastened to the machine, and his bonds are drawn tight. Three times he is asked to confess, and three times he denies the murder; he says that he has told the truth in answer to the first questions put to him. The torture begins. He screams for mercy and cries out that he fired the shot which killed his master, but that Temba forced him to do so. It was Temba, he declares, who forced him to bring red-hot coals from his cabin fire and place them on the roof of the kitchen and of the hen-house.

At the end the officials have wrung confessions of guilt from both negroes. The following document is the argument in defense of the criminals, which is so badly mutilated that it cannot be deciphered except for a word here and there. It is evident that it asks for a definite sentence, for the next paper is the final judgment.

Unzaga condemns the negroes Mirliton and Temba to death by strangulation. They are to be brought out from the prison and dragged through the streets from the tail of a packhorse; each is to have an "esparto grass halter" around his neck, feet, and hands. The town crier is to go before announcing the crime that the slaves have committed. They must be dragged through "the accustomed streets" to the gallows where they will be hanged until dead. At the foot of the gallows, Temba's hands and feet are to be cut off; after his death, his body must remain hanging from the gibbet; his hands and feet are to be nailed on posts upon the public road until they are "consumed by the birds and elements." No one is to take down the bodies under pain of death.

Pedro is to receive two hundred and Marianne one hundred lashes at the foot of the gallows (while Temba and

Mirliton are hanging there), and their ears are to be cut off close. Carlos is to be tarred and feathered and exposed in the streets on the back of a pack beast. The sentence is signed by Unzaga and Cecilio Odoardo. This punishment is given because the slaves are thought to have held back evidence.

On June 20, Andres Almonester certifies that the executioner has carried out the orders of the sentence upon all of the criminals with the exception of Pedro. Temba and Mirliton are dead, Marianne has been lashed and her ears have been cut off; Carlos has been tarred and feathered and exposed upon a pack-mule. Pedro is very ill in prison; there are physicians' certificates to this end, and there is a plea by his owner, Madame de Villemont, that, as the slave belongs to her and is valuable, she be allowed to take him from the prison and nurse him back to health before he is lashed. She states in her plea that to carry out the punishment at this time would mean his death. The last paper in the collection is official permission granted Madame de Villemont to take her slave Pedro from the jail, but the document states that she must return him to the authorities "when convalescent" in order that his ears may be cut off and that he may receive two hundred lashes.

The murder was committed on May 31. Twenty days later, the slaves had been tried, condemned, and executed.

Chapter Nine

CHANGING FORTUNES

IN 1762, by secret treaty, the King of France presented the colony of Louisiana to Spain. Rather a magnificent gesture it appears to-day, for he handed over nearly half of the continent of North America as though it had been a flower. The next year Spain, in turn, ceded Florida to Great Britain —later called West Florida— with the fort of St. Augustine and the bay of Pensacola and all the country east and southeast of the Mississippi. Kelerec, governor of Louisiana, was recalled to France, and the news was announced in New Orleans in October 1764 that Louisiana had passed from the hands of Louis XV into the hands of Charles III of Spain. Alcée Fortier, the historian, says that "the news threw the colony into consternation and despair," and one may well believe it.

Spain was slow to take possession, and revolution was

plotted in New Orleans. Men from the plantations came to New Orleans to help organize a fighting force; but when O'Reilly of Spain arrived in 1769 with three thousand Spanish troops, the colonists saw that their struggle was useless. O'Reilly took charge, executed the ringleaders in the revolt, ruled for a year and departed after turning the colony over to Don Luis de Unzaga. In the last chapter we discussed a criminal trial in Unzaga's administration, and learned something of Spanish justice. The people of Louisiana soon adapted themselves to Spanish rule, and when Don Bernardo de Galvez became governor in 1777, he became a popular figure. He led the Spanish forces against Baton Rouge, which was a part of West Florida, and captured the fort there for Spain. He then led an army against Pensacola, captured it and drove out the British.

A group of Canary Islanders—*Islenos* they were called —followed Galvez to New Orleans, and settled in the marshland near the town. They were fishermen, hunters, and trappers. Their descendants remain to-day in Saint Bernard Parish, adjacent to New Orleans, in a country which is still called the richest fur-trapping region in the world.

In 1765, the first shiploads of Acadians, exiled by the British from their homes in Nova Scotia, arrived at the New Orleans levee. These were a simple farming people of French origin. They remained in New Orleans for a time but soon moved on, going westward along the bayous. Many of them settled in what was known as the Attakapas country—called for the Attakapas Indian tribe, a nation of man-eaters. Others settled along Bayou Lafourche. In 1785 more Acadians joined them. They were a prolific peasant stock,

GRANDEUR, ON BAYOU ST. JOHN, ABOUT 1810

and their families grew with rapidity. Their descendants to-day number approximately one hundred thousand. The term Acadian, or the familiar corruption "Cajun," is used to identify the descendants of these wanderers. They have been made romantic to American readers through Longfellow's poem "Evangeline." Longfellow never visited Louisiana, but wrote his poem from descriptions of the country furnished him by others.

But we Louisianians have a distressing habit of meddling with romance; we are never content to let history remain history, and fiction remain fiction. There was the strange case of "Manon Lescaut," for example—a purely fictitious lady of a French romance. But the writer saw fit to let his heroine die in "the desert of Louisiana." In consequence the lady has sneaked into history. (The driver of a sight-seeing bus in New Orleans once pointed out her grave to me.) So it is that in southwest Louisiana, Evangeline has emerged into a creature of flesh and blood. Let me quote from "A History of the Acadian Country."

Evangeline's real name was Emmeline Labiche. She sought her lover Gabriel for years through the sun-kissed bayous of the Louisiana Eden, so aptly described in the poetic masterpiece of the immortal Longfellow. At last she found him at a country ball where the youth and beauty [etc.] . . . When the loyal girl saw Gabriel (Louis Arceneaux in real life), she sprang toward him. But alas! No love-light answered in his eyes. He staggered back, then told her that, weary with waiting, he had given his promise to another! . . . Gabriel settled near St. Martinsville with his new love and many of his descendants are living there to this day. Evangeline lost her reason and died. Her ashes rest in the little graveyard at the back of the old church.

You may accept this as history or romance, as you see fit. At any event, the name Evangeline is enshrined in the hearts of those who dwell beside the Teche. Lately they have paid tribute to her memory by naming a popular brand of tabasco sauce in her honor.

The Acadians were thrifty farmers. The Teche country is the most tropical part of Louisiana and the roads offer vistas of ever-changing beauty. In another chapter I shall tell something of the old plantation-houses there.

In 1788 New Orleans was destroyed by fire. The French town of wooden houses went down before the flames, and from the ashes rose a stately Spanish city. The old section of New Orleans is that city which came into being at the end of the eighteenth century.

In 1792 a blight appeared on the indigo. It was caused by a worm which multiplied rapidly. In the next three years there were many crop failures. Planters were reduced to poverty, losing all they had gained in successive failures. In 1795 Étienne de Boré planted all of his acres in sugar-cane, and, in the face of dire predictions, attempted to granulate sugar. His experiment was a success, and he realized twelve thousand dollars from his sugar crop. Immediately the Louisiana planter abandoned indigo and put his land in sugar-cane.

A time of prosperity was at hand. Spanish rule had become popular in the colony. The Creole planters near New Orleans began to build finer houses for themselves. This was the Golden Age of Spanish society. In 1798 the Duke of Orleans visited Louisiana. He was accompanied by his brother, the Duke of Montpensier, and the Count of Beaujolais. They were exiles, and no one could have predicted that the Duke of Orleans would become King Louis Philippe in 1830. Grace King, in her "Creole Families of New Orleans," remarks:

The lavish hospitality displayed during this entertainment of Royalty, the splendid banquets and balls to which all the aristocracy of New Orleans was invited, the utter disregard of money expenditure, must have astonished the young Princes, so short of money themselves, even more than it did the simple-minded citizens of that time.

The banquets offered by the Spanish Governor are never mentioned in comparison with those of the splendid Philippe de Marigny—not only in New Orleans but in Fontainebleau, where he also entertained his guests. [Fontainebleau was his country residence across Lake Pontchartrain.]

When the Princes took their leave, they were escorted to Balize at the mouth of the Mississippi by numerous friends and by their host, who added to his other royal generosities the loan of a royal sum of money. . . .

And it may be added that Marigny never got his money back. Years later, the French king entertained him in Paris, but he never mentioned the loan; and Marigny, being a Creole gentleman of the old school, would have died before asking for it, although times were harder for him then, and it is possible that he needed the money nearly as much as the young prince had needed it when it was loaned to him.

It may be interesting to note some of the leading Creole families in New Orleans at the end of the eighteenth century. According to Miss King's book, they were: Marigny de Mandeville, Dreaux, de Pontalba, Rouer de Villeray, D'Arensbourg, De la Chaise, Lafreniere, Labedoyere Huchet de Kernion, De Livaudais, Soniat du Fossat, De la

Vergne, De Boré, Gayarre, Bouligny, Almonaster, De la
Ronde, Chalmette, Cruzat, Jumonville de Villiers, Labillebeuvre, Grima, Forstall, Macarty, De Buys, Canonge,
Charest de Lauzon, Brignier, Tureaud, Garrigues de Flaugeac, de Roaldes, Pitot, Roffignac, St. Geme, Allain, Beauregard, Fortier. There were many others, of course, but these
are significant names of the period. Nearly all of them
owned plantations.

In 1800, by treaty of San Ildefonso, Louisiana passed
back into the hands of France, and Napoleon promptly sold
the province to the United States. Napoleon had two good
reasons for selling it: first, he was aware that if he attempted to retain Louisiana, it would be wrested from him
by either the United States or England, and second, because
he needed $15,000,000 badly to aid him and his allies. The
United States thus came into possession of 900,000 square
miles of territory or about 80,000 square miles more than
the domain of the original thirteen states. That is to say,
the acquisition of the territory of Louisiana more than
doubled the national area. Of course, the present state of
Louisiana formed only a small part of this territory. It extended from the Gulf of Mexico north to the Canadian line,
the Mississippi River being the eastern boundary, while it
stretched westward along the gulf and northwest over an
area vaguely described but not definitely bounded until the
Spanish Treaty of 1819. The territory included the present
states of Louisiana (excepting that part east of the Mississippi, which was acquired from Spain in the Florida Purchase of 1819), Arkansas, Missouri, Iowa, Minnesota,
Kansas, Nebraska, South and North Dakota, and parts of
Oklahoma, Colorado, Wyoming, and Montana. Later, the

inclusion of Oregon (the present States of Oregon, Washington, and Idaho and a small part of Montana) also ceded by the Florida Treaty of 1819, and the annexations of 1848, as a result of the Mexican War, completed the national territory to the west and southwest, and removed Louisiana from a frontier to a central position.

With the Louisiana Purchase came the "American invasion" of Louisiana.

Chapter Ten

AMERICANS IN CREOLE LOUISIANA

AMONG the old diaries and letters examined in preparation for this book, I read a long record of the Nicholls family. Toward the end of the memoir there is a picture of Louisiana in 1805 as a seventeen-year-old boy saw it. It deals with a voyage from Baltimore to New Orleans, and a journey through the bayous and lakes to the Attakapas country.

The memoir was written in 1840 by Judge Thomas C. Nicholls, son of Edward Church Nicholls, first Civil Commandant and United States Judge of the County of Attakapas in Louisiana. Judge Thomas C. Nicholls married, in June 1814, Louisa H. Drake, the eldest sister of Joseph Rodman Drake. He fought in the battle of New Orleans in 1815, and later was appointed Chief Justice or Presiding Officer of the Court of Errors and Appeals; and on the formation of a Supreme Court which absorbed the duties of the other court, he was offered the position of Chief Justice, but was unable to accept it on account of the condition of his health. Three of his sons became judges, and one of them, Francis T. Nicholls, was Chief Justice of the Louisiana Supreme Court for many years; and two of his grandsons have been judges. This seems rather a remarkable record for a judicial family, but as a fighting family it is even more striking. The three sons of Edward Church Nicholls all served in the war of 1812-1815. In the Mexican War the two eldest sons of Thomas C. Nicholls were heroes at Monterey. Another brother served on the border but was invalided home. In the Civil War only two members of the family were of an age to bear arms, but one was killed at Gaines Mills, or First Cold Harbor, and the other lost an arm and a leg.

The Nicholls family is connected in many ways with the history of Louisiana, and consequently this old memoir, never before published, seems of peculiar importance. Only part of it is used, the record of the family's journey to Louisiana and of the life they lived in the Attakapas country.

I am indebted to Mr. Thomas C. Nicholls of New Orleans, the grandson of the writer of the memoir, for permission to use it here.

Upon the election of Mr. Jefferson to the Presidency, my father, who had been one of his staunchest supporters, removed with the family to the city of Washington, with the expectation of receiving some appointment at his hands. Here he continued to reside, in the practice of his profession, until he received intelligence from England that he had inherited an handsome property in Cornwall. This required his personal attendance in England. Preparations were made for the voyage, and our domestic life was consequently broken up at Washington. My mother and family removed to Prince

George's County among her relatives and friends. My father remained in England until he could dispose of the property which he had inherited. . . . Being a gay man, fond of society and having the means of gratifying his tastes, he entered into all the gaities and expenses of a London life. . . . The threatened invasion of Bonaparte into England increased the difficulty of advantageously disposing of his lands. . . . When they were sold at last, my father dispatched a portion of the proceeds to his family in America aboard the ship *Farmer,* but he lingered for a while longer in London. The ship was lost at sea, the bags of gold went to the bottom of the ocean, and the family never reaped the slightest advantage from the inheritance. . . .

My father remained in England until the acquisition of Louisiana by the American government, but this event opened up a bright prospect for him. He hoped to build up his dilapidated fortune and place his family in a state of competence, if not affluence. His intimate acquaintance with the French language and manner appeared to him as peculiarly calculated to success in the city of New Orleans, where he, shortly after possession had been taken by the American government, arrived buoyed up with the prospect of a brilliant future before him. In this anticipation he was not disappointed. Immediately upon his arrival, his golden dreams were more than realized. New Orleans was exactly the theater where' he was calculated to shine. Speaking French with the fluency of a native, and, like the Creoles, fond of pleasure, failure was impossible.

Success flowed in from every side, followed by the most extravagant and enormous fees. The extent of these fees may be imagined from the fact that, notwithstanding his expensive habits and total negligence of pecuniary matters, he was enabled to transmit eight thousand dollars to his family in Maryland during the first year of his stay in New Orleans. He became an especial favorite with the late Governor Claiborne, from whom he received the appointment of Clerk of the Governor's Court, a most lucrative appointment. This position he held until he relinquished it for that of Civil Commandant of the County of Attakapas. He removed to that county following his appointment. This stroke of fortune was all that a prudent man could have desired, as the emoluments were great and the situation was one of the most respectable in the state, at that time, before the territorial government was permanently organized. A Civil Commandant embodied all the law and equity jurisdiction within the limits of his county. In fact, his word was law. Accustomed, as were the inhabitants in Spanish times, to look up to the Commandant as the representative of majesty, the respect and humble submission manifested toward my father could scarcely be believed in the present day.

Finding himself thus comfortably situated, he wrote to his family to join him, informing us that he had permanently settled in Louisiana. Preparations were accordingly made to comply with his wishes, by reassembling the scattered family. My brother, Robert, was at that time a clerk in the Treasury Department of the United States at Washington, which situation he necessarily resigned. I was recalled from Charlotte Hall where I had constantly remained prosecuting my studies, and active arrangements were made to rejoin my father as soon as possible. The family was collected together at Washington City, whence we took our departure in two hired hacks for Baltimore, in a cold and snowing day of December 1804. Our passage to New Orleans had been previously engaged aboard the ship *Comet* commanded by Captain Robert Hart.

After a disagreeable and painful journey, suffering from the intensity of a snow storm which lasted the whole of the day, we arrived at Picks Hotel on Fells Point, late in the evening and nearly frozen. We were ushered into a cheerless room with an unlighted grate, and it required hours before the fire made the room comfortable. To this place we had been recommended in consequence to its proximity to the ship, which was advertised to sail the following day. Here we remained huddled together in no enviable state of mind, in a strange city, without friend or acquaintance, and ignorant of the ways of the world. It was our first night away from home and we were in a dreary state of weather, separated for the first time from friends and relatives; and we were

going we knew not whither, to join my father in an unknown
land. Our feelings can only be appreciated by those similarly situated. Not one of the family had ever been twenty miles from home
before, except myself, then a child; and we were little calculated
to undertake a voyage of this length and under such circumstances.
Yet here we were, and retreat was out of the question.

Everything conspired to make us melancholy and despondent.
On the following day the storm continued to rage with unabating
fury, but we embarked aboard the *Comet* and bid farewell to Baltimore under the same auspices that we had entered it.

After a boisterous passage of thirty days, we cast anchor
opposite New Orleans. At that time it scarcely deserved the name
of a city. To us everything was strange and astonishing, the country, the town, the people. Coming from a cold climate, it was a
matter of mirth and wonder to observe the Creole population wrapped up in their blanket coats, and suffering apparently more in-
tensely, during what we considered a bland and genial spring morning, than we had suffered during the Baltimore snow storm.

The appearance of the city was unprepossessing. Upon the lift-
ing of the fog, which for some time had veiled the city from our
longing eyes, a cluster of irregular, clumsy wooden houses presented itself to our view. Within our range of vision, not one soli-
tary decent looking building relieved the prospect. The levee was
covered with filth, for the refuse of the city was then deposited
there. It was a revolting spectacle and our hearts sank at the
sight.

The visit of Mr. Garland, a friend of my father's, quieted
our alarms and dissuaded our apprehensions. He repaired on board
the *Comet* as soon as she was moored (he being a Naval Officer),
and reported that we had been consigned to his charge. We were
then conducted into the city, carried to his house, and introduced
to his Creole family, consisting of his wife and one little daughter.
Mrs. Garland's aged mother was there, also, and a beautiful Creole
niece, Miss Euphemie Harang. (She afterward married William
Brown, then collector of the Port of New Orleans.)

Our reception was kind and affectionate in the extreme, still our situation was irksome and annoying; not one of us spoke one word of French, and Mr. Garland's family was equally ignorant of English. Our only intercourse was through the medium of signs, occasioning numberless misunderstandings and amusing mistakes. The house was situated on Custom House Street, and as it was small, my brother and myself were placed at a tavern kept by Madame Chabet. It was a wretched wooden tenement at the corner of Chartres and Conti Streets. At that time I do not believe that there was a single pane of glass in the whole city, nor one tolerable building (the Principal excepted). An ordinary brick building, erected by Sam P. Moore, was called "Moore's Folly," and was considered a curiosity. Pavements there were none, the only substitute for them being the gunnels of Kentucky flatboats placed eight or ten feet from the houses, the intermediate spaces being filled with mud and water, diversified occasionally with the carcass of a dead dog, cat, or rat. The novelty and singularity of everything we saw or heard was a cause for unceasing wonder and astonishment. . . .

[Note: It is evident that the writer of this memoir allowed his disappointment in New Orleans to color his narrative, or perhaps he did not see the finer houses of the city. This is not as remarkable at it appears to be, as most of the houses were built in the Spanish manner and presented an austere façade on the street side and centered around a patio or courtyard. He is mistaken with regard to brick buildings, for a brick-yard flourished in 1790, and many brick dwellings were erected directly after the fire of 1788. The old Ursuline convent had been standing seventy years when this young man visited New Orleans, and it remains to-day one of the finest structures in the old section of the city. The "Principal" to which he refers is the Cabildo, which still stands facing Jackson Square. He does not mention the church which stood next door.—L. S.]

During our sojourn in the city we attended one of the grand balls. This afforded us an opportunity of seeing the fashion and beauty of the country. The day was raining and disagreeable, and the ball room was situated at the farther extremity of the city.

How the ladies were to reach the ball room we could not divine, as hacks and public vehicles were then unknown. But the means proved more simple and easy than we, in our ignorance, could have conceived them to be.

I here witnessed a singular ceremony. After the ladies were dressed for the ball—and most finely attired they were—servants were dispatched in different directions to collect their male acquaintances. Each lady then stood in the middle of the floor, surrounded by a ring of lighted candles. Here she underwent the minutest inspection by the assembled gentlemen. Every article of her dress, every fold and ribbon, was critically examined and passed upon. She was whirled around and around until proper judgment should be formed and pronounced. Then she was permitted to retire, to ponder upon, to reject or adopt the various hints or suggestions as might suit her caprice. I was particularly struck with the majestic and splendid appearance of the blue-eyed Spanish brunette who constituted part of our company; she was attired in a court costume and wore magnificent emeralds.

Everything prepared, the order was given to march; when, to my horror and amazement, the young ladies doffed their shoes and stockings, which were carefully tied up in silk handkerchiefs, and took up the line of march, barefooted, for the ball room. After paddling through mud and mire, lighted by lanterns carried by the negro slaves, we reached the scene of action without accident. The young ladies halted before the door and shook one foot after another in a pool of water close by. After repeating this process some half a dozen times, the feet were freed of the accumulated mud and were in a proper state to be wiped dry by the slaves who had carried towels for the purpose. Then silk stockings and satin slippers were put on again, cloaks were thrown aside, tucked-up trains were let down, and the ladies entered the ball room, dry-shod and lovely in the candlelight.

With regard to the habits and customs of the country and its general aspect, everything seemed to us the reverse of what we had ever known or seen. Water, instead of running into the river, ran away from it; and the river itself with its volume of water seemed overtopping the town, threatening destruction to man and beast, life and death hanging in suspence, dependent upon the frail consistency of the mud embankment (the levee), always liable to accident and always exposed to the destructive action of the rains for which the State is celebrated. The people themselves differed in complection, costume, manners and language, from anything we had ever seen. The eternal jabbering of French in the street was a sealed book to us. Drums beat occasionally at the corners of the streets, suspended for a moment to allow the worthy little drummer to inform the public that on such and such a night there would be a Grand Ball at the *Salle de Conde,* or make announcement of a ball of another sort, for colored ladies and white gentlemen. Such were our visions of New Orleans in 1805.

My mother was waited upon by Governor Claiborne and most of the respectable gentlemen and ladies of the city, of American origin; and many of the Creole friends of my father paid her most marked attention during her short stay.

After remaining a few days in the city, it was necessary to decide upon the most proper and eligible mode of conveyance to Attakapas. To embark on keel-boats, the only water craft then used, was out of the question after a thirty-days' confinement on ship-board. None of us could tolerate the prospect of submitting to imprisonment for another twenty or thirty days, exposed to all the annoyances and privations to be expected in such an expedition. To proceed by land was the only alternative. No public hacks were available, but Mr. Garland finally succeeded in engaging a white man to conduct us to Plaquemine, a distance of a hundred miles, in a miserable contrivance drawn by two skeletons for horses. For this accommodation, for which we paid more than the whole would have sold for, we were indebted to the untiring efforts of Mr. Garland; and under these prospects we commenced our journey to the Attakapas.

With such a team as I have described, in winter season, and through a road deep in mud and water, beside the Mississippi, the rapidity of our movements can easily be imagined. Before twelve o'clock each day our steeds were completely tired out and we were compelled to proceed at a snail's pace. No whipping or thumping could quicken the pace of the horses, and at last we were forced to abandon all efforts to advance through sheer exhaustion, after each of us had taken his place on the driver's seat in order to relieve the jaded charioteer.

After a fatiguing journey of five days, we arrived at the mouth of Bayou Plaquemine. Here more obstacles and difficulties presented themselves. In those days it was considered a serious and dangerous enterprise to cross over the lakes and bayous lying between the river and the Attakapas. Regular conveyances there were none. We were told, however, that an Irishman named Blake lived three or four miles down the bayou and could be prevailed upon to cross travelers over, provided that he was paid ten times more than it was worth. We were constrained therefore, to make application to him, and after much solicitation he was engaged to convey us across for seventy-five dollars. We furnished our own provisions. Arrangements perfected, we proceeded in ox-carts to Blake's landing where we found everything ready for our departure. It was understood that we were to camp out for two nights, so our preparations were made accordingly. To our surprise and alarm we found, on the first night, that Blake had provided his men with no provisions, and our scanty store must be divided. Our provisions were produced, and everyone partook. In the night the men were whooping and hallooing like Choctaw Indians. My mother and sister were much alarmed and did not sleep at all. In the morning we discovered that during the night some kind friend had made love to our provisions. This afforded us the agreeable prospect of starving for the balance of the route. However, we were obliged to make the best of a bad bargain, and we proceeded on our journey.

At length, after a fatiguing and protracted trip, we landed in Attakapas in a place called, I believe, Butte a la Rose. It was on the edge of a miserable swamp and the surface of the earth was covered with water. There we were forced to encamp for the night. In the morning, my brother and myself were forced to trudge through the swamps—a distance of six or seven miles—into a settlement to procure means of transportation. In the settlement, our ignorance of the French language was a source of great annoyance. My brother did not understand a word, and I was about in the same situation. It was true that I had studied the language for a short time at Charlotte Hall, but had never attempted to speak, nor had I ever heard it spoken. After fruitless means of making ourselves understood, in order to obtain the means of removing the family and baggage from their unpleasant situation, we lighted on a small planter who seemed disposed to assist us.

He informed us that he had two *charretts* which were at our service, after being told that we were the family of the Judge. (*Le Grande Judge* he called it.) Mistaking the word *charretts* for chariots, we endeavoured to explain to him, in the best manner that we could, the utter impossibility of attempting the journey in such conveyances. We tried to explain that the roads were well nigh impassible. He laughed and shrugged at our misgivings, and finally, nothing better offering itself, we were forced to close with him. Then, behold! To our surprise and delight the two chariots proved to be two ox-carts, into which we joyously embarked and dashed through mud and mire at a furious rate. We were followed by a large cavalcade of Creole gentlemen, on horseback. The whole neighborhood came to do honor to the family of the Grand Judge.

Soon our baggage was hustled into the carts and the family followed. We started on our way, escorted before and behind by the horsemen who yelled and shouted with all their might and main. We soon reached the banks of the beautiful Bayou Teche, and from the other side came cries of welcome. Across the stream was a crowd of men, crying out to us. We crossed the stream on a flatboat, and there before us was my father's house. We were at home once more.

But such a home! How shall I describe it? The best house in the village was, of course, the home of the Judge, but it presented such a dilapidated and miserable appearance that my mother and sister wept with disappointment. We were greeted by my father in the most cordial and affectionate manner. He strove unceasingly to reconcile us to the primitive simplicity of our future home, pointing out the improvements to which it was susceptible, and suggesting various modifications, additions and betterments which he had projected, but had deferred until my mother's arrival for her approbation and aid. And it was true, for in a few days there was a complete change in the aspect of things. By dint of washing and rubbing and scrubbing, and with the aid of lime and paint, our home soon had an air of snugness and comfort about it that we could scarce realize. And the occupation diverted the minds of my mother and sister and kept them from pondering on the dark side of the picture. A week or two sufficed to reconcile us to our situation and made us feel at home.

The Creole families overwhelmed us with kindness, sending us all the little delicacies which season and country afforded: wild ducks, game of every description, and a fine quarter of mutton. The family of Mr. Dillard, the former commandant, whose plantation was situated on the outskirts of the village, was particularly kind and attentive.

Scarcely had the family taken possession of their humble home when we were surprised by a ceremonious visit from a handsome Creole gentleman who announced himself as M. Pellerin. Hearing of the arrival of the family of the Grand Judge he had done himself the honor of calling to pay his respects, he informed us. He soon made himself at home and at his ease, and we were delighted with his mixture of French and English. In the midst of a very pleasant intercourse and growing intimacy, my father appeared, and accosting our visitor in an austere and commanding manner, inquired by what authority was he there, and ordered him to return to jail immediately. Without explanation or expostulation our guest bowed himself gracefully out of the room and retired. Full of wonder and chagrin, my mother requested an explanation of this most singular behaviour on the part of my father. He gratified our curiosity by informing us that M. Pellerin belonged to one of the most aristocratic families in the country, but that he was under sentence of imprisonment pronounced by himself for having resisted the authority of the law. A man named David Reese had received from my father the temporary appointment of sheriff and had executed some legal process against M. Pellerin. This had been resented by

"MARCO," THE TRUE LOUISIANA TYPE,
CANE RIVER, 1820

"HICKORY HILL," ELEGANCE, 1810

the whole Pellerin family as a great indignity and insult. They were indignant that David Reese, a common carpenter, should have been chosen as the organ of communication between the Pellerins and the civil authorities. If any charges should be brought against people of their respectability, they said, it was the duty of the Commandant to have written them a polite note requesting their attendance, a request which would have been complied with instantly; but to send a warrant for one of them by a vulgar carpenter was insupportable. In consequence of their wounded dignity, they had waylaid Reese and had given him a most unmerciful drubbing. For this, our acute guest had been prosecuted, convicted and sentenced to a term in the county jail. The jail was a miserable log cabin near our house, and the confinement was merely nominal. M. Pellerin was never locked up, but generally passed his time on the gallery. He had observed the arrival of the family and with true French politeness deemed it his duty to pay his *devoirs* and welcome, without reflecting upon his situation as a prisoner. Having now displayed the authority of the magistrate, my father soon explained to M. Pellerin the impropriety of his conduct, and the necessity of remaining in jail until his term expired; he ended his explanation by assuring the gentleman that, as soon as his term of confinement had expired, he would be a welcome guest in our house. M. Pellerin did not fail to avail himself of the invitation, and as long as we resided in Attakapas he was a pleasant and a constant visitor in the family.

The population of Attakapas at that time was almost exclusively French; the few Americans we occasionally met with were of the low order, with whom we could have little or no communication. We were consequently constrained to cultivate the Creole families, from whom we received every polite kindness and attention. But as none of us with the exception of myself spoke a word of French (and I spoke but a smattering), and as the English language was totally unknown among the Creoles, our intercourse was subject to many drawbacks, and gave rise to many ludicrous mistakes. Still, they were anxious to please us, and we were not disposed to reject their proffered intimacy. We soon became reconciled to our lot and our stay among them was not only supportable but pleasant. We attended all of the Saturday night balls, entered into all of their innocent amusements, and ended by liking them excessively. I look back now with pleasure to the happy years I spent in Attakapas.

The wide extensive prairies covered the landscape as far as the eye could reach, and were covered with cattle and game of every description. The view was a source of never ending admiration. At that season of the year, the grass having been burned off, the prairie presented a level plain, carpeted with young grass just springing up. From our front gallery we could gaze upon countless flocks of wild geese, leisurely parading up and down and luxuriating in the young herbage until roused to flight by the shot of some Creole hunter. Sometimes herds of wild cattle would sweep across the plain, disturbed in their ruminations by the same unwelcome visitor.

I soon became the very Nimrod of the day and kept the table more than supplied with choice and delicate game. In my early efforts, however, I was much annoyed and alarmed by the cattle, of whose habits I was ignorant. The discharge of the gun would congregate thousands of the mad and ferocious looking animals, which would come sweeping over the waste and rushing towards the quarter whence the sound came, with the noise of a whirlwind, threatening to overwhelm everything that came in their way. To me, these formidable onsets were by no means palatable. No possible means of escape offered, no tree, no bush, to screen me from their attack; flight seemed the only alternative, and that hopeless in the middle of a prairie five miles across. Fear and despair suggested a more sudden protection. Instead of running, I faced about and became the advancing instead of the retreating party. This movement soon brought my assailants to a stand, and their retrograde motion was as precipitate as their advance. Emboldened by success, and the certainty of security, I continued to prosecute my new avocation with renewed pleasure and perseverence.

The balls, however, were my favorite recreation. Regularly every Saturday night, there was a ball in the neighbourhood attended by all who chose to come. The dance continued until the party was dispersed by the appearance of the sun the following morning. The

Creole girls I found beautiful and fascinating and there was a total absence of all parade and etiquette. Each person seemed to have come for the purpose of receiving and communicating pleasure, and everything was mirth and happiness. The young amused themselves with dancing and love making, the old with cards and conversation.

On Saturday evening many *calèches* would be seen on the prairie and on the bayou road. These were wooden vehicles put together with wooden pegs, not a particle of iron being used in their construction; the wheels were without tires, and the body of the carriage swung upon strips of rawhide, and could be raised or lowered at will, as the rawhide strips were wound upon a little windlass at the back of the vehicle. These strange lumbering carriages would appear before sunset, filled with young ladies and old ladies on their way to the coming ball. On the floor of the carriage would be one or two shot-bags filled with dollars, intended by the old ladies to furnish the means of indulging in their favorite game of *vingt-et-un*.

On one occasion, having been invited to a ball on the other side of the prairie, my brother and I started out an hour before dark. We were ignorant of the way, but having received instructions, we conceived it impossible to be lost in crossing the prairie in a straight line. Road there was none, nor did any appear necessary. We thought we had nothing to do but to ascertain the direction and then steer for the house, which we could easily find. Everything prepared, the old horse harnessed to the *calèche,* my brother's violin in hand, we started for the ball. For some time we went on famously, annoyed however by *marais* or *coulées* which caused us to leave our straight path. These *marais* are small ponds or sloughs in the prairie which are filled with rain water. Sometimes they are deep and difficult to cross. We were therefore frequently obliged to drive some distance up or down to find the ford, by which means we lost our reckoning and became perfectly lost. Finally in endeavouring to ford one of the largest, the harness gave way, the horse was separated from the *calèche* which he left sticking in the midst of the *marais* and deliberately walked out. To augment our difficulties, it now became quite dark and there was no prospect of extricating ourselves. The mosquitoes were intolerable, and the weather hot, damp and disagreeable.

My brother with the philosophy of a stoic, submitted without murmuring. Taking out his fiddle, and covering his face with his handkerchief to protect it from the swarming mosquitoes, he commenced playing with all his might and main. To myself this state of endurance soon became insupportable, and without examining what would be the ultimate good to be derived from it, I proceeded to strip off my ball finery, and reducing myself to a state of nature, I plunged into the mud and mire. I reached dry land with some difficulty after floundering in the morass; the horse was found without difficulty, but the state of the harness was such as to preclude all hopes of extricating the *calèche* from its wrecked condition. After several unsuccessful efforts, resignation seemed to be the only remedy. Yielding to the necessity with the best grace I could, I disconsolately retraced my steps, floundered again through the mud, took up my station beside my brother, and resigned myself to sleep to the melodious sound of his fiddle. He never stopped fiddling the whole night through and his nonchalance and unconcern both vexed and surprised me.

A bright sun the next morning enabled us to ascertain our whereabouts and to seek relief. A similar process of stripping and wading brought me a second time to shore, and hastily adjusting my toilet which was in sad disarray, I went to the nearest house, which was scarce a mile away. Upon stating our unpleasant predicament, aid was promptly furnished. A yoke of oxen hitched to the *calèche* promptly dragged it out. After a hearty laugh at our ludicrous misfortune we were informed by the kind planter who relieved us (Mr. Decuir), that we had passed the night almost within hail of the ball, the music of which we might have heard, had we not been otherwise occupied.

It was not long after our arrival that we perceived that my father had not been cured of his habits of extravagance. His office —a lucrative one—was inadequate to make the expenses, and his circumstances were irretrievably embarrassed. My brother was looked up to as the only stay of the family; although, poor fellow, he had not the means of making a dollar. Having been employed all his life in a public office, his pen was his only resource and no opportunity presented itself in Attakapas. The situation of the family affected his spirits and he became gloomy and melancholy, anxious to ward off the coming catastrophe; but seeing no means of doing it, in this unpleasant dilemma he smothered his pride and adopted the only course that remained.

Upon the tract of land where we lived a cotton crop had been planted in partnership with a man named Gration, but as they had but a few negroes between them, my brother determined to aid them in cultivating it. Notwithstanding that he had never done a day's work in his life, he was up early and worked late in performing the offices of a day labourer. Nothing was permitted to interfere with his work, no weather kept him from the fields. We were grieved to see him coming for his breakfast, dripping from the dew and staggering under the weight of a heavy cotton basket. But he knew it to be necessary and he never uttered a murmur. My time was passed in the office copying acts as my father's clerk. It was evident to us all that poverty would soon stare us in the face, that the habits of my father were such that we must depend upon our own exertions for support. Our situation was truly deplorable. We were not calculated to buffet with the world, and we were unhappy in seeing our ruin inevitable; there seemed no possibility of extricating ourselves from it. . . .

About this time, Mr. Morse, a young lawyer from New Jersey, settled in New Iberia and soon became almost an inmate of our family. His attentions to my sister were shortly of that marked description which indicated an intention of paying her his addresses. This circumstance was pleasing to us all. It was true that he was poor, as poor as we were, but he was an enterprising and energetic young gentleman with a good profession, a pleasing manner and a cultivated mind. With him it was decided that I should study law. I installed myself in his office at old Mr. Murphy's—the only tavern in the place—and was soon buried in the learned law of Blackstone.

Knowing the necessity of obtaining a license, I was assiduous and unremitting in my studies, studying hard through the week and figuring at the Creole balls on Saturday night. At one of these I became acquainted with, and formed, as I fancied, a violent attachment to a pretty little Creole of the neighborhood, Miss Emerita Dellahousse. This attachment continued until I removed to Opelousas. . . .

A change in the judiciary system rendered our prospect more gloomy than before. The counties were divided into parishes, and Parish Judges replaced County Judges. My father, through his freedom of speech (and probably through his increased habits of dissipation), had rendered himself obnoxious to Governor Claiborne. My father did not receive the appointment of parish judge; it was given to Judge White, the father of Governor White. My father was thrown upon his profession for his support. Such however were his talents, and so highly was he esteemed, that in spite of his age and infirmities he obtained a fair share of business for some time. Debts were, however, pressing in on all sides, and there were the daily wants of a large and helpless family. These calls were more than his practice could meet, and we grew more and more distressed. Mr. Morse in the meantime had married my sister and was living with us; discovering the incapacity of my father, he took upon himself the entire control. Although his means were limited, I do not know how we could have gotten along without him. . . .

Thinking myself qualified to stand the examination for the Louisiana Bar, I left home with Mr. Morse to attend the meeting of the Superior Court which was in session in Opelousas in the spring of 1809. My notions and knowledge of law were slight and crude enough (God knows), but necessity is a hard master, and necessity required that I should provide for myself. I approached this awful trial with fear and trembling. I was conscious that my fear would mitigate against me, still the essay must be made, and made it was. The court at that time was composed of Judges Mathews and Thompson, the third being absent. After a long and sifting examination I was pronounced competent, and was licensed to my unspeakable joy. . . .

It had been determined before I left home that I should locate in Opelousas and practice law, and accordingly I took board at an old tavern kept by Edmund Johnson and was ready to receive a fee. Unfortunately, however, no fee came.

In the absence of all occupation, I adopted the conduct of the idle young men with which the village abounded. I soon became the idlest of the idle. Had it been the worst result, it would not have mattered so much, but the young gentlemen were dissipated as well, and I was but too prone to follow their example. . . .

The tavern was a large frame house with a gallery in front. One end of the gallery was occupied by the barroom. A long shelf had been placed against the side of the house, and it was the duty of the bar-keeper, at break of day, to garnish it from one end to the other with tumblers containing mint, sugar and a spoon. Hither came all the young men, not only of the house but of the village, as soon as their eyes were opened in the morning, to partake of their "morning bitters"—for so mint julep was called. The usual allowance was ten or twelve glasses each, till called to breakfast.

Stepping from the gallery of the tavern, you entered the billiard room, to which the guests repaired from the breakfast table. We played billiards until the bell rang for dinner, which was hurriedly swallowed that we might return to the game. Supper still found us occupied in the same manner. Afterwards we continued until a late hour of the night. . . . The constant consumption of liquors of all description was, of course, enormous. . . . Such was my life.

At first, it is true, I had no relish for the drinking part, but in the process of time I acquitted myself as well as the best of them. The only excuse I can offer for this dissolute life was my extreme youth, being in fact, a beardless boy, and having no kind friend at hand to warn me of my danger. I had not the slightest disposition to drink, on the contrary, the task was at first disagreeable, and I only yielded to the taunts, gibes and entreaties of my dissolute companions. How I escaped the drunkard's fate, as I look back, appears the effect of a miracle. . . . The habit is so strong, and took so deep a root with me, that I required years to conquer it. And even at this time (I am now fifty-two years old), I can scarcely realize the fact that I have conquered it. How many young men have fallen victims to the same school in which I was so apt a scholar. . . .

And here, unfortunately for us, the document breaks off short. There is a marginal note saying that the memoir was never completed. But those who are interested in the fortunes of this young man may be relieved to know that he escaped at last from the gay young blades of Opelousas, became a famous lawyer and in the year 1840—when this memoir was written—he had been District Judge for many years. This record, set down with no thought of publication, remained with his children and grandchildren in New Orleans. And it is a document of particular interest, as it gives a first hand impression of Creole life on Bayou Teche as the first Americans saw it.

Chapter Eleven

"THE CITY OF SIN"

LEAN Kentuckians, floating down the Mississippi on flat-
boats loaded with merchandise, used to speak of New Orleans as "the city of sin." And at the mention of sweet sin-
ning, they pushed harder at the sweeps, urging the cumber-
some boats downstream. Protestant ministers in far-away
New England preached sermons on the new Sodom at the
river's mouth—a city they had never seen, but of which they
had heard fabulous stories. Each year more men grew curious about New Orleans and each year more men arrived
to see and experience for themselves. Some went away and
told incredible tales of what they had seen, but others liked
it and remained, fascinated with the exotic city which they
found—or for the more prosaic reason that money was
easy to make.

For New Orleans was a city which had been first French,
then Spanish, and which was now Creole, a blending of both.

It was luxurious and gay. The Creoles, at first hostile to English-speaking persons, had gained respect and admiration for the Americans who came down the Mississippi to help save the city from the British. The battle of New Orleans had cemented that friendship, and Americans were now welcome nearly everywhere. New Orleans was never gayer or more picturesque than in the period just after the battle; from 1815, let us say, to 1830. Steamboats whistled on the Mississippi, and the up-river planters loaded their cotton and their families aboard and came to New Orleans in early winter, to attend the opera, the ball, and the circus. Nor did the planter overlook the gambling-houses of Royal Street, where, in softly carpeted room, men played cards by the light of many candles, and where soft-footed negroes brought them wines and liquors in crystal glasses set upon silver trays.

It was a time of extravagant talk, of duels, of quick laughter, and of sudden wrath. Epidemics of disease swept over New Orleans bringing terror and death to hundreds; the river overflowed the levee and inundated the streets; there were strange crimes and brutal punishments; men dreamed curious dreams, and set out to make them come true. New Orleans, bubbling with unquenchable gaiety, offered every refinement of pleasure that the times afforded and every refinement of vice. It was a stronger and more cruel age than ours, and New Orleans was a foreign city; it is impossible for us to judge it by modern standards.

Sunday was a feast day. The Creole population went to mass in the morning, to a cock-fight in the afternoon, and to a ball in the evening. All day long, the Place d'Armes was filled with people, seeking amusement and pleasure.

The saloons were well patronized and the cabarets were gay. In the streets one met Creoles, Frenchmen, Spaniards, and Kentuckians in blue homespun, their pockets heavy with dollars they had earned by their long trip down the Mississippi. And always, like a black thread through the multi-colored pattern of the city's life, the negro slaves shuffling barefoot through the streets.

On Sunday afternoon the public square before the Cathedral was filled with a moving crowd. Along the iron railings were booths where oranges, bananas, sherbet, and ginger beer were offered for sale. Negro women, balancing flat baskets on their heads, cried out their wares—*"Estomac mulatre,"* that ginger cake always dear to children. Along the river-front were the oyster stalls, where men and women waited while the oysters were opened, and ate them fresh from the shell. "The most respectable families" patronized these oystermen, then as now.

Inside the square was the Greek Sherbet vendor, wearing his crimson fez. Naked bronze-colored Indians reeled drunkenly through the crowds. Piquant quadroon girls, wearing their bright-striped *tignons,* moved through the throng, chaperoned by their mothers, who were exhibiting their daughters to the white gentlemen of the town. Old Creole men, wearing knee breeches and carrying gold snuff-boxes, came slowly by, leaning on their canes. Young guards in uniform swaggered, with eyes alert for pretty girls. Young men of fashion, wearing suits of green or gray, flaunted their starched frills, as they paced up and down, discussing the opera, or the duello, or the ball last night. Nuns in black robes and veils passed with quiet steps and downcast eyes.

Beyond the Place d'Armes was the French Market, where all day long crowds gathered buying fruit, meats, vegetables, and flowers from the market men. Here were Maltese, Greek, and Choctaw, Spaniards, Italians, and Frenchmen—even a few Chinese fishermen with shrimp and fish for sale. Here were the vendors of flowers, the sellers of sweet cakes, the women with candied fruits for sale. Here sat stolid Indians, half in, half out of their blankets, staring drunkenly before them as they offered blow-guns, baskets, and feather-tipped arrows and bows in exchange for a picayune.

On the opposite side of the town the negroes held high carnival in Congo Square, as hour after hour they shuffled and stamped in their dances of old Africa, swaying and sweating in the afternoon sunshine while tom-toms thudded their eternal rhythm.

In the side streets were the little cafés where men from the West Indies gathered, constituting a gay and effete group of cynics, well versed in wine, women, dueling, and other dangerous pastimes.

One of the most famous coffee-houses was the Café des Refugiés. It was near the market, between Dumaine and Saint Philip streets. It was patronized largely by those refugees from Santo Domingo, or *Colons de Saint Domingue,* as they were called. Here the famous liquor *le petit Gouave* was concocted, and here in the afternoon and evening the young blades congregated. There was music and singing, on a stage in the courtyard, and here, under the orange trees, the onlookers sat, sipping their sweet drinks. It was gay at the Café des Refugiés, a gaiety not quite French, nor yet quite Spanish, but a mixture of the two.

It must have been a pleasant place, early in the nineteenth century. And the Kentuckians found it bizarre indeed— great strapping fellows that they were—sitting in close proximity to those merry, dark-eyed little men who shrugged their shoulders and rolled their eyes in time with the drumbeats, and who threw their last picayunes at the feet of a dancer who amused them.

Just next door was the Hôtel de la Marine, the rendez-vous of the bold spirits of that time. Pirates and gamblers frequented it; many plots were hatched there. Followers of Jean Lafitte were frequently seen lounging in the sitting-room, or drinking next door at the café. In 1815 the hotel was managed by Mr. F. Turpin, an energetic Creole gentle-man who was also an impresario. He gave elaborate en-tertainments. Some of his old advertisements in the news-papers are amusing. Usually his advertisement was only a small card, printed in both French and English: "The Navy Hotel, Coffeehouse, Public Baths, Table d'Hôte and Boarding House." But sometimes he advertised lavishly, when a special attraction was offered. For example:

ROPE DANCING

Mr. Medrano has the honour of informing the inhabitants of New Orleans and its vicinity that, on Sunday evening next, 6th instant, he will give another exhibition of rope dancing at the Navy Hotel.

He will execute the same feat as on last Sunday, of standing on his head, with his legs crossed, on a pole thirty feet high; but instead of having one circle of fireworks at his feet, he will have three, one on his feet and one on each hand.

He will dance on the tight rope divers steps, and execute many extraordinary feats too tedious to mention. He will appear on the rope in man's clothes; an empty bag will be given him, into which he will enter, when it will be tied above his head; he will then be seen to come out in the character of an old woman of eighty, and in that dress will dance to the tune of Yankee Doodle.

On the slack rope, with fireworks on each arm, he will represent a windmill, and turn with such velocity as to render it impossible to distinguish his form—with a number of feats equally surprising, that can not fail to please the public.

The rope dancing was only one of the entertainments presented by Mr. Turpin. A similar notice of a juggler and thrower of knives appears in the paper a week later. And a Spanish dancer billed only as "Lola" delighted audiences with her "Flame Dance" the week following.

The performances must have been picturesque enough, for a motley crowd gathered in the courtyard of the Navy Hotel when these attractions were offered. The court was extremely large and the hotel extended entirely around it. The balconies leading to the sleeping-rooms enclosed the court on three sides, and the spectators sat in these galleries, and also in semicircular rows of "movable chairs" in the courtyard itself. The performers occupied a low stage at one side. The illumination was furnished by candles and flaming torches.

Nearby, and in the same street with the Navy Hotel, was the Saint Philip Street Theater. Here opera was given, and the nights were gay. At Orleans and Bourbon streets was the famous Orleans Theater, and adjoining it the Orleans ball-room where the Quadroon Balls were held. Many old theater programs have been preserved and it is interesting to see what varied performances were given. Let us take two at random—Saturday and Sunday, November 19 and 20, 1823:

A Second Representation of
Husbands Are Always in the Wrong,
Even When They Are in the Right.
A Vaudeville in One Act,
To Be Followed By a Second Representation of
Rossignol
A Comic Opera in One Act by Mr. LeBrun.

On the following night the program is even more
pleasing:

A Representation of
Brisquet and Joliecœur
A Farce in One Act,
To be followed by
Rouge et Noir
Or the Chances of Gambling.
An Opera in One Act by Tarchi.
The Whole to Conclude With
The Innkeeper Judge and The Hairdresser Lawyer,
A Farce in One Act.
The Curtain Will Rise at Half-Past Six Precisely.

Opera at the time which we are considering was a
much more vital element in the theatrical world than it is
to-day. In New Orleans its presentation was not confined
to the Orleans and Saint Philip theaters, although the most
pretentious productions were made before the French element of the population who frequented those particular
houses. But operas were given also in English at the American theater, which started its career in 1823.

We have an interesting contemporary account of a
performance at the American Theatre in "Travels Through
North America" by Bernhard, Duke of Saxe-Weimar

Eisenach, who indulged in most of the pleasures offered to
a young man of wealth in New Orleans, and who wrote of
it afterward:

In the American Theater [he writes] "Der Freischutz" was
presented under the title of "The Black Huntsman of Bohemia."
This drama so universally known and admired, and which has
followed me even to America, like an evil genius (since detached
pieces of it were sung and played in almost all companies), I had
never yet witnessed. Determined not to remain longer in the rear
of the age, I therefore went to the theatre. The orchestra was
very weak and badly filled. Hardly any of the performers could
sing well. I was told that the handsomest pieces of music are either
abridged or entirely omitted. The decorations, nevertheless, were
tolerably good.

I found the boxes and galleries thronged. In the pit there were
but a few spectators, and these consisted of sailors and countrymen
from Kentucky who made themselves quite at ease on the benches
and cracked nuts during the finest pieces of music, a custom I
have noticed in all English theatres, and from which my tobacco-
chewing neighbors in the boxes did not refrain.

The theatre was newly erected and is arranged not untaste-
fully. It contains, besides the pit and parquet, three rows of galleries, as the French theatre. The boxes are only divided by low balus-
trades, so that you look out as if from a balcony. The second gallery
is destined for the reception of colored spectators, among whom I
saw not a single female, and in the upper gallery the men and
women of the town sit. The salon is lit with gas, and has a very
tasteful girondole.

It is obvious from this passage that opera in English
was attended by a quite different type of audience from that
which was to be found at the French theaters of the city,
which were always the rendezvous of the more respectable
of the population and where the most fashionable women

were to be seen in gala attire, as accounts of the period agree.

Sunday in New Orleans was the day of days. There were balls at night for "the most respectable citizens and their ladies" and, in a hall nearby, the quadroon beauties flaunted their silks and plumes for the white gentlemen, while a line of turbaned mothers sat along the walls, watching their daughters dance. No colored men were admitted, although the orchestra was composed of quadroon musicians. These quadroon balls were held regularly in New Orleans for a period of more than thirty years.

Sunday was a day of respite for slaves, too, and thousands flocked to the Voodoo dances in the afternoon and early evening. At nine o'clock, however, a cannon was sounded and the slaves were not allowed on the street afterward without a special pass from their masters.

Also on Sunday there were strange entertainments held for the edification of any who cared to attend. Here is a typical handbill of the period:

INTERESTING EXHIBITION

On Sunday, the 9th inst., will be presented in the place where fireworks are generally exhibited, near the circus, an extraordinary fight of furious animals. The place where the animals will fight is a rotunda of 160 feet in circumference, with a railing seventeen feet in height, and a circular gallery well conditioned and strong, inspected by the mayor and surveyors by him appointed.

1st Fight:—A strong Attakapas bull, attacked and subdued by six of the strongest dogs in the country.

2nd Fight:—Six bull dogs against a Canadian bear.

3rd Fight:—A beautiful tiger against a black bear.

4th Fight:—Twelve dogs against a strong and furious Opelousas bull.

If the tiger is not vanquished in his fight with the bear, he will be sent alone against the last bull, and if the latter conquers all his enemies, several pieces of fireworks will be placed on his back, which will produce a very entertaining amusement.

In the circus will be placed two mannikins, which notwithstanding the efforts of the bulls to throw them down, will always rise again, whereby the animals will get furious.

The doors will be opened at three and the exhibition will begin at four o'clock precisely.

Admission, one dollar for grown persons and fifty cents for children.

A military band will perform during the exhibition.

If Mr. Renault is so happy as to amuse the spectators by that new spectacle, he will use every exertion to diversify and augment it, in order to prove to a generous public, whose patronage has been hitherto so kindly bestowed upon him, how anxious he is to please them.

The same Mr. Renault who provided New Orleans with the animal-baiting is mentioned as far back as 1808, in the Louisiana "Courier," as furnishing pyrotechnical displays; for attending exhibitions of fireworks was a favorite pastime in New Orleans. Here is a typical announcement:

Mr. Renault has the honor to inform the gentleman subscribers and the public in general that the ascension of his balloon and display of fireworks will take place (weather permitting) on Saturday, the 28th inst. in Fort St. Ferdinand near the hospital.

Mr. Renault, thankful for the confidence reposed in him, has endeavoured to do his best to give entire satisfaction; the fireworks are composed of a triumphal arc, the pillars of which, made in the form of screws, turn alternately.

The arc will exhibit an illumination of 1800 squibs, the whole to be lighted at once by means of a dragon coming from the end of the lot and setting fire to them.

Mr. Renault has thought proper to place in the center of the triumphal arc, an allegorical transparent painting, representing a rare man, distinguished by his virtues and goodness toward his fellow creatures.

The grand illumination will be preceded by the following pieces: The grand Girandole turning on its axis, two grand Girandoles or Caprices, the Chinese whirlwind, a bright star, a glory with the sun in its center, two grand suns turning in contrary ways, the cascade and fountain of St. Cloud, twelve firepots throwing various fireworks into the air, and several rockets.

The balloons will be let loose when the sun is at the horizon, and the fireworks begin at sunset. It will be announced by a discharge of rockets.

Mr. Renault has provided benches and chairs for the use of visitors; there are also tents to shelter the ladies from the dew.

Tickets to be had at his house, Rampart Street, or at the place of the exhibition. The boxes, one dollar; second boxes, six bits; children, half price. There is a private place for people of color.

Yes, New Orleans was gay enough, when plantation people came to town.

Chapter Twelve

A NEW ERA BEGINS

AND always the Mississippi drawing men southward toward the sea.

By 1830 both banks of the river from Vicksburg to New Orleans were astir. The alluvial lands along the waterways of Louisiana were as rich as any lands in America. Fortunes were made in three or four years; men in Maryland, Virginia, Kentucky, the Carolinas, sold their possessions, left their families behind them and came to the shores of the Mississippi. Some came overland in wagons, bringing their slaves with them; others floated down the river on flatboats, carrying their money in ready gold.

It was a strange and picturesque time. Tracts of land changed hands overnight. Men grew rich through speculation. Money was pouring into New Orleans, and the

merchants were ready and willing to finance those land-
owners along the river. The planters bought largely, ten,
fifteen, twenty thousand dollars' worth of farming implements, live stock, hardware, clothing, and other things
necessary for their acres and their slaves. They bought on
credit and repaid the notes with interest.

Slaves were put to work clearing the land. The singing
of negroes and the ringing of axes on the river-bank were
heard by those on board passing steamboats. Great trees
came crashing down. The Indians, amazed before such
activity, shrugged naked shoulders and moved further
away. Levees were thrown up to prevent overflows. Plows
turned the dark soil into furrows; cotton and sugar-cane
fields were planted. Vegetable gardens grew green where
only palmettoes stood the year before. Pecan trees were
set out; orchards appeared. Black men toiled in the earth
taming the soil to fruitfulness. It was as though the very
land itself stirred from its sleep and stretched its strong
black body.

Letters and diaries give the clearest picture of the
times. Here, then, is a letter from a Louisiana plantation-
owner to his old home in Maryland. Colonel Claudius F.
Le Grand is writing to his brother-in-law, Thomas Croxall,
about conditions in Louisiana, along the Mississippi. The
letter is written from "Maryland Bend" near Tuscumbia,
Louisiana, and is dated April 9, 1836.

Dear Thomas: I am at last fixed in this State after examining a great part of the interior of Mississippi and Louisiana. I
finally have located myself on the margin of this noble river. I
found the lands of the interior much cheaper than those I have
bought, but of a quality that must in a few years become sterile,

while those on the borders of the river, which are entirely made of its overflowing, can never be exhausted. I have also noticed the great expense to which the inland planter is put to get his crop to the river, to ship it from there to New Orleans, the common market for all our cotton. Most of the interior lands are much broken; the river lands are perfectly level. Those who live some thirty or fifty miles from the river have to pay from four to six dollars for every bale they send to a shipping port; those on the river can avoid expense. Our gin houses are mostly from fifty to a hundred yards from the river and we can roll our cotton on board the steamboats that carry it to New Orleans without other cost than that received by the boat, which is one dollar per bale. Lands on the river are now becoming very scarce; planters daily more sensible of their real value, and many tracts have been sold for $100 per acre, while the lands in the interior seldom sell for more than from $12 to $20 per acre. These dwellings in this new country are very fine; but on the other hand it is no uncommon thing to see a planter who makes from six hundred to one thousand bales of cotton live in a house so open that he could not by shutting the door keep a dog out. They laugh if you say anything about the uncomfortable way in which they live and point with pride to the fields which bring them in this yearly fortune.

He then writes of his own plantation, recently purchased, a tract comprising 1320 acres, for which he paid $52,800 or $40 an acre. Only forty acres were cleared of "native cane-brakes and palmetto" and the large trees are still standing, but "have been doomed for some time." His slaves are rapidly clearing the land and before long he expects to have three hundred acres in cotton. His fields of sugar-cane are planted already.

If we succeed in our crop, and the price remains at what it now is, our crop will be worth all I got for Portland Manor. I cannot say I am sorry I came here, because I am sure I can do much more for my family than I ever could have done in Maryland. I have had my health very well since I came here; but while at Vicksburg and during my absence in search of land, I lost my poor Nancy. Her loss is severely felt by me, for she was the best of all my slaves. I have also lost some of the infant children from smallpox; my trials in this respect have been very great, and enough to almost make me wish I had never come. My people are now very hearty, and much pleased with their situation; living on the river banks, they have many advantages they could not have had in the interior. I give them the privilege of chopping as much wood as they please, which they sell from the landing to the steamboats that pass daily, at three dollars a cord. Last year the owner of this place sold three thousand dollars worth of wood to the steamboats. I have not had time to enter into that part of the business yet, but shall do so next year.

Coming down the river I visited many of the States that border on this great river, which nearly all our Western States do. On my return I shall go by the way of Nashville, St. Louis, Cincinnati, Wheeling, and Pittsburgh, and will be more able to give you an account of them when I see you next summer. I think I shall leave here in May after my cotton is scooped out. I am anxious to see my dear family, from whom I have been separated now for nearly eight months. I hear frequently from them, and they only complain of my long absence and the very cold winter. The winters here are very mild; but few days have been this season that you could not sit before your door even with your coat off. The sun now is as warm as any time in June, and makes me think of making my escape to the East.

He goes on to tell something of his various slaves, and the following paragraph concerning his body-servant is interesting:

My John does not live with me on the plantation; he was desirous of living at Vicksburg. He lives there at the first hotel. I get twenty-five dollars per month for him and he makes nearly as much for himself. I could get thirty dollars for his services, but the other tavern is not so genteel.

Reverting to conditions in Louisiana, he writes:

Many splendid fortunes have been made here the past three years and many can be made buying these wild lands, clearing them and selling them. Land can be bought for $2.50 an acre, cleared and resold for $20 or $30. This is done daily. My former neighbor, John Weems, went to New Orleans about a month ago to close the purchase of a place for which he was to give $300,000. This sounds big to the ears of a Maryland tobacco planter, but here it is not considered anything. Several places and negroes have been sold since I came here for upwards of $300,000. I was offered one some months past, for which they only asked $500,000, and this was considered cheap at that. Anything under an hundred thousand dollars scarcely takes the attention of a Mississippi River cotton planter. I go on a slower, though perhaps not more sure plan than they do, for where the means is adequate to the purchaser, it is quite as easy to pay the one as the other.

Vicksburg is a flourishing town, and though not nearly so old as Natchez, from its local situation, as it is by a fine rich country, it will soon leave her in the background.

I paid a visit to the great city of New Orleans, and was really more than surprised at its growing wealth; more than I expected to be. It is destined to be the greatest city in the Union, and when the lands on the Mississippi, Ohio, and the many hundred rivers that empty into the Mississippi and carry their produce to New Orleans are cultivated, its ports, though spacious, will not be half large enough to hold the foreign vessels that will be necessary to carry the productions of this great Western country from this Queen of the South.

The levee, or wharf, at New Orleans is now upwards of four miles long, and the shipping are moored all the way along it from six to eight deep. Vessels from every country. I really had no conception of this town until I saw it; the facility of doing business in this country must always induce strangers to settle here in preference to in our cold-hearted towns of the North. It is much easier to get a loan of from twenty to thirty thousand dollars without any security than your word than it would be to get five thousand on a mortgage on the best property in Maryland from the cold-hearted Marylanders; such a State as this and Mississippi cannot help but make their inhabitants wealthy.

Then, with personal messages, the planter closes his letter. It is characteristic of many men who came to the plantations of the Lower Mississippi River at that time. It was a period when men thought in large figures. Fortunes were made in three or four years. Colonel Le Grand speaks of paying for his place with one crop, which, as optimistic as it sounds, proved to be nearly true.

However, this was not a country for poor men. Capital was necessary in order to make a fortune quickly. Everything was done on a large scale. Slave labor, fertile lands, and a ready market brought quick results. Planters doubled their original capital in two years, and paid their debts in addition. Some tripled their investment the third year. There are many instances on record where men came to Louisiana, remained for five or six years and retired to live in the North or East on fortunes made on Mississippi River plantations.

But the majority of the planters remained on their plantations until driven away by poverty after the Civil War, when this whole economic scheme fell to pieces through the loss of slave labor and inability to sell their crops. The case of the Le Grand family is typical.

The letter from Colonel Claudius Le Grand quoted

earlier in this chapter is taken from a family document called "The Journal of Julia Le Grand," privately printed in Richmond in 1911. This journal deals with the Civil War, and consequently has little to do with our story. However, in the biographical sketch which precedes the journal, several letters are quoted, telling something of the arrival of the family in Louisiana after Colonel Le Grand had established a home there. One year the plantation was swept under a crevasse from the Mississippi, and the entire crop was lost. The steamboat which was bringing the furniture and household effects to the plantation exploded and the household possessions went to the bottom of the river. There was a time, following those first flush years, when the Le Grands were almost poor. However, the succeeding year brought large crops and fortune smiled again. In 1850 we find them truly rich.

In the opera season in New Orleans, Colonel Le Grand, with his daughters and a train of servants, would go to the St. Charles Hotel and stay until it was over. In the summers, Julia and Virginia, with their maids and their luggage piled high on wagons, would go to the Springs in Virginia.

There is also an interesting description of the Julia as a plantation belle in the period just before the Civil War. She is described as being very "beautiful and graceful with a suggestion of pensiveness about her," and the writer "remembers her as always in a soft, trailing white gown, full of romantic fancies, and always accompanied by a great dog, the gift of a lover, an absent one, about whom there was some mystery." The Le Grand plantation-house is described as being a very fine one, magnificently furnished.

Miss Julia played upon an old harp "which had a history"; and Colonel Le Grand, the father, played upon a tiny Spanish guitar which he had picked up in his travels. The writer says that the family had once possessed great wealth and were still very rich, although they had lost a good deal, and by comparison believed themselves to be quite poor and tried to economize "or thought they did." Through mismanagement later, after the death of their parents, the girls really lost everything and Miss Julia and Miss Virginia opened a "select school for young ladies" in New Orleans.

The tide of Americans which came sweeping into Louisiana, after the Louisiana Purchase in 1803, reached its climax in 1830 or thereabouts. There was a network of plantations from Natchez to New Orleans and fortunes were in the making. Natchez, Bayou Sara, Pointe Coupée, Baton Rouge, and Bayou Goula were thriving communities, each a plantation center, each a community which drew wealth from the surrounding country. Travelers aboard the steamboats could see an almost continuous stretch of tilled land on the river-banks, and they could see the white plantation-houses set in groves of trees.

The era of building was beginning. The planters, growing richer, were building larger and finer houses every year. The simple house of the pioneer was disappearing; the crude, whitewashed cottages were being replaced by mansions. The Greek Revival was at hand.

Chapter Thirteen

THE PROSPEROUS YEARS

LOUISIANA reached its most prosperous period in the twenty years prior to the Civil War. These in truth were "the good old times." Plantation-owners reaped fortunes from the fertile soil; and the current of the Mississippi carried the commerce of mid-America to the levee at New Orleans. In Natchez, white-pillared houses gleamed at the ends of avenues of moss-draped trees—the homes of wealthy men whose plantations lay in the lowlands of Louisiana across the Mississippi. Natchez-Under-The-Hill was notorious in song and story, a riotous, bawdy section where gamblers plied their trade, and where women of easy virtue laid snares for the sons of rich planters.

Steamboats plowed their way upstream from New Orleans to Natchez, to St. Louis, to Louisville, to Pittsburg. Gigantic rafts floated down the river, laden with merchandise and propelled by sturdy flatboatmen—aggressive males, red of shirt and bronzed of face, men who boasted that they were "half-alligator, half-horse." At Natchez-Under-The-Hill they stopped to drink, to carouse, and to embrace the tawdry girls who waited their coming; but the girls had little financial success with them, for flatboatmen were not paid off until they reached New Orleans.

They were a fearless, hard-drinking, reckless tribe, tall, strong, lean, and bawdy in talk. Their Rabelaisian jokes are still remembered. Their home-loving kinsmen were tilling the farms of Ohio, Indiana, Illinois, Kentucky, and Tennessee. In New Orleans the flatboatmen lingered on the levee to boast and fight, to terrorize the negroes and bring joy to the women of the town—spending in one night of debauchery the hard-earned dollars which their long trip had brought them. Then, penniless perhaps, they would strike out overland for their distant homes.

The full force of the westward movement was sweeping across the continent. Trade was booming. The levee at New Orleans was piled high with merchandise. Scores of up-river steamboats were moored along the bank. Blunt-bowed trading brigs from the ports of Europe, coasting craft from New England, New York, Baltimore, and Philadelphia lined the river-front. The levee was astir. Negroes sang as they rolled hogsheads of sugar and bales of cotton. The old Creole city was beginning to recognize the American invasion for what it was—a commercial struggle to the death. A new city was growing up outside the Vieux Carré, and it was an American city.

On the plantations, the families of the American planters were growing up; the young men and young women were dissatisfied with the simple dwellings and wished for newer and more imposing houses. The era of building was beginning. The finest houses were erected between 1830 and 1860.

Travelers on the Mississippi never failed to wonder before the beauty and prosperity of the river-banks. The light green foliage, the dome-like oak trees shrouded in trailing moss; the fields of sugar-cane billowing in the breeze; the armies of negroes laboring with plows and hoes—these were the things which impressed the traveler, as numerous diaries testify.

The whole "coast" of the Mississippi from Baton Rouge to New Orleans was lined with prosperous plantations, each with its white-columned house standing in a grove of dark trees. At some distance in the rear, midway between the planter's residence and the edge of the swamp, was a massive brick pile with a towering square brick chimney. This was the sugar-house. The cost of these sugar-mills with their complete outfit of machinery was enormous, and the expenses of operation were correspondingly large. Nowadays, with improved systems of granulating the juice of the cane, the yield of saccharine matter is much greater; and nowadays the residue—called bagasse—is used for making paper and wall-board. But not in the old days. Then it was not squeezed dry enough to serve even as fuel, and it was hauled to the river and dumped in. The sugar-mills were operated by large furnaces which consumed an incredible amount of wood, wood which was cut in the swamps by the slaves, and hauled to the sugar-house. Everything was done on a large scale; there were thousands of acres planted in sugar-cane; hundreds of slaves were necessary to cultivate the fields; thousands of cords of wood had to be cut to operate the sugar-house during grinding season.

The planters thought in large figures; they built large houses; they produced large families and large fortunes; they worked hard; they were strong mentally and physically. And it is natural enough to find them generous and hospitable.

The quarters of the negroes usually stood between the residence of the planter and the sugar-house, and constituted a small village. On some plantations, the quarters were arranged in a "street," that is, a long double row of cabins on opposite sides of a lane. On other plantations, the cabins were arranged in a parallelogram, intersected by numerous "streets." The cabins were usually built of wood and were whitewashed. On some plantations the cabins were of brick, but these were the exceptions. The negroes themselves preferred wooden houses—as they do in Louisiana to this day—as they believed the brick cabins to be damp and to cause rheumatism to the dweller therein. Each cabin was furnished with a small plot of ground in which the family was allowed to grow a garden of vegetables for its own use, or to offer for sale.

The earliest type of plantation-house was simple enough, yet it was admirably suited to the tropical climate of Louisiana; it was a dwelling of a single story, raised a few feet above the ground on piers. The framework was of heavy cypress timbers, with the interstices filled with a sort of adobe—a mixture of mud and Spanish moss. Sometimes bricks were used instead, and some of the oldest houses standing to-day were of this type—*briqueté entre poteaux,* as they were called. The high-pitched roof was covered with cypress shingles, hand-hewn. The house was usually four rooms wide and only one room deep. There were wide porches before and behind it, porches covered with the wide sweep of the roof. From a distance the houses appeared larger than they really were.

From this type, the second Louisiana type evolved. The arrangement was the same, except that the house was of two stories. There were four rooms below and four above; there were wide galleries front and back, upstairs and down. Sometimes the galleries extended entirely around the structure. In the second type we find the first floor built of brick, set flush with the ground. The lower floor was also paved with brick, and the gallery of the second floor was supported by brick piers. Sometimes these piers were square, but the majority of these old houses have squat, cylindrical columns, tapering a little at the top and surmounted by a plain capital. The roof was supported by delicate colonettes of cypress, rising from the top of these brick piers. The staircase leading to the second floor rose at one end of the front gallery. The houses were usually white with green batten blinds. Because many houses like this were built while Louisiana was a Spanish colony, they are known as "the Spanish type." Architects to-day speak of them as "the Louisiana type."

But American planters in those thirty years prior to the Civil War would have none of these simple houses. The classic revival had spread from Europe to America, and the Louisiana planter made it peculiarly his own. The neighborhood of New Orleans produced a hundred or more houses of the classic type; scarcely a score of them are left to-day.

"MELROSE," THIS IS CANE RIVER, 1833

It is said that the east bank of the Mississippi boasted the finest houses in the State, and that the traveler was never out of sight of a fine house, from the time he left New Orleans until he reached Baton Rouge—a distance of one hundred and twenty miles. One may well believe it, for even to-day there are twenty-five to thirty magnificent houses remaining there, and within my recollection a score have burned or have caved into the river.

The west bank of the Mississippi was nearly as thickly settled. Bayou Lafourche boasted many fine dwellings. West Feliciana parish was one of the richest communities and has to-day the finest group of houses to be found in the State. Dwellers in East and West Feliciana were luckier than those planters who lived in the river bottoms, for their houses were in the hills, out of reach of inundation by the river. In the same way, Natchez has preserved its old houses. Natchez, of course, is in Mississippi, but many of the houses were owned by Louisiana planters.

The typical country house of 1840 was of the classic tradition, usually surrounded by large white columns, and with galleries on all four sides. It was set in a grove of trees, oak, hickory, magnolia, and bay. An avenue of live-oak trees led down to the front gate, which was a quarter of a mile or more from the house. The dwelling was as solid as huge timbers, brick and mortar, and native talent could render it. While always supervised by an architect, the laborers were usually slaves of the planter. Some of them were skilled artisans. The houses were usually designed by a foreign architect who gave the prevalent French, Spanish, or British touch to the finishing of fine woods, marble, or brass. The impression was of stateliness, of spaciousness. The furnishings were the best that the times afforded; the beds, sofas, secretaries, and so on were unusually large. This was necessary, for the rooms were spacious, and small furniture would have been ridiculous. A bed with posts twelve feet high was not unusual; a sofa seven feet long was the rule rather than the exception. There were few closets. Large wardrobes and cupboards of mahogany were used instead; they were called *armoires*.

The plantation families were fond of flowering trees and shrubs, and, in addition to the large trees, there were many smaller varieties; the pink or lavender or white crêpe-myrtle, the red or white oleander, the yellowish-pink mimosa, the feathery green-and-gold acacia. In the garden one found aromatic plants: cape-jasmine, sometimes called gardenia, the magnolia fuscata, lemon and orange trees. There were roses, and countless lilies and other bulbous plants. Then there were the tropical shrubs: the banana tree, the giant "elephant ear," the yucca or "Spanish dagger," century plants. Vines grew riotously over everything.

There were numerous outhouses: summer houses in the garden, a private chapel, a school-house for the children, carriage houses, stables, the usual farm buildings, and, beyond them all, the negro quarters, the negro church, and the sugar-house. Beyond these the sugar-cane fields seemed to stretch out to infinity.

Visitors were always taken to see the kitchen, a brick structure placed some distance away from the house. It was housed separately for two reasons; first because plantation people lived in dread of fire, second so that the odors of cooking and the noise of the slaves should not prove annoying to members of the family. Nearly one whole wall of the kitchen consisted of a large open fireplace, with a brick hearth extending six feet or more before it. Here all the cooking was done. Steaks were broiled on live coals, cakes and bread were baked in ample iron ovens, the tops hollowed out to hold burning coals. Smaller pots stood on trivets. From the sides of the fireplace hung numerous hooks and cranes. Across the front of the fireplace were the pothooks from which depended the game, the venison, turkey, or chicken, turning slowly on cords, the rich juices dropping into pots set on the hearth below. It was primitive, but the food was delicious.

So lived the Louisiana planter and his family. They were waited upon by their own slaves, physicked by their own physician, their souls saved by their own pastor, and when they died they were buried in their own cemetery. Small wonder that some of them grew arrogant and have been accused of having delusions of grandeur.

Their self-sufficiency seems strange to-day, when distance is so easily bridged; but in those days the houses were remote indeed. Some of them stood a day's long journey from the nearest town. Nearly all of the fine houses are near a water-course, either the Mississippi or some stream flowing into it. This is easily understood, as water furnished the only means of transporting sugar and cotton to the markets.

Miss Louise Butler, writing in the *Louisiana Historical Quarterly* in July, 1927, tells of the manner of life on the plantation:

The children rose early [she writes], were given a cup of *café au lait* and a roll, practiced music or studied until breakfast, after which the tutor, usually a graduate of some Northern college and treated like the gentleman that he was, would instruct them until lunch, which generally consisted of a slice of bread and butter spread with marmalade or guava jelly, accompanied by a slab of jujube paste and washed down with lemonade or orange-flower syrup or tamarind juice. More studies until dinner, then long sunny hours spent in horseback riding, or playing in the large yard, swinging, jumping rope or risking their necks on the joggling board. Twice a week the music teacher would ride from place to place giving lessons. . . . Once a week the dancing master held classes. . . .

Miss Butler has lived all of her life on a plantation, and her forefathers lived there before her. Her stories are authentic, and her description of a plantation ball is enough to make us all long for the good old times. Let me quote a little:

. . . . gorgeous costumes of real lace . . . jewels, plumes. The staircase was garlanded in roses for full three flights. Vases on mantels and brackets filled with fragrant flowers . . . and gentlemen sampling Scotch or Irish whiskey . . . About midnight supper was announced and the hostess led the way to the dining room. On the menu, the cold meats, salads, *salmis, galantines* quaking in jellied seclusion, and an infinite variety of *à las,* were served from side tables, leaving the huge expanse of carved oak, besilvered, belinened and belaced, for flowers trailing from the tall silver *épergne* in the center to the corsage bouquet at each place; fruits, cakes in pyramids or layers or only solid deliciousness, iced and ornamented; custards, pies, jellies, creams, Charlotte Russes or home-concocted sponge cake spread with raspberry jam encircling a veritable Mont Blanc of whipped cream dotted with red cherry stars; towers of nougat or caramel, sorbets and ice creams served in little baskets woven of candied orange peel and topped with sugared rose leaves or violets. . . . Various wines in cut glass decanters, each with its

"BELMONT" DROWSES ON BAYOU MARINGOUIN

name carved in the silver grapeleaf suspended from its neck, iced champagne, deftly poured by the waiters into gold-traced or Bohemian glasses. . . . Illuminating the whole were wax candles in crystal chandeliers, and, on the table, in silver candelabra. . . . More dancing followed supper, and at dawn when the guests were leaving, a plate of hot gumbo, a cup of strong black coffee and enchanting memories sustained them on the long drive to their abodes. . . .

And as florid as it sounds, I know it to be perfectly true. It is small wonder that in three generations, the young sons of the planters thought only of amusing themselves. Money was plentiful. There were slaves to do the work, and overseers to see that they did it, and punish them if they did not.

There can be little question that the children of planters lived lives far too luxurious, and so forgot that life cannot be spent in dancing and idleness without eventual decadence. In the last years before the Civil War there was a decline in taste. The houses were built as show-places, rather than as dwellings; the construction was extravagant, flimsy, and showy. Slaves, no longer under the direct supervision of their masters, were abused by the overseers. The plantation system was showing signs of decay before the first far-off thunder of war was heard.

In 1846 John La Tourette published his survey of Louisiana plantations. It shows the State to be rich indeed. There were many more negro slaves than there were white persons, and an astonishing number of "free people of color." The total figures showed 158,157 white persons, 25,502 free mulattoes and negroes, and 168,452 slaves. The negro population outnumbered the white 35,797. In the northern portion of the State, where people were poor, the population was almost entirely white; but in the rich lands of the river bottoms and in the neighborhood of Baton Rouge and Bayou Sara, there were approximately four negroes for every white person.

Chapter Fourteen

THE STRANGE STORY OF PAULINE

IT was in March 1846 that Pauline was hanged in New Orleans in expiation of a curious crime. She was a mulatto slave who had beaten and tortured her white mistress. The case was widely discussed in its day, and the execution took place before a "huge and heterogeneous crowd." But nowadays Pauline's story lies forgotten among the musty court records. However, as the documents are complete and the daily newspapers furnish a mass of detail, I shall try to reconstruct the story for you here. It is one of the strangest cases in the annals of old Louisiana.

One morning, early in January 1845, Edward Montegut, mayor of New Orleans, received an anonymous letter. The writer stated that a white woman living at 52 Bayou Road was a prisoner to her own slave and that the slave for some time past had treated her "in a most horrid manner."

That was all, but it was enough. The mayor wasted no time, but went immediately to the house to see for himself. He took with him Recorder Joseph Genois and several police officers.

The house was in a good neighborhood. It appeared unoccupied; all of the doors and windows were tightly closed. No one answered the mayor's knock, and he ordered the officers to break down the front door. Leaving one of the officers to guard the entrance, the mayor and his companions searched the premises.

Locked in a "back cabinet" he found a woman and three small children. They were naked, and only a few dirty rags were in the room. The woman lay on a mattress on the floor. Her body was covered with bruises and scars; she managed with difficulty to sit up. Her hair was clotted with blood. Her eyes were discolored. She was shrunken and emaciated.

The children—their ages are given at seven, four, and two years, respectively—were in a similar condition. Their bodies were black and blue; they had many scars and raw sores caused by burning.

When the mayor entered, the woman began to cry hysterically. She was slow to answer questions. She said that her name was Rabbeneck, and that her husband was not in the city. The mayor then asked the cause of her distress, and the woman answered falteringly that she had been beaten.

At this moment, there was a commotion in the hall and a quadroon woman was led into the room by one of the policemen. She was tall and handsome, with large flashing black eyes. She wore gold hoops in her ears and her head was covered with a red *tignon*. Her name was Pauline and she was Mr. Rabbeneck's slave.

The mayor motioned the quadroon woman to stand aside until he finished questioning her mistress, but now the poor woman only cried. The mayor repeated his question and she answered falteringly that her husband had beaten her. The mayor, turning quickly, saw the dark eyes of the quadroon fixed upon the white woman. He ordered the policemen to take her outside until he finished his examination.

The moment the quadroon was led away, Mrs. Rabbeneck began to plead piteously for protection. Her husband, she said, had been absent for six weeks in St. Louis, and Pauline had taken possession of the house and its contents. The first day she had locked Mrs. Rabbeneck in this small room, and had beaten her unmercifully. An hour later she had returned and had beaten her afresh. The first time she used a strap, the second time a cane. The white woman had been rendered helpless by the strength of the quadroon. The children had been beaten in a similar manner. Scarcely an hour passed that Pauline did not come to the room and inflict punishment on one of them. Not content with beating them, she had burned them with hot coals and with a poker. For six weeks this had continued. Pauline had brought them only enough food to sustain life.

The mayor ordered Pauline's arrest. The white woman and her three children were taken to a hospital. There was a preliminary hearing, a few days later, and all of the facts were fully substantiated. Pauline was locked up in the Parish Prison.

The Black Code was explicit. In Section Three we find:

Any slave who shall wilfully and maliciously strike his master or mistress, or his master's or mistress' child, or any white overseer appointed by his owner to superintend said owner's slaves, so as to cause a contusion or shedding of blood, shall be punished with death or with imprisonment at hard labor for a term of not less than ten years.

On the day of the trial—according to the daily paper —an "immense concourse of people" swarmed in and around the court-house to listen to the testimony. Mobs howled outside. An extra guard was put around Pauline as she was transferred from the prison to the court-room.

Judge Canonge presided. He was one of the most famous of the New Orleans judges. He was a brilliant man, a member of one of the foremost families, and a distinguished scholar. Trials were frequently conducted in three languages—French, Spanish, and English. He had been appointed Judge of the Criminal Court by Governor Roman. At that time the Criminal Court was unique in character; from it there was no appeal. At Pauline's trial he insisted that there should be no intimidation, and that she should have a fair chance. He appointed N. Z. Latour to defend the prisoner.

The members of the special tribunal, six in number, were called to the book and severally sworn by the judge, upon the oath prescribed by the Code, the judge being in turn sworn in by one of the jurors as the presiding officer. The prisoner was then arraigned and entered a plea of "not guilty."

Her attorney stated that Pauline was ready for trial. The district attorney read the indictment. He then explained to the jury the law of 1814, under which the prosecution was instituted and which inflicted the penalty of death upon any slave who struck his master, mistress, or any of their children, so as to cause "contusion or shedding of blood." He then read an amendment to the act, passed in 1843, giving the jury privilege to commute the punishment to imprisonment at hard labor.

Peter Rabbeneck, the owner of Pauline, has not returned to New Orleans, nor does his wife know where he is. She is well enough to come to court, although she is still weak and her face is scarred. She is placed on the witness stand. Pauline is brought into court and the two women face each other. The quadroon woman looks squarely into the white woman's face, but says nothing. The judge asks: "Do you know this negress, Pauline?"

"Yes, she is my husband's slave. . . . "

Mrs. Rabbeneck then testifies that she has been married for nine years, and that before coming to New Orleans her husband, Peter Rabbeneck, was employed as overseer on the plantation of François Robieu, a short distance from the town of Natchitoches. They had lived there for some time, where Rabbeneck enjoyed a good reputation. Three children had been born to them.

Early in 1844 her husband had purchased the woman Pauline from his employer, François Robieu, saying that the quadroon was to act as nurse for his children. Later, a dispute arising between Rabbeneck and Robieu, her husband had left his employ and had brought his family to New Orleans where he had rented the house on Bayou Road. She had discovered subsequently that Pauline was her husband's mistress, but when she taxed him with this, he had ordered her to be silent.

Pauline is then called to the stand and asked if what the white woman says is true. Pauline says that it is true in part. When asked to tell who she is and where she came from, she makes the proud answer that she is a Virginian and a quadroon, that she was once the property of President Monroe, but that she had been sold to a slave dealer and brought to New Orleans where Mr. Robieu had purchased her, along with several other slaves, and had transported her to his plantation near Natchitoches.

She testifies in a defiant manner and says that she has nothing to reproach herself with, that her mistress is insane and that it was necessary to keep her confined. Her master, Rabbeneck, has charged her to control his wife, and so on.

Mrs. Rabbeneck is recalled to the stand and her evidence continues. She tells of a family which lives next door in Bayou Road. The name is Isenhart. She says that when she discovered that Pauline was her husband's mistress, she cried and begged that he put the slave woman out of the house. Her husband refused, struck her and embraced Pauline before her eyes, whereupon she grew hysterical and cried for help. The Isenhart family hearing, her husband assured them that his wife was insane and had delusions. He told them that they must pay no attention to her cries. She testifies that when the Isenharts withdrew, her husband forced her to witness his love-making; that he drove her from his bed and gave her place to Pauline. That a short time after, her husband having business in St. Louis, he departed up the Mississippi on a steamboat, leaving the house in charge of Pauline and giving her two hundred dollars. As soon as her husband was away, Pauline locked her in a room, stripped her and tortured her in various

E H Suydam.

"ASPHODEL," EAST FELICIANA, BUILT IN 1835

"THE SHADOWS" REFLECTS ITSELF IN
BAYOU TECHE, 1830

ways, beating her with a cane and with a strap, burning her with a poker and dragging her about by the hair. The children she treated in a similar manner, and Mrs. Rabbeneck was too weak to aid them. Pauline cursed the children, beat them and forced them to hand her whips and canes with which to beat their mother.

There follows the testimony of a negro slave woman called Dinah, who, at Christmas time, had been employed by Pauline to work by the day and wash clothes. On the second day of her employment at the house on Bayou Road, she testified, Pauline returned from market to find that a biscuit was missing from the breakfast table. She charged Constance, the seven-year-old girl, with the theft. The little girl denied stealing, whereupon Pauline stripped her naked and lashed her with a leather whip, drawing blood. As the child lay upon the floor, the woman kicked her repeatedly. She then forced the child to break a brick to pieces with a hammer, and place the rough pieces of broken brick on the floor. Pauline forced the child to kneel on the broken brick, striking her afresh whenever she cried out with pain.

A few days later, Dinah testifies, she heard Pauline beating some one in the back room, and upon the latter leaving the house, Dinah went to see who was confined there. She raised a mosquito bar and inquired if she could render Mrs. Rabbeneck any assistance, but the woman only moaned in pain. "So I paid no more attention to her but went on with my work."

On another occasion Dinah heard Pauline in the cabinet abusing her mistress, cursing her, and telling her that if she did not get up and scrub the floors that she would beat her to death. Pauline then dragged her mistress out of bed by her hair, beating her in the face with her fist. The white woman screamed so pitifully that Dinah remonstrated with Pauline, urging her "to act with more mildness," but Pauline attempted to close the door of the cabinet. Failing to do so, as the body of the white woman was lying against it, she commanded the child Constance to hand her a cane, whereupon the child, "all of a tremble," did so. Pauline then lashed the white woman in a most cruel manner. Dinah then testifies that, on the same day, she informed a gentleman, for whom she occasionally worked, of the barbarity in the house on Bayou Road, and the next day the gentleman addressed an anonymous letter to the mayor. This led to the arrest of Pauline.

The mayor's testimony follows, and that of Dr. Beugnot. They describe the condition of the sufferers when discovered, and repeat what Mrs. Rabbeneck had told them.

Catherine Isenhart, the daughter of the man living next door, is called as a witness and testifies that she heard cries, but that Mr. Rabbeneck told her that his wife was insane. She had frequently heard Pauline abusing her mistress, but she had never seen her beaten.

The case was submitted to the jury with argument. After being instructed by the court in regard to the law, they returned the following verdict:

"We, the undersigned freeholders, forming the special tribunal which was convoked and sworn to try the slave Pauline, belonging to Peter Rabbeneck, accused of striking her mistress so as to cause the shedding of blood, do unanimously find her guilty and agree to sentence, and do hereby sentence the said Pauline, belonging to Peter Rabbeneck, to death, and do hereby unanimously fix and appoint the 21st day of February, 1845, between the hours of 10 A.M. and 2 P.M., as the time when the said sentence of death shall be carried into effect, the place of execution to be opposite the Parish Prison. And inasmuch as we are given to understand that the said Pauline is now *enceinte* and this sentence can not be carried into execution while she is in that situation, we, in such a case, do further unanimously order that said sentence of death shall be executed at the same hour and place on the 28th day of March, 1846."

Pauline's behavior during the trial was extraordinary. She is described as "proud but entirely passive"—a tall, handsome quadroon with piercing black eyes, staring straight ahead of her—and never heeding the crowd which shouted curses and threats at her, as she passed, under guard, from the prison to court and back again. She wore always a "sulky, stubborn, and revengeful look," but she said nothing. On the last day of the trial the mob in the streets was so threatening that she was hustled into a cab and driven to prison, as it was feared that she would be taken from the officers and killed then and there.

The day after the trial a committee of physicians was appointed by Judge Canonge to examine the condition of Pauline. She succeeded in convincing them that she was to become a mother, and named Peter Rabbeneck as the father of her unborn child. But as the months passed, it was found that she had lied. No child was born. During the period of her imprisonment it is said that she appeared indifferent to her approaching execution. She admitted, in a casual manner, that she had lied in order to prolong her life.

While Pauline was awaiting execution, Mrs. Rabbeneck found herself alone and without money. Her husband did not return and she was without means to support herself and her three children. A family in the town of Plaquemine offered her a home, so she went there and remained, taking her children with her. We have only one last picture of her, a faded clipping from the Plaquemine "Gazette":

The miscreant who ill-treated his wife so outrageously in New Orleans last fall, and then left her and children to the tender mercies of the slave Pauline (now under sentence of death for her barbarities toward her mistress and children), was found prowling about the premises of one of our citizens Thursday night, and was very properly arrested and put in jail. His object in hanging round the house in question was to see his wife, but whether with good or evil intent it is difficult to tell. He will hardly find a lawyer in this place who for the sake of a fee will undertake to shield him from justice.

And so Peter Rabbeneck disappears from the record. What became of him, we have no way of knowing. His wife and children remained in Plaquemine, with the family which had offered them protection.

Pauline was executed on March 28, 1846. We have a description of the execution by Henry C. Castellanos, an eye-witness. He writes:

Orleans Street, in front of the prison, was blocked up by an immense crowd as early as 8 o'clock in the morning. At 11 o'clock she was robed for the execution, confessed and took the sacrament. At 12:15 she was taken from the cell and conducted to the scaffold, erected on a platform connecting the Parish Prison with the Police Jail. I have witnessed executions of different kinds, but I never saw such a perfect example of firmness as that which she displayed.

Some would have called it indifference, but such was not the case. She died not only penitent and resigned, but exhibited great moral courage. When seated on the chair, the Abbé Louis said a prayer in which she joined with apparent eagerness and devotion. When asked whether she desired anything, she replied in the negative—nothing except a crucifix and a glass of water. The question was then put whether she was ready, and she calmly answered "Yes." The drop fell, and she suffered three or four minutes ere she expired. When her form was drawn back to the scaffold, it was found that her neck had not been dislocated, and she must have died from strangulation.

There were no less than 5,000 persons to witness the execution, among whom serious and sorrowful faces strangely contrasted with the boisterous and merry. Bedizened courtesans flaunted their charms in open carriages; women of all description were there on foot, young and old, of all colours. Loud was the laugh and merry the jokes which provoked mirth among the lookers-on, and as I contemplated the swinging and circling form of the expiatory victim and the stolid indifference of that huge and heterogeneous crowd, I thought that a public execution was a beastly and barbarous exhibition—a brutal privilege of the law to satisfy the morbid appetite of those who delight in scenes of cruelty. . . .

After hanging about twenty minutes, the culprit was pronounced dead, and the body lifted to the platform, whence it was taken back to the prison for interment. The sheriff and officers under his direction performed their duties well, and the press gave them much credit for the dignified and orderly manner in which the stern but just mandate of the law was obeyed. . . .

And so ends the story of Pauline, and surely it is one of the most curious which came out of slavery in Louisiana.

Part III

LEISURELY TIMES

Chapter Fifteen

A YOUNG MAN OF FASHION IN 1850

AMONG the documents examined in compiling this book, I found the diary of a young Creole gentleman of fashion, who lived on a plantation on Cane River near Natchitoches. The young man was studying law, and it was necessary for him to write fluently in English, although he preferred writing and speaking in French. So he wrote, as an exercise, a complete account of his daily life for three years, beginning in January 1850, when he was twenty-two years old.

This diary I found fascinating. Although it was extremely difficult to decipher, due to fading ink and yellowing paper, I read one thousand closely written pages. It was my original intention to use parts of it—the more, let us say, exciting incidents—and let the rest go; but as I read I realized that the fascination lay not in the incidents themselves, but in the placid passing of the days; the details of plantation life, the visits to this one and that, the trips to town, the dances, visits to the convent to see his cousins who were being educated there—a score of things unimportant in themselves, but building up a picture of the times which I have never seen elsewhere. Consequently I have not deleted the diary; I have taken the record of the first three months exactly as the young gentleman wrote it. This diary is the most perfect picture of Creole antebellum life that I know. I have not quoted more than one sixth of it.

Here we have young Lestant Prudhomme at home after four years at college; he has returned with the intention of studying law, and has arranged to read with a leading lawyer in the town of Natchitoches. At home he assists his father a little in the management of the plantation, but only a little. There is an overseer who does all that, and the men of the family have plenty of time to amuse themselves. Every day they ride on horseback to visit "Aunt Benjamin" or "Uncle Cloutier" who live on adjoining plantations. The neighbors—who are all cousins—come nearly every day to visit. They eat dinner in one house and supper in another; they return home for an evening *soirée,* then go in a body and spend the night in a fourth house because "Aunt Phanor" is alone and lonely. The young man enjoys games of *maroc* and glasses of wine; quiet evenings by the fire; talks with the governess; games with his little brother Serdot. On Sundays the family goes fifteen miles to Natchitoches in order to attend mass and visit the convent afterward to see daughters and cousins who are boarding there while going to school. Steamboats pass, carrying cotton and cotton-planters to New Orleans and home again.

Jenny Lind sings in New Orleans and the family goes down to hear her. There are parties, weddings, funerals. And life goes on its placid way.

The picture becomes more complicated when one realizes that nearly every person mentioned is a relative. At the time that this diary was written in 1850, the Cloutiers, the Lambres, the Prudhommes, the Metoyers, and the rest had been neighbors for a century in a sparsely populated country. They had intermarried until they constituted one large family; they were a close-knit social group in themselves. It is interesting to note that Lestant Prudhomme, in writing, never criticizes one of his own group; they are never boring, never tiresome, never dull; they are always "pleasant and agreeable." The only criticisms that he makes—and slight criticisms at that—are of strangers, or men and women outside the circle. These guests he sometimes finds dull, or he thinks that they talk too much. It is only his own group which interests him. He never thinks of going away, and seldom thinks of changing anything in the existing order. He has been born to luxury, as luxury was counted in those days, and he thinks nothing of it. He has lived on a plantation all of his life, and is so accustomed to the goings and comings of the negro slaves that he never mentions them, except in the most casual way; one would think that he did not see them at all. And yet we know that he had his own personal servant, a body-servant so-called, who awakened him in the morning by bringing coffee to his bed, who did the thousand and one things which he wished done, and who accompanied him frequently on his trips over the country. Never once does he tell us of this man; never does he mention his name. The negroes did not exist, as far

as he was concerned, any more than the furniture around
him. They were part of the picture. One would never know
that they were there, except for the occasional mention of
buying or selling them.

The overseer attended to the business affairs, and the
young men were never so occupied that they could not take
any amusement that offered. There is constant movement;
life was spent in preparing to go somewhere, going; preparing to return, returning; unpacking and getting settled;
then it all began over again. There was only one fear—the
fear of being alone for even an hour.

Nowadays it seems a life altogether incredible. The
reader may ask: was the writer of this diary typical of his
time? Were all rich young Creoles as lacking in interest in
the affairs of the world? And my answer must be that young
Prudhomme was typical of his time in every way, except
that perhaps he was more intellectual than most of the
young men around him. He read more, and he was studying
law. The only quarrel he ever had with his mother—whom
he loved devotedly—was because she thought he was not
gay enough! He was too studious; he did not go about
enough with young people. I could hardly credit my senses
when I read that part of the diary, yet there it was, in black
and white, and set down in all sincerity.

This must not be taken as a criticism of the young man,
for it is not. He had come of a long line of men accustomed
to leisure and ease, and he was typical of the class which
he represented.

The diary follows. It is written in a large book, entitled "A Record of the State of the Weather, the Daily

News, and My Occupations and Amusements," by P. Lestant Prudhomme. With the exception of minor changes in punctuation, made for purposes of clarity, the diarist's style has been retained in all its florid peculiarities.

Chapter Sixteen

THE YOUNG MAN'S DIARY

FOR the last fortnight we have had wet weather: the rain incessant and the temperature high. From news received it appears that it was the same on Red River, and the natural consequence of so much rain was that the waters commenced rising at a rapid rate, and frightened many planters who had but a few months ago experienced the effects of the unprecedented rise of '49. Many commenced gathering their cattle so as to be ready for the emergency. However, although a great rise above has been reported, the inhabitants of this section of the country need entertain no fears, for the water has almost stopped rising and before the second freshet is felt here the water will be low enough for the channel to contain the surplus.

Having finished my course of practical surveying with Mr. Walmsley, deputy surveyor, and afterwards having assisted on the 21st at the union of Miss Aspasie Lambre and Simeon Hart, I this day resumed my study of law and commenced again reading

Chitty's Blackstone from the first beginning. I am studying under J. G. Campbell, an eminent lawyer of Natchitoches.

Yesterday, during the whole morning, wild pigeons passed from one swamp to the other. It was really a most astonishing thing to see so many large flocks flying over with hardly any interruption. Many of them were killed, for such persons as had any gun in their possession made use of them, and this fact was the cause of my not commencing my studies yesterday as I had concluded to do.

This evening, at about five o'clock, just as I had put away my law book and had taken my stick and reading book to go and take a walk, I heard of Edward Cloutier's arrival from Louisville where he had gone to study the profession of dentist, and had been so unfortunate as not to be able to find an institution nor any dentist that would consent to teach him. Immediately my designs were changed; I had my horse saddled and I went to see the new-comer. Everybody was surprised at this young man's return but when the causes became known, it was well conceived. His father, however, seemed not to enter in the same spirit, and appeared much troubled at his return.

WEDNESDAY—30TH

This morning there was a very good and heavy frost; the weather was clear and beautiful the whole day.

This afternoon I drew a cask of wine of three hundred bottles. Father was unable to assist, feeling unwell.

Before returning from my walk this evening I stopped a moment at Mr. Phanor's where I was engaged to remain for supper, which invitation I declined, being unable to remain on account of my studies which I had neglected during the day, and for which I wished to make some atonement by studying tonight.

Upon my return home I informed my sister, Julie, that I had been requested to let her know that her presence would be agreeable at Mr. Phanor's, and she, expressing the desire of complying with the engagement, I accompanied her, and returned immediately to tend to my studies.

The water fell about an inch last night and about as much today.

We were gratified today with the visit of my aunt Benjamin Metoyer, and this is the first time she has been able to leave home for a long time, having been constantly confined to her room with a malignant cold or kind of catarrh.

THURSDAY—31ST

The cold gave place to a warm and windless day.

In the morning we had the visit of Mrs. Cloutier and her son Edward; the former went to spend the day at Aunt Benjamin's and the latter remained with me.

In the evening, after my studies were over, we both went off from here on foot to pay a visit to our Aunt Benjamin.

The water is still falling, a circumstance that pleases everyone, as a strong rise is reported above.

In the evening on my way to my aunt Benjamin's I met my aunt Baptiste, upon whom, not without some trouble, I prevailed to come and spend the night at home.

Felix Metoyer accompanied my cousin and me back. The evening was spent most agreeably, everyone appearing to be in fine spirits. The conversation and the little games and amusements going on were so animated no one thought of retiring before eleven o'clock. We had also to enliven the party the company of Mr. and Mrs. Adolphe Prudhomme.

SUNDAY—FEBRUARY 3RD

I got up earlier than usual, put on my Sunday go to meeting clothes, performed my sabbath devotions and then sat at a breakfast table well covered with several fine and delicate dishes (such as are not found everywhere), such as tamales, tortillas, sausages, and blood pudding.

FEBRUARY 6TH

Mr. Harris, a school teacher, who, on account of the bad regulations and the low state of the finances of the public school, has received no pay for his troubles, and keeps the place so as to have it at the next appointment, and who is a man of family and now troubled and very much broken down with the fever that comes on him frequently, being in a somewhat destitute situation came here to buy some meal, but humanity would not justify the selling of food to a man in need of it. He slept here and the next day at 1 P.M. he went off laden with provisions and thanking his benefactors a thousand times for their generosity.

FEBRUARY 7TH

I was touched with the unfortunate condition in which this man is, and cannot conceive how his neighbors who are certainly able to entertain him, whose interest it is to do so, and who if they have any humanity to feelings should supply the wants of the unfortunate.

At about half past five P.M., just as I had shut up shop and put my book aside, I got a note from Mrs. N. Prudhomme requesting me to come and spend the night at her house, Mr. N. not being at home. I immediately took my stick and went off. Upon my arrival I was pleased to find G. Prudhomme, who had just come, and for the same purpose spent the evening very pleasantly and remained over night.

FEBRUARY 8TH

After breakfast, to quit the table and form the happy family circle around a good and hot fire place was done by unanimous consent, then went on the ordinary conversation of the general news, home and foreign, things that are of importance only in small places or in the country were in their turn talked of, such as the most important subject of where each one present intended to spend the day. Mrs. Phanor's trip to town and also that of her sister, Mrs. Archinard, when their return, etc., etc., when to the satisfaction of all present Mr. Phanor walked in and helped to adorn the circle, the conversation never, however, tarrying and new subjects being constantly brought on the *tapis*.

In the meantime, I had my horse saddled, however without knowing which way to go and spend my Sunday, but the arrival of Emile and Gabriel Prudhomme soon settled the question, and I spent the day at home, entertaining my company as well as possible. A little shooting with the blow-gun and a fowl piece was practised. At about 11 o'clock A.M., Phanor went home, there to receive his company, and had a real *diner de garçon*, no ladies being present, and, to increase the pleasure of the guests, the steamboat passing by put out a barrel of fine and nice oysters. At four in the evening I went off with my two friends, paid a visit to Narcisse Prudhomme, where my companions found their parents. Thence I went and supped with them; some time after supper I went off to go and see why John and Edward had not come home Saturday evening as they intended. However, I found no one up at Mr. Cloutier's (my uncle) and was on the point of returning home when the door was opened by a servant bawling out the apostrophe, "Misier di vous entre." In I stepped and was introduced without any ceremony into the bed room. My uncle then got up, took me in the parlor where we sat in *tête-à-tête* before a good fire and talked and puffed till about half past ten P.M. when I took leave of him and returned home, with once in a while having a cold N.E. wind full in the face.

N. B. Last night, reading a New York paper, I saw a northwestern passage had been found and also a new continent which, however, was not approached very near, the cold being too excessive.

SATURDAY—FEBRUARY 9TH, 1850

The wind was high the whole night and blowing from the North West. Before the rise of the sun the whole surface of the earth was covered with a dazzling white mantle, which, when the bright luminary of the day appeared, seemed to be strewed with diamonds. Towards noon the wind abated a little and it got warmer.

After sitting at a breakfast table covered with the best of dishes, to which we paid great attention, everyone got ready for a hunting expedition.

Walking, running, and blowing in the field we kept on hurrying, all anxious to come to the charge. At last, after about two hours' walk, we came to a field covered with high grass which prevented high prospects for a good hunt. There to our great delight we found that the game we were hunting were all assembled, all certainly unconscious of the fate that awaited them. We were not long before opening our fire on them, and pointing our guns in all directions as well as our blunderbusts to receive their terrible charge. *Pin, pam, pow, bow,* was in a moment heard in every direction. The affray had commenced and our weak and tired enemy fell like hay before the mower's scythe.

After two hours' chase, we started for home loaded with the plunder of the enemy and shouting with joy as we drove our 86 prisoners ahead of us to be sacrificed at the best of altars, the kitchen, to satisfy our highly finished tastes as epicures.

At Mr. J. B. Cloutier's, the place of rendezvous, a sumptuous dinner was awaiting us, in honor of our victory.

Mr. J. B. C's lady not being at home, we determined upon assembling the young men and making an always agreeable *souper de garçons.*

The whole evening and the *veille* were spent, some conversing on the topics of the day, and others playing at different games of cards. At 12 P.M. the company retired.

SUNDAY–IOTH, 1850

Felix and myself left in the morning after breakfast to go to town and meet Mrs. Benjamin and Mr. and Mrs. Adolphe. I assisted at Mass. The church was full. There was no preaching, the regulations to be followed during Lent were read and some remarks, and very appropriate ones, on the manner the regulations were to be fulfilled.

After Mass I started with several persons to go to the Convent and see my cousins, but just as I was going to enter, perceiving there were many persons present, and consequently fearing not to have a seat where I wished, I came back. Afterwards I was sorry for not having entered for I heard that instead of one parlor as before there were two and that there was sufficient room.

I found the town very dull and did not know what to do with myself and played one or two games of billiards to while away the time.

I had the pleasure of spending a pleasant *soirée* at Dr. Kerell's where I and others had been invited. We had some music part of the time. I was troubled with both of my feet that I had hurt yesterday at the hunt, and wound however being slight, but notwithstanding painful, so I did not dance but one set.

MONDAY—11TH, 1850

The steamboat *Doswell* got in Natchitoches about 11 A.M. There was a man on board returning from California after an absence of 10 months during which time he made $10,000 selling liquor. He bought as a present to Mr. Melony (Constable) a fine cane with a heavy gold head made of California gold; it is worth $50.00.

I left town at 3 P.M. and on the way I prevailed on E. Cloutier to come with me. We played cards till 11 o'clock at night.

TUESDAY—12TH, 1850

Mardi Gras

It rained the whole night and continued till 5 P.M.

Several young men and I intended to go and spend the day at Theophile's and stay there over night to feast the day, but the inclement state of the weather prevented us.

The *Doswell* came up at 11 P.M. She stopped here to put out some freight and I put a letter on board for a young man, J. Bolwing, from Baltimore, who has come to New Orleans with negroes he has to sell, and has written to me to know whether any member of my family would take them. I could not give him any positive answer, and begged him to wait a few days when I would be able to give him positive information. My uncle Adolphe spent a part of the evening here; my father had sent for him to know if he would not buy two or three of the whole lot (twelve) of those negroes—he buying the rest. The wind at 6 P.M. turned to the N.W.

WEDNESDAY–13TH, 1850

At 3 P.M. I had some fire made in the school-room where I repaired to write. Edward came with me, and he amused himself with my blow-gun shooting at little birds that came to eat the meal he had thrown on the ground near one of the windows.

FRIDAY–15TH

This morning a white frost spread over the earth, and ice was to be seen in small holes of water.

I returned from my uncle's at 11 P.M. I left him taming some wild mules.

Father went to his plantation and in the evening, shortly after dinner, mother went at Phanor's where the children went to meet her after school. Thus I was left alone in the house quietly reading the dry and uninteresting Blackstone. The Governess remained in her room, and I had not the pleasure of seeing her before the family returned. For several days past the river has been rising pretty fast. It has already attained what it had lost and is still rising. From 3 P.M. yesterday to 4 P.M. today it has risen 7 inches.

This evening I had a little trouble correcting one of the slaves who attempted to run away from me and bruised my hand a little and sprained my thumb. Thus it seems that in this world we must constantly suffer; my toe is hardly cured that I must hurt some other part of my body.

SATURDAY–16TH

There was a fine white frost this morning, and the sun was bright. I made a good fire in the school room where I intended to study, but about 10 A.M. John Cloutier came here to go to his brother-in-law's, and as he did not know the way, I had to lay

my book by and start off with him. We spent the day very agreeably there, and got back at about 6 P.M. After supper we played
at the game of Ramps till very late, and we were very much amused
at Bag Dad.

SUNDAY—17TH

The day was most charming; it was neither too cold nor too
warm.

Some persons had been invited to dinner to eat the snipes I
had killed, and although all the persons that had been invited did
not come, the party was pretty large and gay, and, as all the guests
proclaimed with one unanimous voice, the most excellent.

My grandmother is at A. Prudhomme's. She has been there
for the last two or three days. She is very much frightened at
the news about the water and on that account is to return immediately to town. The water is rising here at about the rate of 2
inches in 24 hours and a rise of 15 feet is reported.

MONDAY—18TH

I spent the evening at Phanor's. The steamboat on which Phanor
and his lady and Leonce Rocques were to descend to New Orleans
was expected today, but till sundown no signs had been seen of it
and so it was not expected before two or three days. However, a
short time after supper, while the whole company had formed the
always pleasant family circle around the fire, the boat was announced by one of the servants and it was found to be quite near.
Mrs. Phanor was much surprised, she was on the point of not
going, but being pressed a little by those present, in a moment
every thing was ready.

Leonce alone who had not yet packed his trunk was not ready,
and believing he had no time to prepare had given up all idea of
going when I succeeded in deciding him to go, assuring him he
might fix everything in five minutes. At that very moment Felix
arrived, and in a second Leonce was prepared to start. A moment
after the passengers were aboard and the boat was off.

Upon my return from the boat, I found all the children crying which is very natural, but it did not take them long to be reconciled with the idea that their mother and father were gone.

The *veille* was not interrupted, it continued till 10 P.M. when my sister and I left the company to return home, where we found mother and father alone in the sitting room playing Ramps; and although it was late they played several games after that. The day was a most charming one, somewhat cold and damp.

TUESDAY—19TH

The weather was somewhat warmer, with very little wind, and the sun shining.

I intended this day to resume my studies I had left last week, and was about getting to work when Mrs. Metoyer, accompanied by Felix, arrived here; the former to spend the day, and the latter to go snipe hunting. Being invited by him to participate in the sport, the day being beautiful and the idea of going to shoot snipes again took me from my studies. In a moment the horse was saddled, I was as soon ready and off, both of us went anticipating a glorious hunt. Unfortunately, contrary to our expectations, we found but very few, and very wild snipes; I had the good luck of killing eight or nine but my companion was entirely disgusted, not having been able to shoot more than once or twice.

We got back at Phanor's after the dinner was over, but the table was soon set, and after partaking of a good dinner we were treated with two or three dozens of fine oysters.

After dinner Felix and Adolphe went to Theophile's; the former with the intention of spending there two or three days. I accompanied my aunt here and started out hunting again. I met with very little success, seeing but few snipes, and I returned home wet to the waist.

I got my newspaper tonight. I had not received any for the last month, and I spent the *veille* reading the news, and also a prospectus of the Western Military Institute, where my brother is at school.

WEDNESDAY—20TH

The day was cloudy and windy. Father bought four mules at $80.00 apiece. He had to go at his plantation, having been sent to see a sick girl.

I read a little in the morning, and gave an hour's lesson to my sister. After dinner I read a newspaper and slept till 4 P.M. Adolphe had a hot fever which had been on him the whole day. Mother represented to me the position of my aunt alone with her husband sick, telling me I ought to go and spend the night with them. Accordingly, after supper I took my cane and told everyone good night and started. I found my aunt alone by the fire reading the news. We stayed up till 9 P.M. playing Ramps and eating candy.

THURSDAY—21ST

It has been ascertained that the rumor about the fifteen foot rise is false and the water is now falling here. It was on a stand two days ago.

My uncle Adolphe got up this morning without any fever, but yellow and weak. He, however, tended to his duties. This evening after I had got through with my studies, I took my book and came to take a walk; I had not got very far when I was overtaken by a storm and heavy shower of rain, and I just had time, making very good use of my legs, to arrive at Phanor's, where I got sheltered from the rain which lasted about an hour and a half.

SATURDAY—23RD

The weather was cloudy. The heat was oppressive.

The whole company that had agreed upon going to town to-day met here at about nine o'clock and started for the place of destination. Mrs. Archinard and her small daughter, Mrs. Deblieux and Julie (my sister) were in a carriage, and my friend Felix and I followed on horseback. We stopped a moment at my uncle Cloutier's on the way and got to town at about 11½ A.M.

The Young Man's Diary

Immediately upon my arrival in town I went about transacting
some little business I had, and repaired at Mr. Campbell's office
to stand an examination on the passages I had read. This examination finished at 3 P.M., I was then very hungry, having fasted in
the morning, and I went directly at Mr. Phanor's where Mrs.
Archinard had the kindness to have a dish of eggs prepared for
me and gave me some sardines, but nothing in the line of fresh
meat, this being one of the ember days. With these different dishes
I made a very sumptuous dinner; though had it been another day
I would have liked very much a piece of fine beef-steak or of
roasted beef, and would have been able to enjoy them well, my
appetite being great, no breakfast and a late dinner.

SUNDAY—24TH

The weather was again cloudy but there was no rain. I spent
the day most pleasantly and agreeably paying visits to different
ladies and to the priest, Mr. Martin, whom I had heard spoken
of very highly, and who came up to my expectations. I found him
to be a polite gentleman, entertaining and receiving his company
admirably well. He showed me a fine collection of natural curiosi-
ties, and though I have visited many museums, I found things I
had never seen. After spending with him about half an hour very
pleasantly, I took leave, highly pleased. He has been here about
six or seven weeks, and preached a sermon during Mass which
the whole audience pronounced excellent. It was profuse with deep,
profound, conclusive, and convincing reasonings, beautifully worded,
and delivered in an audible and plain voice, with appropriate and
oratorical gestures.

At dinner we had the ever agreeable company of three or four
young ladies with whom Felix and I spent our time most pleasantly.
At about eight the company went to the convent to assist at the
Benediction of the Blessed Sacrament, after which we had the
pleasure of seeing several young ladies, some my cousins (all
charming and beautiful), and spent with them several hours. During that time Felix, Ursin Lambre, and I were taken through the

whole establishment by the superior, Mother Landry, whom we had the good fortune of delighting with our (as she expressed it) modest deportment in the chapel. The establishment is spacious, the study rooms are large, the dormitories comfortable and orderly and adorned with neat and good beds, the play grounds vast, everything well calculated to promote the happiness and comfort of those lovely creatures that are there to be secluded from the world, till they come out to be the pride and glory of society.

MONDAY—25TH

We were to return this morning, but Mrs. Archinard wishing to have her daguerrotype likeness taken together with that of her younger daughter to give them to her elder daughter that is in the convent, we were detained the whole morning and left town only about half past eleven. We dined at Uncle Cloutier's and got home in the evening. We stopped a moment at the public school to see John B. Cloutier who this day commenced teaching.

The heat was very oppressive. It almost gave me the spring fever. It made me feel dull and wearied so that I was very glad to get home. I spent my *soirée,* while the others were playing Ramps, writing my journal up to date.

N. B. On our way to Natchitoches we met Mr. Hart and his lady, who were coming on their first visit in the Island. This lady is a relation of ours and was coming among her relations to introduce her husband. We were sorry that we should be going when they were coming, but were better reconciled when we heard they would stay a couple of weeks with us.

TUESDAY—26TH

The weather was cloudy and the heat oppressive. Before setting to my studies after dinner I killed about two dozens of black birds and went to pay a little visit to my aunt and uncle Adolphe. They appeared somewhat uneasy on account of Phanor's youngest son whose leg was stiff in consequence of a bruise he had received on the knee. Mother and Julie went at Phanor's to see my aunt Benjamin who had sent them word to come and see her.

I commenced reading at 4 P.M. and did not come out of my room before 7. I retired suffering from headache.

WEDNESDAY—27TH

I commenced reading very late, having after breakfast repaired to the garden with mother for the purpose of trimming some young fruit trees.

I stopped reading this evening sooner than usual, so as to go and spend the night at my uncle Theophile's. I had to go up two of the bayous to get there. I met, at my uncle's, Felix whom I expected to find there, and besides Mrs. Simeon Hart, who had gone there to take a boat for New Orleans. I spent the evening very pleasantly and played a few games of cards.

THURSDAY—28TH, 1850

We had a beautiful spring day. Many trees are budding, some are in blossom, and others again are covered with leaves. I started from my uncle's after breakfast and got here about 9 A.M. I went at my studies, took a short recreation after dinner and commenced again, and did not leave before supper.

The *Hecla* came up a little before that; she looked magnificent in the dark, her lights shining like as many diamonds, and the cinders flying out of her pipes forming huge and tortuous columns of fire that cast a luminous light far around.

We heard from Phanor and Lize; the weather, it appears in New Orleans, is very inclement, and little favorable for amusements.

After supper I got a newspaper and read it to Father and Mother till we all retired at 10 P.M. Julie spent the *soirée* at Phanor's.

FRIDAY—MARCH 1ST

Since yesterday, Father has remained almost constantly in my room reading Clay's Ten Resolutions proposed to the Senate to settle all the difficult points now agitating the country and threatening a dissension between the North and the South, if not a total dissolution of the wonderful and admirable Republic, the admiration of the whole world.

This evening, a short time after I had commenced my studies, Achille, Gabriel, and my aunt Neville arrived here, and as a matter of course I had to go out of my room and see them. My aunt Adolphe came about five, and the consequence of all these visits was that I had to study till 10 o'clock at night and be deprived of my *veille*. Julie went off on horseback with Achille to spend tomorrow at his house.

SATURDAY–2ND

I immediately after breakfast shot and killed many black-birds. At 9 I commenced my studies and had a hard day's work with it. Reviewing what I had read during the whole week, that is, writing the answer to all the questions, I was occupied till 7 P.M., having taken but a short recreation after dinner, and notwithstanding I lacked about 15 pages of getting through.

My aunt Huppe arrived from town this evening with my sister Odilie who had been in town two weeks for her health. After getting very healthy and fat, she again a few days ago took the fever and had it even today. Julie came with them. My aunt Benjamin, Eloise, and Eugenie went to town this morning. My aunt Adolphe started this evening with Phanor's children. Angella went with her to see Odilie in town and they unfortunately crossed on the way.

SUNDAY–3RD

This morning I heard that four or five young men had spent the evening with my uncle Adolphe, and I was sorry to have missed such a fine opportunity of amusing myself.

Today the weather was most enchanting and beautiful. I spent the day most pleasantly at home. A numerous and agreeable company of relations took place here and every one of the guests being in fine spirits the party was pleasant to every one. We were twenty-five grown persons at the table and seventeen children. My uncle Janin, who was of the party, stayed over night.

After every one was gone, at about 5 o'clock, the governess, my sister Julie, and I accompanied on foot Aphalide and her brother Felix half way home.

On my return I mounted my horse to go at my uncle Cloutier's and see his son Edward who has been confined to his bed for the last fifteen days. I spent the evening very pleasantly in company with Mr. Hart, Mrs. A. Lambre, Mr. and Mrs. Cloutier and their son, John, and got back home at 11 at night.

N. B. The governess (Mrs. F. Leech) got a situation; she is going after leaving here to teach at my uncle Neville's.

MONDAY—4TH

The lottery ticket the governess and Julie took together was received and upon examining the newspaper . . . can you imagine what was seen? The ticket had won no prize.

Pretty late in the evening my aunt Adolphe and Felix went off, my sister Julie accompanying them to spend the *soirée* with them. I wished to go but, being at my studies, I was prevented from going then but went a little later. I spent my time while there very agreeably and got back home about 11 o'clock at night.

TUESDAY—5TH

Everybody (the ladies) retired pretty early, and Father and myself remained on the gallery talking about instructive subjects till about 10. I did not retire until 11, being occupied with the Blackstone.

WEDNESDAY—6TH

This morning at 6 the weather was cloudy and prognosticated badly for our trip to town. In consequence, instead of starting before, we started after breakfast. However, it was not long before the sun appeared and shun beautifully for the rest of the day.

My mother, my grandmother, Julie, Angella, Odilie, Coline, and

I went to see the performance of a circus and were all very much pleased with the performance. It had represented the night before and this was the last time. Some of the feats were most wonderful. The circus was the general topic of the day, and all agreed on the opinion that it was the best that had ever visited Natchitoches.

I have seen many feats performed at circuses, but several of those performed here I had never seen. I spent the day taking *le tout ensemble parfaitement bien*. The steamboat *Doswell* got in town at 11 P.M.

N. B. I had my hair cut.

THURSDAY–7TH

I passed my weekly examination at Mr. Campbell's and succeeded so well in answering the questions that he complimented me on my success. I paid several agreeable visits, particularly that at the convent together with my mother and sisters. My mother called for several young ladies, who were not allowed to come, it being contrary to the rules of the establishment. We were taken through the establishment and when we came to the study room all the young ladies were there in a row, and such of them as know mother came out of the ranks and conversed a few minutes with us.

We left town at 3 and, as we paid a visit, we did not leave the ferry before half past 4. We stopped at my uncle Cloutier's about fifteen minutes. His son, Edward, is better and able to get up.

Before getting home, hearing that several young men on the coast had gone to the circus that was to represent at T. Chalair's, immediately upon my arrival I got ready, took another horse and started. I arrived just as it commenced, and though it was the second time I had seen the performances, I was delighted, and much amused at the remarks of astonishment made by the audience.

FRIDAY–8TH

At 6 P.M., while yet at my studies, I was sent word that Gabriel Prudhomme was here; I immediately went to see him and was very much pleased at learning his intention of spending the night here.

As all the young ladies were assembled at Phanor's, it was not natural that two young men should have remained at home (especially being so near by), and consequently we went to amuse ourselves with the young ladies; and it is useless for me to say that the *soirée* was extremely agreeable to both of us.

The steamboat *Hecla* passed here at half past 11 at night.

SUNDAY—MARCH 10TH

I was to go with Gabriel who wished to go at Theophile's and dine there, but our projects had to be given up for all the young ladies that had spent the night at Phanor's came here to spend the day. However great might have been our disappointment, we were not sorry that things had turned out as they did, for we amused ourselves very well. In the evening, all the company started to go at my aunt Hertzogs, the ladies in carriage and the young ladies and gentlemen on horseback. After spending a couple of hours agreeably there we started on our return, just as the rain was commencing. By riding fast all got here without getting wet, but as I did not like to have the ladies alone, I followed the carriage and got home well drenched. This little excursion was pleasant and amusing for the young spirits, and a good cup of Creole coffee a short time after our arrival with some fine cakes set everything right. I went and spent the night at Gabriel's father's and spent the *veille* very pleasantly. The weather got very cold after the rain.

MONDAY—11TH

I got back home at about 10 A.M. I found my aunt Neville here, and amused myself speaking with her till I heard that my aunt Huppe had waited for me to take her at my uncle Theophile's but seeing I was not coming, she had started alone with a little negro boy; when I immediately begged to be excused and started. I met my aunt at Phanor's ferry. We arrived but a short time before dinner, the road being in a most awful state. I dined there, and got back at about half past three.

TUESDAY—MARCH 12TH

I studied right hard the whole day, even at night, not having done much since Thursday, when I last passed my examination.

My uncle Cloutier who had gone to accompany Mrs. Hart and her sister at his brother's-in-law, passed this way on his return home and spent about an hour here; say from 4 to 5. He appeared to be very gay and amused us very much. He could not be prevailed upon to remain here till morning.

THURSDAY—14TH

The weather was most beautiful but the heat somewhat oppressive. I took breakfast at Phanor's. My uncle Theophile, his lady, and Mrs. Hart spent the day here. Octavie and Leonce came about 12. Shortly after dinner my uncle Adolphe came, and shortly after my aunt Benjamin also arrived, and so the company was pretty large. Julie went off with my uncle Theophile and his lady and also Mrs. Hart. The company that went out hunting last Monday returned today. They met with pretty good luck, and amused themselves exceedingly. I could not get to my studies in the evening on account of the company. I expected to go to town tomorrow in carriage with father, but I learned tonight he had changed his mind; to my great disappointment. I would have put off this journey till Saturday, but as I had prepared everything for tomorrow and I wished to be here on Saturday, I did not alter my mind.

SATURDAY—16TH; SUNDAY—17TH

Those two days were, by me, spent most pleasantly, and I think I can say with truth that it was the same with all of those that participated in the party. Saturday, Felix and Leonce got there. The latter went off at night saying he would return in the morning, but did not do so, I expect, because of the weather, as we had a pretty good shower in the morning. The time was spent conversing, principally with the ladies, making music, dancing, and turning the lathe. I made a pattern for a fish-trap, which my aunt Huppe had requested me to make for her to send to her son, who resides at Pointe Coupée.

One of the most important, if not most interesting topics of conversation was upon the Holy Bible. I maintained it or defended it against the charges which the other gentlemen made, or entertained against this most splendid of all works, as it must be when we consider the infinite power and boundless wisdom and goodness of Him who is its author.

We got home just as the *Doswell* went up this morning.

TUESDAY–19TH

How strange . . . how wonderful! how incomprehensible this climate. Last night most beautiful weather. The wind coming from the north. The firmament studded with millions of bright luminaries, darting forth their brilliant and sweet light, to guide the weary traveller during the absence of the powerful emperor of the day.

Nothing in consequence is expected but a white frost in the morning. But lo, to everyone's surprise a change in the night was operated, and long before day-break the reservoir of heaven overflowed and the earth is bathed in the tears of angels, whose mourning for the sins of men are heard like the distant thunders, far off in the west.

I spent the morning in my room with Edward Cloutier, whom I entertained on the subject that occupied the principal part of my time Saturday and Sunday. Proof I was looking for, and proofs I found so natural, and so convincing, that if the works whence I derived them had been at hand, I would have maintained my position with more success and demonstrated its correctness with so much force as to overthrow the great opposition against which I was arguing.

Soon after dinner, perceiving the smoke of the *Hecla* that was coming up, Edward and I went to Phanor's landing where we presumed she would stop. The cotton reported falling, and the favorable and masterly speech of Webster, which it is supposed will bring the slavery question to an amicable conclusion, was received. Before returning we spent some agreeable moments at the house with my uncle and aunt Adolphe, who were alone. When we were about leaving, Leonce and Felix arrived, which circumstance detained us a little longer.

After our return, I got at my studies and read till 7 o'clock at night. Leonce and Felix came here and spent a part of the evening. They came with Father who had gone a moment at Phanor's. It was agreed that Edward and I, and perhaps Julie, would go to sup at Phanor's and spend the *soirée*. However, Julie did not wish to go, Edward was afraid to expose himself as the weather was inclement, so that I also would not have gone, but had to do so, having to see Felix to know at what time in the morning we would start for our premeditated fishing party, but only went after supper and did not stay long.

Leonce and Edward said they also would come, and all four of us were in good spirits, proposing to ourselves fine fun.

WEDNESDAY—20TH

Early this morning the weather was cloudy, and so we started only after breakfast. However we had some fine fun, and succeeded in catching a very good number of fish.

Adolphe came to meet us and fished a while. We got back at about half past 11 A.M. Felix and Leonce, after going at their homes, returned for dinner and spent the rest of the day with us. The angling of the fish was fine sport, but the eating of them was very pleasant and more substantial sport.

The Doctor got here while we were at table. He came to see the governess, who, since yesterday, is sick and unable to teach school.

When Leonce and Felix started, Edward and myself accompanied them part of the way for the sake of taking a walk.

Julie, Edward, and I, after supper, went at Phanor's to spend the *veille* and we spent it very pleasantly, talking, playing cards and dominoes. We returned at 11 P.M. Felix came with us to spend the night.

THURSDAY—21ST

The day was beautiful, and the heat was more oppressive than it has been this year.

According to an understanding yesterday, we were to go today to fish crawfish, and accordingly we (the same that were out fishing yesterday) went out and met with pretty good success, and above all amused ourselves very well.

Felix, Edward, and I, as there were some fish, tried with the recipe to make what is called in French *bouillabaise,* which is nothing more than a kind of fish gumbo. We did not succeed but, notwithstanding, out of the failure we got another dish which was most excellent as I was told, for this being Lent, and a meat day, I could not enjoy the fruits of my labor. For this I was somewhat recompensed in seeing with what pleasure the others had in eating it. Strange consolation this, one might say, but it is the consolation of a cook who has a great satisfaction in seeing the others flatter his dishes by their great attention to them. We spent the *veille* making music and playing cards.

At ten o'clock we made plans to go on the premeditated fishing party tomorrow. Father, Felix, Edward, Leonce, and I were to compose the party, and a breakfast on the banks of the bayou was to be taken.

FRIDAY—22ND

About midnight there was a heavy rain which continued until about 3 P.M.

The fishing party, to the great sorrow of everyone, could not take place today and it was put off till tomorrow. According to the present prospects it will again fail. First, the weather will hardly be favorable, and, secondly, Felix is to accompany Mrs. Archinard and Mrs. Ben. to town, and Leonce, I think, will go at my uncle Cloutier's.

SATURDAY—23RD

I went fishing at Attaho with Edward Cloutier, and we succeeded in catching a pretty good mess.

We returned at about 1 P.M. but still arrived in time; the dinner having been delayed on our account. Shortly after dinner, I started with my sister Julie to accompany her to town, where she intends to spend Holy Week; Edward came with us in the carriage and we left him at his father's. We got to town about dusk. I slept at Phanor's where I acted as protector to Mrs. Archinard, Mrs. Ben., and her sister who were there.

SUNDAY—24TH, PALM SUNDAY

The weather was very good and most delightful. I attended church in the morning and vespers in the evening. The time not thus occupied was spent most agreeably as I was in company of the ladies, with John and Edward Cloutier who came this morning.

We all left town together in the evening, and got at my uncle Cloutier's a short time before supper. I intended getting home, having to go out surveying in the morning, but as Edward was to accompany me, and he was just recovering from illness, I thought proper to remain till morning.

I spent the *veille* very pleasantly. My uncle Neville enlivened the society by his presence. Theophile and his lady were on a visit, having come the day previous.

MONDAY—25TH

I got up early with my companion, Edward, and got here before breakfast. I immediately made my preparations for the occupation of the day, and soon after breakfast Father, Edward, and two negroes coming to haul the chain accompanied me to father's other plantation, which I was to survey. This occupied us the whole day. We got back a little after dusk, and upon our arrival I was shown a note written by Felix Metoyer, in which he stated he was alone with his mother and would like my companion and myself to come and spend the night with him, to which request we acceded, and we spent a very pleasant *veille*. We got at my aunt's after supper, but we were given one.

TUESDAY—26TH

I wanted to return this morning to calculate my field notes which I had taken yesterday, but Felix would not consent to it, and sent a

"ROSEDOWN" LIES DEEP IN A GARDEN, 1835

negro boy to get what I wanted to make the calculations. The boy
went several times before I got the things, and then he did not bring
them, but they were sent to me a little before 12 M.

Felix and Edward spent the day reading, and I marking several
household articles for my aunt and making my calculations. In the
evening, mother came and spent a couple of hours at my aunt's. I
returned home at about five in the evening, and after supper I continued my work, and with the assistance of Father, a little before
midnight the whole was finished. The steamboat *Doswell* went up
this morning at 8 A.M.

WEDNESDAY–27TH

Felix came to meet me and he, Edward, and I started off for
Natchitoches. Edward remained at his father's and we got to town
at about 6 P.M. I went to confession to make my Easter duties. I
spent the *veille* at my grandmother's, where there was a rehearsal
of holy music for the festival days.

HOLY THURSDAY–28TH

This morning there was a heavy frost. All the cotton that was
growing was killed. Very little injury, however, was done, for very
few planters had any grown cotton, and if any very little. The seed
that was in the ground was not hurt. The corn was frozen to the
ground. It was already from six to twelve inches high. Many young
and tender fruits were frozen, many blossoms were destroyed, and
the leaves of fig, catalpas, china trees, and many others were all
killed.

There was grand ceremony in church in the morning and in the
evening, and at night the Stabat Mater was sung. I was one of the
young men who accompanied young ladies along the aisles to gather
some money for the use of the church. There were some fifty odd
persons who took communion at High Mass. My mother, the governess, and the children got in town this morning. I spent my *veille*
both at my grandmother's and at Phanor's.

HOLY FRIDAY–29TH

The weather was again beautiful, and a white frost made a good fire place feel comfortable. I spent the day with regard to church, as I did yesterday. I spent my time very agreeably, as is always the case when persons from the coast are in Natchitoches. I spent the *veille* at Phanor's.

HOLY SATURDAY–30TH

It was cold early this morning, but towards the middle of the day it got to be pretty warm. There was service in the church this morning; there was none in the evening. My aunt Benjamin, Leonce, my uncle Cloutier, and his son John came in town. We were seven in a very small room at Phanor's called *le garçonnière,* and as all did not come in together, we did not get to sleep before midnight, and as out of three beds we had to make room for seven, none slept too much. I went to confession to go to communion tomorrow.

EASTER SUNDAY–31ST

The weather was delightful. I got up at five o'clock to hear Mass at the convent with Mrs. Archinard and my sister Julie, all three of us receiving the Blessed Sacrament. I again attended to High Mass, and the church was crowded. The pastor made a very good sermon. I spent the day most delightfully. Many persons left town to return to their homes. Enough, however, remained to render the *veille* that was spent at my grandfather's very agreeable. The company was delighted with some very fine pieces played on the piano, violin, and flute; and two or three cotillions were danced.

After vespers Joseph, Janin, Felix, and I took a little ride on horseback in the pine woods. The woods looked beautiful, the trees being covered with their fine green robes, and the shrubs ornamented with their many and variegated flowers, all pleasing to the eye with their thousand different hues, and presenting a most beautiful tableau to the admirer of nature. The *Hecla* got in town last night and left at about 12 M. today.

MONTH OF APRIL—1850

MONDAY–1ST

I left town this morning in company with Leonce Rocques, and both dined at my uncle Cloutier's, who was in most excellent spirits. In the evening I went with Edward to fish for crawfish; my companion continued on his way home. We met with very little success in catching crawfish. When I returned my uncle had had a young calf killed and prevailed upon me, in consequence thereof, to remain and take supper. I got home at half past nine at night. Everybody in the house had retired.

TUESDAY–2ND

I intended to resume my studies which I had discontinued for the two weeks, but just returning from promenade I did not feel like getting to the task, and kept putting it off from hour to hour till the day was spent, and I had employed it recreating my mind in historical reading. I paid a very short visit to my uncle and aunt Adolphe late in the evening. Mother, Father, and Julie spent the *soirée* playing Ramps.

WEDNESDAY–3RD

At about 12 M. Mr. and Mrs. Adolphe sent word here inviting us all to go and dine with them and participate in the delights of a good fish dinner. The fish had been taken by Felix, Leonce, and my uncle Adolphe.

Father and I went and indeed the dinner was most excellent. We had not only fish but many other delicate dishes, and a fine dessert at which everyone took some champagne, several bottles being offered.

All the guests did honor to the meal, and rose from the table in fine spirits and humour. Then the next thing was to whiff a good cigar, seated in arm chairs at the coolest end of the gallery, and enjoying social conversation.

My little brother Serdot had a very violent attack of fever to-

day; and this gave mother some uneasiness, fearing he might have a
fit, which has already happened in a similar circumstance.

THURSDAY—4TH

The weather was more or less cloudy the whole day. However,
there was a beautiful sunset. Yesterday I agreed with Felix Metoyer,
Leonce Rocques, and John Grimmer to go out fishing this morning.
I accordingly did so; left early, had to go alone and meet the party,
for they passed before I was up, and as it was not certain I would
go, they did not wait for me. We met with very fine success, and
took breakfast with some little provisions we had taken with us, and
returned about half past eleven.

In the evening, feeling sleepy, I threw myself on my bed and slept
so sound when I got up it was five P.M. I commenced the reading of
Blackstone, and at sun down I took the book and went out to take
a walk. At dusk I went to get my sister Julie who had gone at
Phanor's, and met her on the way with uncle and aunt Adolphe and
all the little children. My sister wishing to spend the *veille* at
Phanor's, I took the children home and after supper went to meet
her. We returned together at about half past ten. Leonce came before
we left. He had spent his *veille* out. Father went to town to take his
notes, as he intends shortly to go down to the city (New Orleans).
He got back at about 6 P.M.

FRIDAY—5TH

Immediately after breakfast I took my law book and went at the
end of the alley where I read for about an hour and returned to the
house. Felix Metoyer paid us a short visit this morning. Father went
to his plantation on the Rigolet Bondieu.

Toward five in the evening Matthew and Emile came here to be
ready in the morning for a preconceived fishing party. Felix came and
spent the *soirée* with us, and when he left he took John Cloutier with
him. John and Edward came a little before supper also for the purpose of participating in the fishing party.

We spent a most pleasant *veille*.

NEW ORLEANS CLOSES IN UPON THE
SARPY HOUSE

SATURDAY–6TH

Early this morning everybody was up and making preparations for the fishing excursion. The weather was most beautiful, and consequently appropriate. All those who intended participating in the party got on the banks of the bayou Attaho in good time, and all in fine dispositions for amusing themselves. The only thing that was wanted to complete the whole were young ladies, there being but two present. However, we amused ourselves exceedingly well; fished with great success and very good luck; and made a most excellent fish breakfast.

After this we left for home, and there the whole company spent the remainder of the day in a most pleasant and agreeable way.

Those participating in the party were: my mother, my aunt Neville, my sister Julie, my cousin Harriette Hertzog, Messrs. J. B. and E. Cloutier, Matthew and Émile Hertzog, Leonce Rocques, Charles Hertzog, Felix Metoyer, Joseph Janin, and I. (Father, Ben Metoyer, and Adolphe Prudhomme came to enjoy only the pleasure of breakfast.) When all started, John and I remained and caught a fine string of fish before returning.

I accompanied John and Edward at my uncle Cloutier's to go on another fishing party in the morning, but which was to be on a smaller scale, only a few gentlemen going.

When I left I took leave of Father who intended going to New Orleans on the *Doswell,* which went up to Natchitoches this morning but had not yet gone down. Leonce and Felix went with us at my uncle Cloutier's where they spent the night.

SUNDAY–7TH

This morning early, John, Edward, and I got up ready to start early on our pleasure party. Felix and Leonce did not accompany us, wishing to return. Sometime after getting to the place of *rendezvous,* the bayou, we were met by Achille and Octave, besides two strangers who came with them. These are mechanics who are building a house for Achille.

The whole party had then arrived and we all got fishing but

with the worst kind of luck, as it was rather cold till about ten or eleven o'clock, when we succeeded in catching a sufficient mess to take our dinner; which was not according to our mutual desire for we had come to take breakfast. Thus in our luck and our meal we were disappointed, and to make the thing yet worse, we found out, but too late, there was neither sufficient lard to fry the fish nor bread to eat them. However, we made the best we could of it, without either one of us satisfying his appetite, for we were very hungry, not having had any breakfast, and having taken a great deal of exercise.

After this meal, all being tired, wearied, and disappointed in the bright expectations we had entertained, we left the bayou (not, however, without having amused ourselves) for our respective homes. Achille took a good dive in about twelve feet of water, having slipped off a log on which he had placed himself to fish.

John, Edward, and I returned at my uncle's where we remained till about five or six P.M., during which time we played a few games of Maroc. The weather was very fine during the whole of the day, but in the evening it got cloudy and commenced raining just as I was leaving for home. However, as I was obliged to return, father having this day left on the *Doswell,* I started. Before reaching home, the skies got very black, the thunder rolled heavily, and the flashes of lightning were frequent and so brilliant and vivid that my horse would stop short, and for a few seconds I would be perfectly blind. However, I got home safely, and the threatened storm passed off in rain. I got home at about half past seven, pretty wet.

MONDAY–8TH

This day I intended to renew my studies, but I had to accompany my sister Julie to Hippolyte Hertzog's, where I left her and returned with Hippolyte who was going to town as far as my aunt Hertzog's, where I dined, and got back home at about 2 P.M. I found Mr. Blane here and, consequently having to entertain him, I could not attend my studies. At about 5 P.M. I went with him at Narcisse's to see my uncle Noyrit who has lately come there from his plantation on the Rigolet. The day was most charming, though a little warm.

TUESDAY—9TH

At about 9 A.M. Mr. Blane left for Mrs. Benjamin's where he went to get some medical plants and returned at about 11 A.M. He remained here till about 2 P.M., and having gathered some more medical plants in the garden he went off, to my satisfaction for he was not much company for me.

WEDNESDAY—10TH

Phanor having written from New Orleans that he would be up by the *Hecla,* this boat was anxiously expected, and many, for the last two days, kept constantly on a lookout. Today at about 11 A.M. I saw the smoke at last and at 2 P.M. it got at Phanor's, where I repaired to receive the newcomers, and spent about two agreeable hours in their company. I find Phanor and his son much improved, but as for his lady, I think she does not look as well as when she left. Phanor had left for the city on the 18th of February, and thus returned after an absence of nearly two months. This time appeared very long to all his friends and neighbours who were very much rejoiced at his arrival. Narcisse returned from New Orleans. Bishop Blanc came by the boat.

THURSDAY—11TH

I read Blackstone for about an hour, and then went at Phanor's where we had been invited to dine. There was a pretty large concourse of persons there, and I spent my time very pleasantly.

The whole evening I entertained myself very agreeably with my ancient teacher, about Europe, the United States, the condition of France, its politics, human nature, Natural Philosophy, Chemistry, and many other entertaining subjects.

I was presented by Phanor with a fine and delicate little hatchet for the purpose, as he said, of surveying. I received it with pleasure, not only for the value of the thing, for it will very well answer the purpose for which it has been given to me, but because it pleased me to recognize the friendship of my friend Phanor in the presentation of this little article. Felix who had spent the day at Phanor's came here and spent the night. We played cards with mother and my sister Julie till about ten, when we retired.

FRIDAY—12TH

I had to entertain a large company of ladies and gentlemen who came here to spend the day, which was naturally for me a very agreeable and pleasant thing.

When the company started at about 6 P.M. I went with Felix and Leonce as far as my aunt Benjamin's and returned before supper with Felix who came to spend the night here and be ready to go in the morning fishing with Leonce and me. The school finished here today.

SATURDAY—13TH

We had to wait some time for Leonce after having got up, but we started still pretty early. The overseer (Mr. Gavin) accompanied us. We met with great success, and thus enjoyed the sports, and enjoyed still more the breakfast we took on the banks of the bayou. Leonce shot several alligators. We got back at 11 A.M. I did not feel well after my return, and had no appetite so that I could not enjoy the fine fish, nicely dressed up, which were on the table. I took a good nap in the evening.

Ephalide and Lize came here in the evening, and when they went off, Mother, Mrs. Leach, Julie, and I accompanied them a part of the way. Leonce, when we passed before Phanor's gate, came and met us. Lise, mother, and Mrs. Leach did not go far, but the others continued as far as the lane. I got back a little before supper with Julie.

SUNDAY—14TH

I left very early this morning to go to town, and had breakfast at my aunt Clarice's, where I found everybody preparing to go and assist at Mass, the bishop being in Natchitoches; and learned that many persons from the coast either had gone or were going for the same purpose. I found Theophile and his lady in town.

The ceremony at Mass was very long. The sacrament of confirmation was administered to a large number of persons. I assisted at vespers, and two young men and I answered the psalms, the musicians not having come to the evening office.

I left town at about half past five with Edward and John. I paid a visit at Achille's on my return, and got home at about half past seven. Many of the persons who had gone to town remained for the ceremony at the convent. The confirmation of many of the young ladies was to take place. My aunt Benjamin and Ephalide went to town this evening to be present in the morning.

Between here and Natchitoches, many of the inhabitants are dissatisfied with their crops. The weather not being favorable and the cut worm being very destructive, several have had to plant both corn and cotton entirely over.

MONDAY—15TH

I commenced reading Blackstone early this morning, and before breakfast, taking my book with me, I went at Phanor's. What I read then is all I could read the whole day. A bricklayer came soon after breakfast to finish the cistern, and before I could get him everything that was necessary it was nearly twelve. At about 2 P.M. the *Doswell* arrived, and as she had a great deal of freight on board for the plantation I was busy the best part of the afternoon, and as I had to entertain Dr. Kerell, who arrived while we were at dinner, the evening went off without my being able to come to my studies.

Dr. Danglasse came here to hold a consultation with Dr. Kerell about the governess who, though she teaches school no longer, remains here. After the doctors had left I wrote a long letter to my father to send by the *Doswell*.

The overseer told me this day he would have to replant nearly the whole crop of cotton and that there was much corn missing. This is generally the case everywhere; the crops have come up very badly. Wherever the cotton is up it looks green, but the seed and roots are perfectly rotten. Adolphe went to my father's plantation on the Bondieu, and this evening when he came back he told me the cotton had to be planted entirely over and there were no seeds, but that

the overseer here had told him he could spare as much as would be
necessary. Upon this I immediately dispatched a boy to the plantation
to tell the overseer to come over in the morning with sufficient hands
to transport some cotton seed.

TUESDAY–16TH

I was kept busy the whole morning, tending to the plantation
business.

At about five Leonce and Felix came here on a visit, and left
at about six. Just at that time my aunt Adolphe arrived with
Phanor's children, but the boat which I had been expecting the
whole day was coming around the point, and as I had letters which
had been written here and others that had been sent to me for the
same purpose, I repaired to the bank. The Captain, to whom I had
spoken yesterday for the letters I would have to put on board, did
not stop, but passed at full speed and thus I had to throw the stick
upon which I had previously attached the letters. It fell on board but
unfortunately bounced back and fell overboard. It being soon sent to
shore by the waves, I lost no time but took a horse and cut across
the next point where I got before the boat, but she passed so fast
and so far from shore that again I was disappointed; the stick not
reaching it; then there was no other chance remaining, and when I
had succeeded in getting the letters, which was not without trouble,
I started on my way home much disappointed, and far from admiring
the Captain's kindness to whom I had previously spoken, being anxious
not to miss the present opportunity. I felt much more sorry on account of the other letters, which were business letters, than for mine.

When I came back there was no one here, all having gone at
Phanor's to receive the Bishop and the Parish priest, who came to
spend the night. I got ready and went to meet the company. I got
there while they were at supper, and my disappointment having taken
away my appetite, and hence not wishing to disturb them, I waited
on the gallery till the meal was over. I spent my time pleasantly,
but it would have been more pleasant had I succeeded with my letters.
We returned at half past ten.

A peddlar stopped here today. The bricklayer went at Émile Sompayrac's to commence a cistern.

The sun was scorching, and even in the shade the heat was oppressive.

Just as I had commenced my studies this morning, the bricklayer arrived to finish his work, and to get hands to work with him took me some time. After that I was occupied with the Indian who came for provisions, and before I had got through with him, up drove a carriage filled with ladies. Mrs. Narcisse, Miss Ryan from Alexandria, Mrs. Boyce, and her sister Miss Roubieu. To assist them out of the carriage was my first care, then to entertain them for nearly two hours was my next pleasant and agreeable task. They then started to go and dine at my aunt Benjamin's, and they got my sister Julie to accompany them.

This morning, having been told by the bricklayer there was not sufficient sand to finish the work he was at, and being unable to get some at the neighbours' as they had none, I spent the whole evening with him searching in vain for the article, and came to the conclusion of sending for some in Natchitoches, as he (the bricklayer) told me he had some there.

At about half past six Lise, Octavia, and the children came here. We accompanied them back as far as the lane and met on our way Phanor, Leonce, and Felix who were coming to meet us.

I spent the *soirée* very pleasantly on the gallery with Mother, Julie, and the governess, and was the best part of the time defending myself against the charge brought against me of having the preceding night and some time in company appeared lonesome.

Mother started early this morning to go and see Mrs. Hippolyte Hertzog's who has been sick with the fever for several days. After breakfast, desiring to see Adolphe I went at Phanor's and remained after having done what I wanted, in the school house, to see how the school was going on; and there wrote a letter to my brother Anthony, who is at the Western Military Institute, Blue Dick, Kentucky.

I had not yet got to the house when I was met by a negro boy who wanted something. A few minutes after having satisfied him I was again disturbed by others, and thus kept busy till near 11 A.M. And then retiring to my room I there endeavoured to make a hair line, but only succeeded after dinner, soon after taking that meal having resumed the task. I then commenced reading Blackstone, and took a long walk alone, but on my return I met some ladies and gentlemen who were also taking a walk, and I thus returned in company. I sent a little boy to town in order to have some sand brought by the market cart that is to come tonight. The hands have not yet commenced sowing the cotton, being busily engaged replacing the corn.

FRIDAY—19TH

Mother and Julie went at Phanor's to question the young scholars on what they had seen during the week, thus making a kind of revision or recapitulation. I remained alone the whole day with Mrs. Leach, the ex-governess. I got up early reading Blackstone, and read very attentively the whole day, being but little disturbed.

At about 9 A.M. the bricklayer returned and got immediately to work. Tonight mother did not return but remained at Phanor's on account of my aunt Adolphe who was sick with child. We had great company here; Leonce, Felix, and Mrs. Aliede Buard having come to spend the night. The evening was consequently spent in a most agreeable way. The overseer commenced sowing the cotton on this side of Cane River.

SATURDAY—20TH

Felix and Leonce started at about 10 A.M. to go and spend the day at my aunt Benjamin's. Mrs. Aliede soon after felt so much indisposed that she had to keep her bed and my sister, of course, did not leave the room. Mrs. Leach remained in bed in her room and so I was left alone. Not feeling like studying, I went with Phanor's

A PLANTATION DINING-ROOM,
WITH OVERHEAD FAN

E H Suydam

"GREENWOOD," THE CLASSIC REVIVAL,
IN WEST FELICIANA, 1840

boy, Alphonse, to fish in the river, but spent a couple of hours without having the luck of catching a single fish.

After dinner I retired to my room to take a nap, but did not sleep. Leonce and Felix came here. Some time after their arrival they went in the garden to take a walk, and I came up with them just as they were coming out of the garden, and we kept on to the end of the lane and returned. The *veille* was spent very gaily. The *Hecla* was heard coming up at about 9 P.M. She got here at half past eleven. The ladies had retired but Felix, Leonce, and I waited for her. She put out some freight at this place, and I learned by letters that came that Father was to come up by the return of the same boat. The bricklayer finished the cistern. They got through sowing the cotton on this side of the river.

SUNDAY—21ST

All the company left to go and spend the day at my aunt Benjamin's and I remained alone, intending to spend the day at home, notwithstanding the pressing invitations I received to go at my aunt's.

At about eleven I went to see Narcisse, whom I had not yet had time to go and see since his return from New Orleans. I was by him requested to stay at dinner, but excused myself on the plea that I had to go at my aunt Benjamin's. I got there at about half past twelve and spent the day very pleasantly. I returned with Leonce, Felix, and Octave, the latter of whom we accompanied part of his way, and on our return stopped a moment at Narcisse's.

We got here at about half past seven and found the family in the house, mother having returned from Phanor's, as the alarm created by my aunt Adolphe, or rather on her account, was thought false.

We again spent a pleasant evening. Leonce and Felix spent the night here.

SUNDAY—22ND (WRITTEN IN FRENCH)

Aunt Adolphe's baby was born shortly after my mother left her yesterday; the news caused us much merriment. We made some pretty good jokes about it. We fired a volley in celebration of the new arrival, and our shots were answered by other volleys from adjoining plantations.

WEDNESDAY—24TH

The weather was damp, rainy, nasty, and sloppy the whole day. Yesterday and today fire felt quite comfortable. All the planters needed rain very much and were crying aloud for it, but now that it has commenced it seems there is no end to it. They begged too hard, and their prayers must have been too fervent.

I got two letters last night from the best friend I had at college and I was so much the more pleased with the reception of these epistles, as I had been several months without receiving any. The letter I wrote in reply is eight pages long, and had I had time I would have completed a dozen.

By the communication I received I was apprized of Joachim Antunez's [a college friend's] marriage. He is only about twenty-two, but I think he has done right, for as he is very rich he possesses the means of supporting a wife and family. He is from Alabama and is engaged to a young lady of Iberville, La., Miss Euphrasia Demellier. May they be happy is the prayer of a friend. It is short, but fervent.

I have been reading Blackstone pretty attentively since the beginning of the week. A few days ago I discovered that some whisky had been taken out of the lock-room and that the perpetrators of the theft, as the better to hide their action, had mixed what was left with water. Sometime before supper I mentioned this to mother and we got into a long discussion about the way things were run. Towards six o'clock in the evening the rain increased and kept on nearly the whole night.

THURSDAY—25TH

It rained again from 6 A.M. till about 4 P.M. almost without any discontinuation. No one came here and I spent the whole of the time very assiduously at my studies. In the evening I removed with my books from my room to the study room, where I had some fire made and studied very comfortably, and as quietly as can be possible for one who has a part of the business on the plantation to attend to, till supper time. After supper I returned again to my studies, and left them at about 9 P.M. In the meanwhile the market cart from town had arrived and brought a speech of Hon. Isaac E. Morse, a representative from the State of Louisiana. It is on the President's message in relation to California. It is a pretty good speech, but cannot be admired after the productions of the great and wise heads of the country have been universally read, throughout this vast Republic.

While I was thus occupied, my sister Julie and the governess reading, we heard a great noise like something that had fallen, and then a shriek was heard, showing that something had happened to my little brother. The two ladies immediately left their books and ran into my mother's bed room to see what was the matter. I remained alone, continuing to read, presuming my brother had only fallen out of his bed and, more frightened than hurt, was caused to fret. I was not mistaken, for it happened just as I thought, but he fell out of mother's high bed instead of his low one. Shortly after this occurrence all the ladies retired, but Serdot, after his fall, did not wish to go to sleep and he was brought to me. I kept him very quiet while I was reading, so that the youngster soon felt his eye-lids coming down in spite of his endeavours to keep them up, so that he desired to see his nurse, into whose hands I immediately placed him and he was soon asleep.

Shortly after, it being eleven o'clock, I retired to my room, where I was not long before giving way to the lulling caresses of Morpheus.

FRIDAY–26TH

After dinner, before resuming my studies, I took a walk in the field, and was very much pleased at the appearance of the two staples, the corn being high and green, and the cotton full of life, and the seeds ready to send their pumola to see the light. I returned from my walk quite pleased, but suffering from the heat.

Julie and Angella spent the day at Phanor's. Mother went to meet them at 5 P.M. Felix came here at 7 P.M. and only remained a short while, having to return at his mother's and make the preparations necessary to go to town in the morning together with Adolphe.

Mother remained to stay up with my aunt Octavie's child to-night. Angella and Odalie went to spend the night at Narcisse's with the little daughter. During and since the rain the river has been rising very rapidly. After supper Mrs. Leach and Julie got to playing the piano, and I amused myself perusing the Baltimore "Sun" I received last night.

SATURDAY—27TH

I crossed over this morning to go and see Lafille, an old woman, to whom my grandfather has given her liberty, and who nursed me when I was but an infant baby. She has been with the fever for some time and for the last six months has been always unwell. Her disease is old age. The fever has reduced her to a rather low state, and fears are entertained for her life. I found her better this morning, having no fever, and a good face. On my return at the house I sent her some little delicacies or dainties and marked a quilt for a girl to sew, and then it being nearly dinner time, I sat to the piano and recreated myself a little playing some few tunes I know. After dinner I got at my studies and kept on till about ten but not without interruption. For, according to my orders, I was called to put up my lamp I had given to clean, and, a very essential screw being lost, I spent a good while looking for it, to-gether with the boy that had cleaned the lamp. After having given myself a great deal of trouble I left and returned to my studies, hoping that in the morning I would be more successful in my searches.

I did not enjoy my meals very well, taking them, contrary to my habit, all alone, and though I was busy the whole day I found the time passed on very slowly. I remain alone tonight, mother having been prevented by the rain from coming. The water is rising very fast. It has risen at least eight feet.

SUNDAY—28TH

It was cool the whole day. I found the screw that had been lost yesterday, and was very glad to have been successful. It would have been trouble to not have found it.

The overseer took breakfast here with me and remained till 11 A.M. I then got ready to go at my uncle Cloutier's, expecting mother would be there, and started at about half past eleven, I stopped a while at Phanor's, not having gone there for nearly a week, and paid a visit at Achille Prudhomme's newborn girl. When I got at my uncle's the company was at table. I spent the evening very pleasantly, having found all my companions. I came home with Edward Cloutier, Ursin Lambre, and Felix; the latter was on his return from town, accompanying his sister, Mrs. Phanor.

We spent the *soirée* very well, and at about half past ten all retired with good dispositions.

MONDAY—29TH

I woke up very early this morning and woke up my companions, who desired early to return to their homes and resume their occupations. I spent nearly the whole morning in leisure, reading, and in the evening studied Blackstone; which I had to leave long before night, having told Felix we would take a ride in the evening. We went at his mother's where we spent about an hour.

In our ride we saw the smoke of a boat in this river, and the *Hecla* being expected we presumed it was she coming. We were not mistaken, for just as Leonce and Felix, who had supped here, were starting, the noise of the boat was plainly heard (though before we had several times come out of the house to see whether we could hear her and had not been successful), and my father being expected these gentlemen remained to await the arrival. At half past eleven the boat came up to the landing, and father was welcomed home. Felix and Leonce started soon after and we retired after midnight.

Father reports that the Mississippi and the Missouri rivers are very high; Black river also is very full.

TUESDAY—30TH

Early this morning Father distributed the presents he had brought from New Orleans. I got several fine books, a silver pencil, some most excellent smoking tobacco, and a bottle of absinthe.

Phanor and Adolphe paid us a visit.

I spent nearly the whole morning verifying the bills of lading, and found only one or two articles missing, which I presume were put at Natchitoches or at the plantation on the Bondieu.

I felt very dull and unwell the whole day, a thing I cannot account for, as the joy and satisfaction I experienced at Father's return could not have been productive of such consequences.

I came to my room at half past four P.M., and taking my book containing an analysis of what I have read of Blackstone, my cane and hat, I started on my usual recreative walk, both for the purpose of studying and taking exercise. My dog accompanied me as is his custom.

MONTH OF MAY–1850

WEDNESDAY–1ST

Already has the bright, the lovely May arrived. The month in which nature is in all her verdure, her freshness, and her beauty. When the trees are adorned with their rich foliage and covered, some with blossoms, scenting the air with their delicious perfumes; and others possessing no odour, but pleasing the eye with the brightness of their various and multiplied colours.

Nature that remained so long in a state of desolation, of apathy, begins now to recover her lost strength and commences to live. The weather was rather cloudy and in the evening at about five o'clock there was a little shower. A good rain would have been beneficial to the crops. I spent the whole day studying right hard to go in the morning to town, and pass an examination of what I had prepared in Blackstone. Felix came to spend the evening with us, and remained till morning. I left my small room today for the large, spacious, and commodious school room.

THURSDAY–2ND

I got up early this morning and started on my journey. I met two companions on the way, Edward Cloutier and Octave Metoyer.

I did not find Mr. Campbell, he being at Shreveport. I returned at my uncle Baptiste's at 6 P.M., and together with his son John I spent the evening very pleasantly at Achille's where we found Émile Hertzog.

At half past nine we went at my aunt Balsin's, who had gone to spend the night at Achille's, and found Rémy Lambre and Ursin, whom we had to awake, and stayed up very late. We amused ourselves playing cards. Weather was pretty fair.

FRIDAY—3RD

Although I had returned pretty late, I got up somewhat early. I spent the day at my aunt Balsin's, paid a short visit at my uncle Baptiste's for the purpose of getting his son to come with me. Both of us then went at my uncle Neville's where we spent about an hour very pleasantly, and then brought a young colt hardly tamed to Ursin who was to come with me.

This young man was afraid to ride his horse, and I got on him. The horse jumped and reared a little with me, then his owner took him, and we got home at about 7 P.M., having paid a visit on the way to my old school master, Mr. Leroy.

We spent the evening very pleasantly and retired at about half an hour after midnight. The steamboat *Doswell* passed by here at about 6 P.M. on her upward trip.

SATURDAY—4TH

Ursin, Edward, and I accompanied my three sisters at Achille's, to be present at the christening of his child, now about fifteen days old. We found many persons present, and consequently spent the time very pleasantly, singing, dancing, and drinking wine.

All that had left here returned at about six or seven and Felix came a little later. The *soirée* was spent agreeably and at nine, the ladies retiring, I went to my room, together with the young men that were here, and soon after we played several rounds at cards and went to bed.

SUNDAY–5TH

Father, mother, and all the family going to town, I went also and left here with Edward who intended going no farther than his house, and Ursin, who was going with me to town.

Three miles from here we met my uncle Cloutier, his lady and family coming in the Island, and this circumstance caused Edward to leave us and return on his steps.

We got in town some time after Mass had commenced, and repaired as soon as possible to church. I paid several visits and left with Ursin at 3 P.M., both having found the place very dull.

He accompanied me near home, and meeting John and Rémy who were returning, went off with them. I tried in vain to get them to come home, where several young men had told me they would come and spend the evening. After I got there I went at Phanor's a moment and returned home with Felix, Leonce, and Edward. We spent our time very gaily, took a good supper, drinking, and making a very laughable concert. One played on the piano, the other accompanied on the flute, the third beat the drum, and the fourth accompanied with cymbals, that were nothing more than coverlids of some culinary utensils. The drum was a settee covered with a good strong leather, on which the drummer pounded with his fists. Sometimes, that is, once in a while, we sang some comical and innocent songs, and then some romances, accompanying ourselves the whole time with our four instruments. The whole was no extra music, no wonderful performance, but it was comical, farce, and laughable. We went to bed happy.

MONDAY–6TH

It has almost become a puzzle to understand the rotations of the seasons this year. May has come on, and winter seems yet not to have relinquished her despotic and destructive way. Yesterday the cold was severe as in the winter. Not only nature, but men, governments, the whole world seems to be reversed; contentions and strifes everywhere; subversion of governments; rivers overflowing in every part of the world; everything in fine acting in a different way from what it has done heretofore, and appearing to indicate a total dissolution of the end of the world.

I breakfasted at Phanor's, the young men who were here wishing to do so; but we got there after breakfast, and another table had to be set for us. I was kept there till 10 A.M. doing some little work for Mrs. Phanor. I returned to dinner and at three I got home, with fine dispositions to commence my studies, but hardly had I commenced when a young man of my acquaintance came to spend the evening with me. Felix came here a moment after 6 P.M. and mother, father arrived from town at about seven. Shortly after the young man left, my uncle Janin who is now paying his farewell visits, having returned from Theophile's where he had spent the day, got here together with Leonce, my aunt Cloutier and her son Edward. They all got back at 6 P.M. and came with Theophile, his lady, and baby.

Felix and Edward came at about eight and spent the night with me. We retired at 11 P.M. after a *soirée* of cards and music.

TUESDAY—7TH

I went after breakfast with Edward at Phanor's. He went off fishing with Leonce, and I, having my occupations, could not participate in the sport, and returned to my studies. My aunt Cloutier spent the day with us. Edward came here at 11 A.M. having had no luck in fishing.

Theophile stopped here a moment on his way to his plantation. His lady came at about 12 M. The weather was more or less cloudy and cool. At about 5 P.M. there was a little drizzling rain, which lasted but a moment. At half past seven or eight, however, there was a pretty heavy shower accompanied with thunder and lightning. Theophile came back pretty early this evening from his plantation and accompanied my sister Julie and his lady at Narcisse's. My aunt Cloutier left pretty late for her home, together with her son Edward. I studied till supper and again after supper, preparing myself to go to town tomorrow.

Theophile and his lady spent the night here. Ever since I have removed to this room this is the first night I find myself alone; every night one or some of my friends spent the night with me.

THURSDAY—9TH

I went to Mass very early this morning and received the Sacrament. I would willingly have remained in town to assist at High Mass, this day being the Assumption, but a dinner was to be given to my uncle Janin (who is about to leave for France) at home and Father desired me to return.

I accordingly left town after breakfast together with Joseph Janin and we got home a little after eleven A.M. The house was full of persons, every gentleman along the coast having answered the invitation. The company was numerous; only three ladies were present, and from twenty-five to thirty gentlemen. Everyone was well disposed for amusing himself and as a matter of consequence the day was spent gaily.

At about 5 P.M. the company commenced to retire and at 7 some had not yet gone. I accompanied Mrs. Hippolyte at Phanor's where we remained better than an hour. The *veille* was gay, Hippolyte, Theophile, their ladies, and Joseph having remained, not intending to leave before morning, and Felix having come to spend the *soirée*. There was music on the piano, flute, and violin and a little dancing. We retired at half past ten.

FRIDAY—10TH

At nine this morning Theophile, Hippolyte, their ladies, and Joseph had all left, each one for his respective home. Mother started at about 10 A.M. to go and spend the day at my aunt Benjamin's. Father and I went there at about half past twelve. Having to return home early we came back before three.

Not having studied any in the morning, I commenced immediately upon my return. A rise is reported above, and as the river is pretty full and rising here, though the rise at this place is presumed to have been occasioned by the rain, planters are fearful of an overflow; which if it happened would complete the ruin already commenced last year by the water which came to a height never yet heard of, and coming in the month of August destroyed all the crops. My sister Julie came back this morning from her visit, with a hot fever.

SATURDAY—11TH

A little drizzling rain prevailing once in a while, I spent the best part of the morning fixing different things in my room, and finished reading Webster's speech which in my humble opinion is a most masterly piece of eloquence. His ideas are just, correct, and elevated. He favours no party or sectional division but speaks mainly, openly, and impartially, giving the North and South their respective merit, and unfolding most judiciously their mutual wrongs. But as a thrice Senator, a learned scholar, and patriot, he shows the wrongs, the evils, and the dangers, and then reveals the course that must be pursued to remedy the one and avoid the other. He speaks of a peaceable secession as a thing utterly impossible, and his reasons for maintaining this opinion are clear and convincing to every reasoning mind not carried away by politics or fanaticism.

Narcisse Prudhomme came here this morning to bring his little daughter and had to remain on account of the rain. Felix came here in the evening and left to go and take Leonce, then return to get me to go and sup at my cousin's, J. B. Prudhomme's. However, the rain commencing again we changed our minds, and did not go.

Having the news, by an express sent purposely, that Mrs. Balery Deblieux had been delivered of a fine boy, there was a salute of twelve or fifteen shots at Phanor's and I answered here.

MONDAY—13TH

I amused myself before and sometime after breakfast shooting at some cherry birds, and then went to my studies. At about 6 P.M. I left on my way to town where I had to be in the morning to transact some pressing business. I had the rain part of the way. I spent the evening very pleasantly and retired at about 10 o'clock. The steamboat *J. T. Doswell* went up at about 1 P.M.

TUESDAY—14TH

I left at my uncle's after breakfast and at 11 A.M., having got through with my business, I started back to dine, according to my promise, at my uncle Cloutier's. There were several young men there who had come for the same purpose, so that I spent my time very pleasantly. I left at about 7 P.M. with Ursin Lambre, supped with him at his mother's, and started at 9 P.M. for home, where I arrived at ten and found nobody up. I retired to my room, and at 11 P.M. consigned myself to the care of Morpheus who soon lulled me into a calm and profound sleep. On my way home tonight a shooting star cast such a vivid light that my horse was frightened and I was myself surprised.

WEDNESDAY—15TH

The weather cleared off at about ten last night, and the firmament again, after an absence of several days, was studded with its thousands of bright and luminous gems. Consequently this morning the sun rose in all its magnificence and we had a most delightful day, a circumstance which comes very much *à propos,* as the crops have suffered very much from the inclement weather we have had.

Fears were entertained by the planters of another overflow, but the news reporting that the rise is not a regular one, and that the river above the raft is extremely low has quieted their troubled spirits. However, the river being very much swollen here and the Mississippi very high, a regular rise might easily cause an overflow.

After breakfast I went a moment at Phanor's. He and his lady had left this morning for town, and consequently I was deprived of the pleasure of seeing them, but I found other persons there.

I commenced my studies at 10 A.M. When I got back home there was no one at home. My sister Julie had gone at my aunt Benjamin's to meet mother and spent the day there, and father had gone at his plantation. Consequently at about 12 M., not wishing to dine alone, I was just starting to go and dine at Phanor's when Father got back, and after a little detention we started together. We partook of a good dinner and after spending a couple of hours most pleasantly we returned home between three and half past. I got to my studies and at about 6 P.M. I went at my aunt Benjamin's where I found Leonce and Felix and saw Ben Metoyer's child there, two days old. I returned at about seven o'clock and a moment after I was surprised to see Felix and Leonce arrive, having parted with them at Phanor's. We spent a most pleasant evening.

Mother remained again tonight at my aunt Benjamin's, my aunt not having returned from Grand Ecore where she has gone to see her daughter, Mrs. Balery Deblieux.

THURSDAY–16TH

I studied right hard the whole day and at 6 P.M. went alone to take a ride on horseback, training a horse for my father.

FRIDAY–17TH

The fair weather seems to have set in now; it is indeed highly time, for the crops need the heat of the sun to resume some vigor and life.

I got up very early, and wishing to prepare a sufficient number of pages in Blackstone before four this evening, to go to town this evening with Felix and Leonce, I lost no time and got to work as soon as I had got through with my toilet.

I took a short recreation after breakfast and again resuming my mental occupation, I did not leave till half past twelve when the bell rang for dinner. Edward got here from Theophile's a little before dinner and left soon after. Soon after dinner I again took up my work, and finally succeeded in getting through with my task, and having studied several chapters upon which to-morrow I will have many questions by Mr. Campbell, the gentleman under whom I am reading law.

At the private school at Phanor's the monthly examination took place this morning. Father, Mother, and Julie assisted to it, and I think the parents were pleased with their children's progress. Between four and five P.M. I left for town in company with Felix and Leonce, the latter of whom is to take a tour in the East and North, and thence perhaps going to see his parents in France.

We enjoyed each other's company very well all the way, and got in town at about 8 P.M. I spent the *veille* at my grandfather's with several young gentlemen.

SATURDAY—18TH

Not being able to pass my examination, Mr. Campbell having a great deal of business to transact and expecting to get off to tend the Caddo court, I left town with Felix Metoyer at about 10 A.M. to go at Mr. Balery Deblieux's. There was a pretty numerous company at the house, so the day was spent in a most pleasing way, and we saw the gentleman's first born (a boy). My aunt Benjamin and Aphalide Archinard were there. The former of these left in the evening a little after we did on her way home. The water commenced falling at Grand Ecore last night.

SUNDAY—19TH

The weather was again most delightful and I spent it agreeably. At about nine I, together with other persons, accompanied my uncle Janin and Chaupin and Leonce Roques to the boat *Hecla* which had come up in the night, having been eleven days on her trip. Between eight and nine A.M. the bell gave the signal for the departure of the boat, and I took final leave of my travelling friends. They all appeared to leave with regret, and on the part of those they left behind the separation was no less painful. I assisted at Mass, and the pastor's sermon produced universal satisfaction on all the congregation. I left town with Edward and Ursin at about 6 P.M. Supped at my uncle Cloutier's and went to spend the night at my aunt Balsin's. We stayed up pretty late, and after a pretty animated conversation on the different mode Creole and American children were raised, in which conversation my aunt participated extensively, we played a few games of cards and retired. We were four young men, all of opinion that the American way was better, discussed against my aunt, whose opinion differed from ours.

MONDAY—20TH

Again the weather was most beautiful and the temperature was about the same as yesterday. This is very beneficial to the crops which circumstance, added to that of the river's falling, tends to quiet the troubled spirits of the planters and give them once more a little hope.

I left pretty late at my aunt's and got here at about 10 A.M. I found two ladies from Cloutierville home. They left soon after. I felt miserable the whole morning and thus dispensed with the perusal of Blackstone.

At 3 P.M. I resumed my studies. At six, I had my horse saddled and took a ride at my aunt Benjamin's, whence I returned with Felix who had gone there, and parting with him at Phanor's I got home a little before supper. I spent the whole time, from supper till 10 P.M. talking upon and discussing on the gallery with Father certain interesting subjects.

TUESDAY—21ST

After breakfast I left with my book and returned at about 10. During this time mother had occupied some servants cleaning under my room (the school house) and throwing under it and in the apartment small pecan tree bushes in order to chase off the fleas which dogs and cats by frequenting the place had brought in. I continued in my room till dinner. After dinner at about half past one I commenced working at my compass which needed some repairs, then I left to accompany Julie at my uncle Theophile's.

The water has commenced falling here. The weather continues fine and warm, and consequently the crops appear to have more life and have already assumed a pretty good appearance.

Planters now entertain the hope of making the regular crop. The heat was, this day, more excessive than it has yet been.

Felix, by previous notice, came to accompany my sister and me at my uncle Theophile's. We were pretty long on our way, having to go a pretty good distance up the bayou to cross, it being too deep where the road passes for a lady to ford without getting wet. Felix and I got back at about half past seven and spent the evening with father who was alone with the children, mother having gone to spend the night at my aunt Benjamin's.

The *Dolphin,* a government boat, passed here about 10 P.M., and the *Doswell,* about two hours later; both running up. The *Dolphin,* I presume, is to be engaged clearing the passage by the lakes around the raft, an impassable part of the river which is clogged up with logs for many miles.

WEDNESDAY—22ND

I spent my time studying till about 5 P.M. when I left to go and get my sister Julie. We returned about 7 P.M.

A moment after we started on foot to go and meet mother, whom we supposed on her way from Phanor's, and coming up with her Julie returned and I continued my walk. When I got back the supper was over, but this did not prevent me from taking my meal.

Everybody retiring early, the moon shining most beautifully, I started up the road, directing my steps towards Phanor's, where I had before leaving heard the sound of music. When I got there everyone had just left the parlour, so that I went to Felix's room, who came out with me, and both of us seated at the end of the gallery, enjoying the sweets of a delightful cigar, conversed upon matters in general till half past ten when I took leave, bidding him a good night's rest and returned to my room, where I was not long before falling in a profound sleep.

THURSDAY—23RD

I kept at my studies minus the recreation I took after dinner till about half past six, when coming out of my room with my valise in one arm and my staff in the other hand, to leave for my uncle Cloutier's having to survey there tomorrow, I met with two gentlemen, N. Deblieux and F. Vienne (the assessor)—they remained but a short while. I went out of my room to see them just as they were mounting their horses.

I supped at Achille's and got at my uncle Cloutier's at about 9 P.M. I found only the young men up.

Breakfasting early, we started on our hunting expedition and came back at 11 A.M., having killed a large doe. We had a fine joke on two of our friends that participated in the hunt, and it amused us very much to tease them about it, particularly as it seemed to vex them much.

We played a little at cards in the evening and left to come home, for Felix and I came home and Theophile, his lady, Edward, and Ursin went home. I found Mrs. Leach here. She had spent the day at this place and remained over night.

The weather was again dry, beautiful, and warm. The planters are complaining of the grounds being already too hard, and would like to have a little shower. This morning several persons were here, and went off as they came, one or two at a time. At about 12 M. father and I went to dine at Phanor's. Mrs. Phanor was not there, having gone to Natchitoches the day previous, together with Julie. There were my aunts Adolphe and Neville and a pretty good assembly of gentlemen present. I spent my time very agreeably and returned at about 6 P.M., a little after father, to get my horse and go at Narcisse's where we remained till pretty late, and both of us returned each one to his respective home.

I worked the whole morning calculating the field notes I had taken last Friday, and finding some errors which I could not account for, I, at last, after searching in vain to account for the mistake, remembered my chain had been broken, and examining it I found it was incorrect.

It was then nearly 1 P.M. and I determined after correcting my chain to go on the spot and survey the land over. Leaving here at 4 P.M. I got at my uncle's at about five, and at sundown I did part of the work; a small cotton field, which work balanced, as I proved immediately upon my return from the field. Ursin Lambre spent the night there, and we amused ourselves playing the game of Maroc.

WEDNESDAY—29TH

I got up early this morning to accompany my grandmother at cousin Prudhomme's where we breakfasted. I had left home with the intention of returning there, but wishing to pay a visit to Mrs. Plauche and Emile Sompayrac I continued. When I wanted to take leave of the company at the latter place, I was so much pressed to remain at dinner I remained till 4 P.M. I then left and went at my uncle Cloutier's to get his son Edward to come home with me, but could not succeed, and was here prevailed upon to remain till morning, though I intended to return after supper. The weather was threatening and very warm.

THURSDAY—30TH

The weather was fair (after a light shower about day-break) till about 1 P.M. when the clouds hid the sun; the whole atmosphere looked dark and gloomy, the lightning was vivid, and the thunder rolled heavily. Then two or three thunder claps which caused the house to shake, then came a heavy rain, accompanied with a strong wind, which luckily terminated immediately, for not only would it have thrown a few limbs down, as it did, but would have prostrated both cotton and corn. The rain continued, lasting till about 9 P.M. with some short intervals between the showers, which were not heavy but just hard enough to do the good necessary to the crops, which stood much in need of it. Thus all the planters were pleased and joyful and an end was put to their perhaps justifiable fear of the too long drought. I came from my uncle's at about 9 P.M., together with Edward, and we got home just in time to accompany my sister Julie at my aunt Benjamin's. After remaining there a short time Edward and I came at Phanor's. He remained there and I came home, but returned for dinner.

We spent the evening most delightfully and came home together with Felix at 7 P.M. This was after my return from my aunt Benjamin's where I had gone to get my sister, and stopped again at Phanor's. Phanor was then there, having just returned from town where he had gone in the morning.

We spent the *soirée* most agreeably, being delighted with several fine duets on the piano and flute. Father had the fever this day.

FRIDAY–31ST

I spent the morning here with Edward. At half past 11 A.M. we left to go at Theophile's, and we returned at about 5 P.M. He remained here a moment, then leaving I accompanied him as far as Mr. Leroy's where I stopped to pay the gentleman a visit.

After my return I went on foot at Phanor's to see Felix about the premeditated drive of tomorrow, and returned immediately. Mr. and Mrs. Lecompte were there. They were on their way to Natchitoches from their plantation.

MONTH OF JUNE–1850

SATURDAY–1ST

Long before sun up my uncle Adolphe, Felix, and I started for Theophile's place (the lieu of *rendezvous*). After a short time we found ourselves at the desired place, where we found Edward and Ursin who had come to participate in the drive.

Taking breakfast early, all mounted and started in good humour and finely disposed for the sport. Notwithstanding these fine dispositions, and great ambition of killing, we were not successful. Not a single gun was fired, and hunting till about 2 P.M. after having been eaten up by the mosquitoes and gnats, perfectly dissatisfied with the very thing we expected would give us great pleasure.

At first the dogs would not hunt, chasing rabbits, hogs, foxes, etc., but they were broken from it and then took the deer trail, but then there was another impediment. The driver drove so awfully bad, through negligence or dissatisfaction, that all the deer would run out of the drive instead of passing towards the huntsmen. It was a complete failure. We all remained at Theophile's till 7 P.M. then all starting together but soon separating. Ursin and Edward going one way, Felix, Adolphe, and I going the other.

SUNDAY—2ND

Mother, Father, my sister Julie, and the children went off to go and spend the day at my uncle Neville's, and I remained alone till about 11 A.M., then left for the same destination the others had. I took Narcisse on the way and left him at his brother Achille's and continued as far as my uncle's where I got at about 12 M.

A short while after my aunt Cloutier arrived accompanied by her son Edward. We all participated in a most glorious dinner and spent the evening delightfully. When I left at about 6 P.M., Edward intimating to me his desire of accompanying me, I went to take him at his house. But did not leave before seven, as we were expecting his brother, John, and Ursin that had gone in the morning to town. Edward, Ursin, and I got here at 10 P.M. and finding everyone had retired we repaired to my room where we enjoyed ourselves conversing and drinking wine till 11 P.M. and then retired to take a good night's rest.

The weather was beautiful and the heat excessive.

MONDAY—3RD

The day was beautiful and the heat perhaps more sensible than yesterday. I got up early for the purpose of drawing a barrel of wine with which I got through at about 10 A.M. This prevented me from entertaining my friends as well as I would have wished before their departure which took place shortly after breakfast. At this meal we had the pleasure of an old acquaintance's company, Mr. Bishley, who did not make a long stay. John Janin, who sometime past had left for Kentucky, returned last Saturday on board the steamboat *J. T. Doswell,* and this evening I went to see him. Upon my return I got ready to go to town and tend court, and was detained a little by the arrival of Mr. McAlpin and Mr. Latier, who were on their way to Natchitoches. I excused myself and left, but was stopped on the way to participate in a rural collation and then kept on. I spent the night at my uncle Cloutier's, and hearing there what someone had said about certain young men and myself I was pretty much vexed.

TUESDAY—4TH

I left at my uncle's after breakfast in the company of Edward, and as we travelled slowly we got in town at about 10 A.M. I heard a great deal spoken or said about the fair which had taken place last night, and was to be again continued this evening, and in addition to the buying and selling a little dancing was to be performed. This fair which had been got up for the purpose of raising sufficient money to buy a house and lot, well situated on a little elevation near town, and well adapted for the object in view, that of having a college which is to be given to the Jesuits.

Much opposition was raised against this, some stating it was calculated to weaken the public school system; others say they would not like to have it under the superintendence of the Jesuits; and others again that the time chosen for holding the fair had not been well selected as the times were hard and money scarce, the crops having been destroyed by water, and many other reasons useless to mention.

However, all these objections seemed to have vanished when the time arrived. No one thought then of the validity of their reasons, but of the enjoyment which was thus presented to the citizens of the little town of Natchitoches, which has grown very dull and consequently requires but little amusement to attract the whole public.

The ladies who had undertaken the management of this money making invention were very successful, making about eight hundred dollars in two nights. I did not attend this evening for several reasons, one of which is that my sister, not having been able to come, I did not think right that I should go without her.

There were some small suits of very little consequence transacted in court. There are more persons in town than I have seen for a long while. It gives the place a little gaiety and business-like appearance. Father came to town to attend the police jury.

THURSDAY–6TH

Several showers took place in the evening. Leaving town, I was caught in one of them and detained about half an hour, and though the skies looked low and dark I continued. Supped at my uncle Baptiste's and got home at 10 P.M. Father, though he desired coming, could not do so, being detained by his business. The reason of my returning home is that the court adjourned this morning till Monday next, and I did not wish to remain so long in town without my occupation.

Joseph Janin and I drew a barrel of wine for my grandfather. I went to the convent with father; Lise and Phanor were there and also Mrs. Plauche and Mrs. Victor Plauche, and there spent an hour most pleasantly. At the Police Jury a law was passed to allow hogs to run at large in all the districts where it was not permitted. This law found but few supporters in the public, but few being pleased with it. A petition by the planters to have it repealed was much talked of.

SATURDAY–8TH

The weather was beautiful and warm. Some of the young men who had assembled last night went off after the *soirée* and others this morning. John Cloutier and I remained till 11 A.M. today and went at my uncle Cloutier's where we remained till 5 or 6 P.M.

All of us left in the evening; went at my aunt Benjamin's a moment and returned home to spend the evening, which was agreeably spent, being delighted part of the time with some beautiful duets on the piano and flute.

During the whole morning I suffered with a violent headache, which luckily (after I had taken a short nap and a little brandy and sugar) left me free from the acute pains it produced.

SUNDAY–9TH

My uncle Cloutier and family got here before breakfast—after this meal they went off to go and spend the day at my aunt Benjamin's, and a little after mother left for the same purpose. Before these departures had taken place, Adolphe had arrived to pay a visit. Father, John, and I remained to go later and join the company. During this time Ursin came and at 11 A.M. we started for our intended destination. Father did not accompany us, being then suffering with a sore throat.

MONDAY—10TH

I spent the day pretty pleasantly, remaining in court to see the business carried on. I came from home this morning and was caught in the rain which falling so light did not wet my clothes through.

TUESDAY—11TH

Father and Phanor came to town to act as witnesses. Attended the court a great part of the day, and paid several pleasant visits. The grand jury was dismissed this morning. There are less persons in town than there were last week, but I amuse myself.

WEDNESDAY—12TH

I spent the best part of my time in court, and there a thing of very rare occurrence happened. A man by the name of J. Frank who has been accused with the murder of an individual (presumed to be Hobly) whose corpse was found very much decayed. This man Frank been confined in the parish prison for ten months not being allowed a trial, there being no judge when court was to take place. His trial was to come up this session, and was to commence this evening. The Judge, lawyer, and all persons interested in the case had already assembled at the court house, and everything apparently was ready to give the prisoner a fair trial when it was ascertained that the bill of indictment was missing. In spite of all the searches made it was not found, and the court proceeded to other suits.

Conceptions and suppositions were raised about the mysterious disappearance of the bill. These were numerous and various. All pitied the prisoner, who if the bill did not happen to be found before the jury was discharged, would have to remain six months more in confinement.

He, the prisoner, is a poor man, father of a family, and was, before the accusation of murder was brought against him, always considered to be a quiet, good, and honest man, and as the facts of his guilt are not clear and apparent, he is generally supposed to be innocent of the charge brought against him.

FRIDAY—14TH

My aunt Baptiste and her son Edward came to town, and this evening I left with them to go and spend the evening with them. Father also came with us; he had been in town since Tuesday morning. Octave Metoyer, who was at my uncle's, invited Edward and I to go and spend the night with him and we did, as he was alone.

SUNDAY—16TH

After breakfast I started from my uncle's with Ursin and we got to town at half past eight. We immediately made our preparations to assist at Mass and we were delighted with a sermon which was preached by Rev. Mr. Martin.

In the evening at about four o'clock grandfather had a fit, but when I left, about an hour after, he was to all appearances well, although the Doctor in attendance was doing something to relieve him entirely and prevent the occurrence of another.

I got here at about 8 P.M. Mother was absent, being at Narcisse's, whose lady was last Saturday made mother of a large boy.

MONDAY—17TH

Edward Cloutier, who is to leave in a couple of days for Baltimore where he goes for the purpose of studying dentistry, came here at about 9 A.M., bidding farewell to all his relations.

I felt unwell nearly the whole day, and everyone tells me I look very lean, that I have not improved during my stay in town. This did not surprise me; I attribute it to change of habits and food, and also of life. I had, during my stay in Natchitoches, to eat in order to live. I had no appetite and found no relish in eating.

In the evening I paid several visits with Edward, and we returned home. Felix spent the *soirée* here with us.

TUESDAY—18TH

The weather was cloudy in the forepart of the day, but it eventually cleared up and the firmament looked bright. Edward left after breakfast; I accompanied him part of the way and took leave of him. The separation was painful, but its being useful and necessary made it somewhat easier.

I resumed my studies, but being unwell (and I have been so for the last two or three days) I studied but little. I took a bath which did me much good; I restrain my appetite, which is, however, not good and drink some tisane. I find by following this course that I am better. In the evening I took a long walk along the river, reading till it got too dark to see, and on my return, Julie being at Phanor's, I stopped and supped there. We got home between nine and ten o'clock.

Mother and Julie spent the evening at my uncle Neville's. There are several persons sick at that place. The *Doswell* went up at about 11 P.M.

WEDNESDAY—19TH

The weather was most beautiful but the heat warm.

We had company today. Mrs. Moreau and my aunt Benjamin and Lise came to join the company. I felt somewhat better today, and took another bath, which I hope will produce the desired effect.

I studied very hard the whole day, and even after the family had retired I had to come and finish what remained unfinished, having to start tomorrow with mother, Julie, and the children on a tour towards Campti.

Julie and I accompanied Lise, Mrs. Moreau, and the children as far as Phanor's gate.

For the two or three last days I have felt very dull, both on account of my health and the sad and deep reflections in which I have been plunged.

The *Doswell* went down by the Rigolet.

Chapter Seventeen

LES BELLES DE LA CÔTE JOYEUSE

THE diary which precedes this chapter is but one sixth of the whole manuscript; it is far too long to quote in its entirety. To me, it seems a nearly perfect picture of Creole plantation family life in that flush time just before the Civil War. When I had finished reading it, I made a search for other documents which would throw more light on the life of "the joyous coast" of Cane River. In my search I found an old song-book; many yellowing sheets of music bound together and stamped with a date—1850. It had been lying at the bottom of an old trunk, forgotten and neglected, for sixty years. It lay hidden beneath old clothes, old hats, faded artificial flowers—beneath a hundred souvenirs of the past. The song-book once belonged to Miss Eulalie Buard of Natchitoches, and it now belongs to Mrs. Blanche Greneaux, a descendant, who still lives there.

Fully a hundred songs are bound together, sentimental

ballads mostly, about doves, moonlight, nightingales, and bowers of roses; the young ladies of the old songs are all sad, they swoon with love and die of sadness. There are "exhibition pieces" too—probably played to rapturous applause at the graduation exercises at the convent—with imposing names, such as "The Shower of Pearls" and "The Fire-Fly Polka." The latter, according to the faded printing on the cover, was "composed in the city of Natchitoches in 1849," but was printed in New York by Hall & Son.

But the most interesting sheets of music in the collection are two groups of waltzes: "Les Belles de la Rivière Rouge," and "Les Belles de la Côte Joyeuse." They were composed and dedicated to the belles of Red River by J. Grimmer, and published in Cincinnati by Peters, Webb & Co., in 1850. The first group is made up of several short selections, each one dedicated to some girl whose name seems to-day as remote as the waltz itself: Laure, Nizilda, Clothilde, Felecie, Attala, Cornelia, and Eda. Some of the waltzes are grave and slow, others are frivolous and gay; and one might suppose that the composer tried to give an idea of the character of each of the young ladies. The other waltzes, which are dedicated to the belles of the Joyous Coast, honor young ladies by the names of Odalie, Julie, Cecile, Estelle, Henriette, and Aurore.

In finding this book, I felt that I had come upon a group of old acquaintances, for these were the friends and cousins of Lestant Prudhomme. They are the "doves, angels, little loves" that he describes as immured in the convent. And Mr. J. Grimmer himself has wandered in and out of Lestant's diary. Julie and Odalie are Lestant's sisters; Aurore is his cousin. Nearly every girl mentioned appears in the diary at one time or another.

Turning over the brittle pages I found the "Grand Valse de la Société Philharmonique des Opelousas," also written by the versatile J. Grimmer, and published by F. Zambilli at 197 Royal Street, New Orleans. It is dedicated to Miss Nizilda St. Amant of Natchitoches, evidently the same Nizilda who inspired one of the first group of waltzes.

And it is highly probable that these convent girls carried this music book with them when they went to spend the day at Phanor Prudhomme's—that day when Lestant joined them there and enjoyed himself so much.

Somewhere in this volume that you are reading, you will find a drawing of Phanor Prudhomme's house— Bermuda Plantation—and it might be well to turn now and look at it, for it was here that the belles of the Joyous Coast assembled for an evening of music. It is a charming old house even to-day, and it is still occupied by the direct descendants of the Prudhomme family.

The parlor is large and square, with plain white-plastered walls and fading family portraits—the same that hung there in Lestant's time. The portraits are those of Lestant's grandparents, the old planter and his wife, painted in Paris while the Prudhommes were on a visit there. The old gentleman is pictured with a cotton boll in his hand, for he was proud of the fact that he was the first planter of Red River to make a success with a cotton crop. In Lestant's time, the room was furnished with carved mahogany furniture, upholstered in black horsehair; the curtains were of red brocade; there was an old square piano of rosewood. And even nowadays it is easy to think of the belles of the Joyous Coast assembled around the piano, with the music-book open before them, singing like a cage full of mocking birds. And so Lestant must have seen them, as he came into the room, wearing a black stock around his throat, and carrying his cane in one hand, and the inevitable copy of Blackstone under his arm.

And how Lestant loved the ladies! Let us look into his diary again: On August 10, 1850, we find him exclaiming: "Oh the young ladies! Where there are young ladies, there is also happiness and amusements, pleasures and divertisements reign supreme!" On August 18, he writes: "I am enchanted with the young ladies, their conversation pleases me, they are charmingly mannered, they are altogether beautiful and lovely." And these are his three cousins.

The girls have come home from the convent for their summer vacation, and there are dances every night; in the afternoons the young people ride about on horseback from house to house. Usually there are ten or twelve in the party. Lestant is never happier than when he and Miss Aurore are together. He tells of making a fan for her, from the tail feathers of a wild turkey he has killed. She was "pleased and surprised and blushed deeply" when he presented it to her. It is all as naïve and old-fashioned as a lace-paper valentine.

On another day he took his cane and his copy of Blackstone and set out for a walk, accompanied by his dog. Miss Attala and Miss Aurore rode by on horseback, and his description of their charms takes up a full page in his diary. In fact, the month of August is filled with incidents as fragrant as an old bouquet. He dines with Desirée, rides with Attala, dances with Amelie, and encourages his sister,

Julie, to invite the whole group to his plantation. They come and spend the day and Lestant grows lyrical in his happiness. One day when the young ladies are assembled, a thunder-storm comes up; immediately there are screams, "fainting fits," and great excitement. The young ladies prove themselves typical of their generation by "swooning" time after time. It seems to be the fashion to faint during thunder-storms, for even "Aunt Theophile was very much frightened by the noise of the thunder, and it had produced such an effect on her that she had, after the rain, to give up the keys and management of the house, and retire to her room and get into bed."

Vacation is over all too soon, and the "little loves repair to the convent to resume their studies." Lestant goes to town to make a series of last farewells, and later goes to dine with some male acquaintances at Lacals' Hotel.

"We all indulged a little in champagne [he writes], and that most treacherous of wines made us all sick. I had consequently to go to bed, and so did my friend, John, and after the effects of the beverage had passed, we met again, but it was too late to start home, as it was our intention to do."

They go home the next day, but Lestant suffers as a boil is troubling him. He arrives at home to find that the whole family has gone off on a visit. He is desolate indeed. "The house looked vast and empty, but I assured myself that I had good companions in books. I read until about noon and then could stand it no longer. I went at Phanor's."

But now, at home, he finds himself thinking of the

young ladies at all times. Finally he decides to go to the convent to see his sister Odalie. The other young ladies come into the parlor to see him. The nuns must have left him alone with them for a moment—although he does not say so—for he writes with some pride: "I demanded the *privilège de cousin,* which was granted immediately amid blushes, and I had the pleasure of imprinting upon their rosy lips a warm and sweet kiss." Well pleased, he rode home singing. What is a ride of fifteen miles to a young man in love with love?

On October 7, he remembers Blackstone, and writes: "There having been so much amusement and attractions on all sides while the young ladies were home from the Convent of the Sacred Heart, I neglected Blackstone and amused myself. The vacations being well over, I this day commenced again." But he was interrupted almost immediately by his Aunt Adolphe and Lise, who ask him to take a walk. He cannot bring himself to refuse. "We went together to a place where victuals is cooked for the hands, all except myself took a collation at that place and found the food for the slaves toothsome and well cooked." He mentions casually that the hands have been picking cotton for a month; but all the cotton is baled and weighed now and soon will be shipped on a steamboat to New Orleans.

And now we reach a point in the diary which gives an interesting note on family affection. His "Aunt Huppe," a widow with one son, has come to visit Lestant's family. She has been a guest in the house for months, as her son Bernardin has gone to act as manager for a plantation in Pointe Coupée. There are references to the son's approaching marriage to a wealthy Creole girl. This marriage will restore the fortune of Aunt Huppe, which, since her husband's death, is diminishing. Let me quote from Lestant's diary for December 12, 1850:

Upon my arrival home I found a gentleman and his lady to whom I was introduced; a short moment after two other gentlemen and their ladies arrived. Phanor and his lady came for supper; others came for the *soirée*. The first gentleman mentioned had with him a young daughter, a fascinating young lady of sweet sixteen; she rejoiced in poetic beauty. . . .

But my pleasure and that of my parents was soon marred upon the reception of a letter which told us of the unexpected death of Bernardin Lafon, who was carried off by cholera in the short space of 48 hours. We were all thunderstruck and grieved at the reception of such painful news; and, to increase our sorrow, there sat his mother, my Aunt Huppe, gay, laughing, entertaining the company, unconscious of the great misfortune that had happened to her. We were compelled to hide our grief and appear gay. We dared not tell her, for her son was her only hope, and she saw in him the only consolation for the loss of three husbands. In Pointe Coupée her son was doing well, had fallen in love with a charming and agreeable young lady, the sole heir to an immense fortune from an old aunt of hers; he had obtained her hand and was soon to marry her. Eighteen months ago he had spent a few days with his mother and had explained his plans to her; she was to join him for his marriage celebration and remain and live at his new residence.

But the news of his death could not therefore be told his mother without preparing her for it, and the occasion was not appropriate. Ah, it is hard, when one is grieving at the death of a relative and friend, to converse and laugh and that in the presence of a person who is the deceased's parent! Great violence must be exerted to overcome the natural feelings on such occasions.

The next day he writes:

Letters were written to different members of the family to apprise them of Lafon's death, and two or three came to help prepare the mother to receive the unfortunate news. Her health, however, would not permit it, and it was determined to tell her nothing of it until she would be better. I was mournful, and the family sobbed behind doors the whole day. My poor aunt, alone, was gay. A spectacle indeed to pierce the heart!

Two more days pass, and other members of the family arrive, but Aunt Huppe is not told. Finally she begins to suspect that all is not well. She asks questions. They deny everything. Finally they decide that she must be told the following day. A whole week has passed. On the following Monday, he writes:

This day was very cruel on all the persons in the house. At about nine o'clock several persons of the family having arrived, the painful tale was told my aunt who immediately fainted and during the day had many fits which followed each other in rapid succession. Her grief was great and her cries and lamentations so painful that everyone present could not but sympathize with her, and in the whole house, both blacks and whites were bathed in tears.

Her grief continues. For the next week he writes that she "went from collapse into collapse." Lestant abandons Blackstone entirely for a time, as the sadness of the household precludes concentration. Christmas comes, but the household is so deep in mourning that they do not celebrate the day. Lestant cannot bear it, and goes into Natchitoches on Christmas morning, but "a poor Christmas it was, there were no amusements of any kind, no family dinner, no meeting of friends, not even an egg-nog in the *comme il faut* taverns to welcome the customers." He returns home and writes on New Year's Day: "A new year has commenced, and all we have gained by its arrival is the unpleasant certainty that we have only grown one year older."

The days pass, and the visiting begins again as before. There are notations of family councils regarding the division of his grandfather's property. A neighboring planter, Mr. Robieu, dies, and his slaves are sold at auction on January 13. This was the same Mr. Robieu who had once owned the infamous Pauline, of whom I have written in another chapter.

On January 14, Lestant writes: "Phanor and Mr. Victor Sompayrac came here and estimated my grandfather's negroes and afterwards divided them into eight shares. They were at it the whole day." Lestant is given the task of surveying his grandfather's plantation so that a division can be made. This takes more than a week, for the place is very large. On January 28, he is still working on his calculations, and writes: "I was engaged until 11 A.M. drawing sketches from the plat dividing my grandfather's plantation into eight equal parts, and stopped only because Phanor and my father came into my room and remained until dinner time."

On Monday, February 17, he writes: "Many young ladies and other persons have gone down to New Orleans to see the famous Jenny Lind, and some have gone on board the *Saxon,* a new, large, and beautifully commodious boat that passed this evening at 2 o'clock."

On Tuesday, March 11, the whole family went into Natchitoches to see a circus—all, that is, except Aunt Huppe, who is "still prostrated." Lestant writes that he likes the performance "pretty well. The clown, who is the life of such representations, was amusing in his remarks, and was very witty. The feats of the company were pretty well performed. The amusement concluded at half past ten, and all retired to their homes, the madams accompanied by their husbands, and the young belles by their beaux." They all enjoyed it so much, in fact, that the family remained in town and attended the circus again in a body the next day. They returned home and found Aunt Huppe preparing to go to Pointe Coupée to attend to her late son's affairs. "She is better and is resigned to her condition."

The family visits begin afresh. The boys go hunting nearly every day. Sometimes at night they have parties— *souper des garçons*—at the overseer's house where they make merry until morning. A man passes by selling lightning rods, and all the Prudhommes invest in them. At night sometimes the young men hunt coons with torches and packs of dogs. The next day the family enjoys coon gumbo, and relatives come from near and far to partake of it.

March passes and April comes with its high water and the eternal fear of an overflow. The negroes plow the fields. Lestant goes fishing nearly every day. Blackstone is forgotten again. He goes into Natchitoches for Holy Week and attends church every day. On Easter every one is gay. The church is packed full.

All the fine dresses came out; the young ladies were loving and looked angellical, and the beaux were dressed up tip-top and had a noble, strapping appearance. The deportment of all was distinguished and delightful. We delighted in the company of the many sweet and charming belles that had this day met in Natchitoches. There were, in honor of the feast, many family dinners at which many persons attended, and who delighted in the pleasures of the good repast and gloried in the companies of young ladies where pleasure and amusement were foremost.

There was a ball at night.

Lestant describes the weather with true poetic enthusiasm:

The beautiful and ever charming month of May has already come upon us, but this time it does not come with the congenial and mild heat of spring, for the weather is extremely cold for the season; so much so indeed that fire is found to be comfortable, and the smoke with its graceful curves rises this morning from every chimney. The destructive winter appears to give up its power with reluctance to its successor.

May gives place to June and June to July. And life on the Joyous Coast continues in its eternal round of visits and good times. In August the young ladies from the convent come home again, and Lestant abandons even his diary; he sums up a month in this fashion:

The vacations of the young ladies of the Convent of the Sacred Heart commenced on the 20th of July; only a few days more are left and the classes will again begin. These vacations have been the source of general recreation, young and old all delighting in pleasant entertainments. Promenades on horseback nearly every evening, dinners, and parties very frequent, in all of which gaiety reigned supreme. During the week before the last from Tuesday inclusively till Saturday night there were dinners at which no less than from forty-five to fifty-six persons were assembled, and that exclusive of children who were some fifteen or twenty in number. During these parties the jovial dance was introduced in spite of the heat and was no less gay for that; as all generally participated in it and appeared to enjoy

"OAK ALLEY" ON THE MISSISSIPPI,
ABOVE NEW ORLEANS

themselves heartily. The day was spent at one place and the evening at another, so that for one week there was no stop at all. These vacations have consequently been very gay and it is unfortunate they should be so short; indeed the six weeks which they lasted have flown around with the rapidity of lightning.

But it is, in the order of all perishable things, a natural consequence that all things must have not only a beginning but also an end. The end of the vacations is nearly on us, and though it may be regretted, yet it will come, and the little doves shall again return to their occupations for ten or eleven months more. After spending six weeks so pleasantly, one can return to his work with courage and satisfaction.

On September 4, he writes:

On the first of September the youthful beauties, our jewels, our sweet little doves took their flight towards the town of Natchitoches, there to enter the Convent and remain imprisoned for one long year, to the great regret of their numerous friends and relations of which I am one. The beginning of school was not very triumphant, nor to the satisfaction of the nuns. Is it not natural that the parting of children from their loving parents and friends should cause them to grieve and prevent them from their studies, or at least beginning their studies with spirit and alacrity? Ah, but it was more than this. Ah, but it was more than this. The cause of the dissatisfaction has become known, for the nuns have rebuked them, upon their return to the convent, for having danced the waltz during vacation—and that with their parents' consent! And for a little harmless diversion, the girls must now go about bathed in tears. It is not fair, neither is it just. . . .

Winter again with its hunting and bachelor suppers, the incessant family visits, the trips to town; Christmas with its family party; New Year's Day comes around again.

Getting up at about 7 A.M. my first occupation was to get the New Year's gifts for the young ladies and children of my acquaintance, and the distribution of them was a pleasant task, particularly when the gifts were presented to the young ladies, who, according to an old custom still existing to some extent in this part of the world, upon receiving the present allow the donor the privilege of taking a kiss from their sweet, beautiful, and rosy lips. . . . This being New Year's day the young ladies were allowed to leave the convent and spend the day with their parents. I, being at Natchitoches, amused myself very well. . . . At six in the evening I witnessed an affecting scene at the gates of the convent. All the young students together with their parents and guardians were present, making a pretty large assembly even without including those who had only been drawn to the spot through curiosity; and while this large meeting was busily engaged in many conversations, and all the pupils looking bright and satisfied with the manner in which they had spent the day, the convent bell gave notice that the moment for entering had come. Then in an instant the whole scene changed, a mournful and sad countenance was placed on every face, the parents kissing their children, embracing in the most affectionate manner, and grieving at the painful separation. The bystanders felt, through sympathy, the effect of this grieving so that all present were more or less affected with a general source of regret. When all the students had entered the convent, the persons who had been present walked off silently, sorrowfully, and sadly, each one to his residence or occupation. The bustling day was over and all was quiet and sad; everything looked more calm than ever.

The year 1852 began like other years, but to Lestant it was to bring an unwelcome change. His father decided that his son was not progressing rapidly enough with his law studies, and on March 22 Lestant left home and went into the town of Natchitoches to live. Or, at least, that was his intention. His departure was regarded as a tragedy, nothing less.

This day having been selected for my departure from home in order to follow up my studies more closely, I got up this morning, sad and pensive at the idea of the cruel separation which was to take place, and the new life I was about to commence. After breakfast I got bundling up all my books and clothes, assisted by my sister Julie. It was a painful occupation. . . . I would have given way to my grief had I not seen every one around me grieving at my departure. Not wishing to increase their sorrow, I mustered up all the courage I could in this trying moment, though inwardly my soul was sad and my heart bleeding. At ten everything being ready I bade goodby to all and mounted my horse. My father accompanied me, traveling a mile with me. . . .

When I took leave of my mother and sister, the tears which they had thus far restrained, could no longer be held back, and flowed down their cheeks in rapid streams. At this touching sight I mingled my tears with theirs. . . . I rode off in an agony of grief. . . . After my father had left me I was defenceless, a prey to every sad reflection possible. . . .

And all this because he was going for a short time to live in a town only fifteen miles away! His diary continues, day by day. The very first week-end he goes home and remains for four days, and after that he spends at least half of his time visiting his home or the plantations of Phanor or "Uncle Cloutier" or "Aunt Benjamin." And in town he finds gay companions. The young ladies, too, cause him sleepless nights, and sometimes he indulges in a *souper des garçons* at Mr. Lacals' hotel. In the summer he returns home for weeks at a time. Mr. Campbell remarks to Lestant that he is afraid that the copy of Blackstone must be worn out by this time; and Lestant comments in his diary that he is afraid that Mr. Campbell is sarcastic. In November, the diary breaks off short with plans to attend another wedding and a ball which will follow.

It is highly probable that there was more of the diary, but if so it has been lost. I made inquiries concerning the later life of Lestant, and to my great surprise I found out that he never practised law, nor did he ever marry! He continued his social activities to the end of his days, spending his declining years with his sister Julie, who had married a Mr. Deblieux and who lived on a plantation near Red River.

Chapter Eighteen

THE NEWS OF THE DAY

THERE are many references to the Natchitoches newspapers in young Mr. Prudhomme's diary, and it may be
interesting to look for a moment into the old files. Let us
take "The Natchitoches Chronicle" for November 8, 1851,
for it was on that day that he tells of reading Henry Clay's
letter on the Compromise Measures, and sets down that
fact among his daily "occupations and amusements." Sure
enough, here it is, six columns of closely set type. It is the
leading article in the paper; it may be said that it is the
only article in the paper that week, except for brief notices
and advertisements. But I shall not go into Mr. Clay's
remarks, for they are well known and have been recorded
elsewhere. Rather, let us look at the lesser news and see
what we can find.

On the first page, in the column next to Mr. Clay's
speech, is an advertisement of British periodicals: "The

Farmers' Guide, The London Quarterly Review (Conservative), The Edinburgh Review (Whig), The Westminster Review (Liberal), and Blackwood's Edinburgh Magazine (Tory)." This seems to show that the planters of Natchitoches read English magazines and newspapers as well as those from France.

Another advertisement tells of "Great Importations" from New York. Various drugs are listed and one's attention is also called to the "fine new window glass and paint brushes, Havana segars, chewing and smoking tobacco and patent medicines of the approved kinds." They are offered for sale by T. Lacoste, "opposite the Steamboat Landing."

Just below, Henry Wakefield advertises a "beautiful beverage" for curing "all invalids at this season of the year," especially those suffering from "billious, yellow, congestive, or typhoid fevers." There is a note appended which states that he has also received some "fresh tamarinds" which he offers for sale at his store on Washington Street.

In the next column to Mr. Clay's letter, we find several of the usual advertisements for runaway slaves. These advertisements vary little; they are usually printed twice, first in French, then in English. I shall quote one of them here, but the reader must remember that there are many of these announcements:

RUNAWAY IN JAIL

Was committed to the jail of the parish of Natchitoches a runaway negro who says his name is William and that he belongs to Alfred Lofton of Sumpter County, Alabama, formerly belonged to a Captain Roberts. Said negro is about five feet seven or eight inches high, has two scars on his upper lip, underpart of his left ear bitten off, weighs about 150 or 160 pounds, is jet black and seems about 28 or 30 years of age. The owner is requested to come forward, prove property and pay charges in order to take him away, or he will be dealt with according to law.

The notice is signed by S. M. Hyams, sheriff, and is dated Natchitoches, October 28, 1851. Below, the same notice is printed in French. Each, according to custom, is decorated with a small woodcut of a negro running, a bundle tied in a handkerchief swinging from a stick over his shoulder. Old newspapers of this period are filled with such notices. The French heading is interesting: "Marron en Prison," or "Marron" or sometimes "Detenu à la Gêole."

There is a whole column filled with the cards of lawyers and commission merchants, and a small notice informs the public that S. P. Page "has returned to this place and is prepared to attend to all duties of the dental profession at Lacals' Hotel."

On the last page of the newspaper we find a notice which interests us particularly as it deals with the Prudhomme estate mentioned in the diary. The notice, signed by C. F. Greneaux, clerk of the court, gives notice of the succession of Emmanuel Prudhomme and his wife Catherine Lambre, the grandparents of Lestant Prudhomme. Phanor Prudhomme, whose name is familiar to those who have read the diary, is named administrator. This notice is printed in both French and English.

There are numerous advertisements for patent medicines; notable among them is "Dr. Christie's Galvanic Necklace," which seems to cure everything.

A crude woodcut of a stage-coach appears above an advertisement of Simon Cockrell, manager of the Grande Écore and Sabine Stage Line, who also advertises his "unsurpassed livery stable" from which he can supply the traveling public with "the finest of stages, private hacks, horses, wagons, teams, and in fact with every kind of conveyance."

The paper is full of the names which have become familiar to us through the diary: Metoyer, De Blieux, Greneaux, Prudhomme, Lambre, Sompayrac, Robieu, and so on. A notice states that Mr. Robert McAlpin has lost a gold ring and offers a reward for its return. Mr. McAlpin's name has been mentioned in the diary; for he lived many miles down Cane River, beyond the Prudhomme plantations, and sometimes on his way to and from Natchitoches he stopped for the night, as was the custom of the time. It is well for the reader to remember that name McAlpin, for we shall speak of him again.

Under the heading "Daguerreotypes," we learn that "Mr. Rhodes has taken Rooms at Mr. de Monfort's, on Trudeaux Street, where he will be pleased to furnish all who may call upon him with Likenesses and Lifelike Portraits, put up in Cases, Lockets, Bracelets, &c."

On the inside pages we find advertisements of the Red River Weekly Packet, embellished by a woodcut of a steamboat belching forth great clouds of black smoke; we learn that the passenger packet *P. F. Kimball* leaves Grande Écore every Tuesday morning at ten o'clock and leaves Natchitoches at noon the same day. There are also notices of the *Doswell* and the *Hecla* already familiar to us.

An advertisement signed "Louis Duplieux, importer," tells us that he has "For sale on the arrival of ship *La Jenny* from Bordeaux, 40 casks of good claret wine; 100 boxes of red and white wine. All subject to drawback in the stores of the Custom House in New Orleans."

Among the news items we have a detailed account of the election returns showing that Mr. Isaac E. Morse has been elected to the United States Senate by a good majority. There is also announcement of those elected to the House of Representatives, and to the office of sheriff, and other offices. It may be of interest to know that Mr. Simon Cockrell, owner of the livery stable and stage lines already mentioned, had been elected coroner.

There is brief editorial comment on Henry Clay's letter, and an editorial urging the young men of Natchitoches to continue giving their *soirées*. "Another has been spoken of. This is as it should be, and the young ladies will not be too chary of their charms to attend if the ball is properly conducted."

The only social note pertains to a bachelor dinner. Mr. Lacals has entertained several gentlemen at his hotel; the party was given in honor of the officers of the Jockey Club. The editor himself attended, and closes his note in this delightful manner:

The company was quite a large one; many speeches were made and many toasts drank. We had intended to chronicle some of the good things said; but our memory is as frail as the glass in which we sipped our wine, and things to be remembered, though they sparkled like our champagne for the moment—have become flat in the repository of our memory and—forgotten.

Just below this editorial is the notice of a "Public Sale of Valuable Property" in which we find that the estate of Dr. S. Douglass will be sold at auction. His plantation lies "between the plantations of the late F. Robieu and J. F. Hertzog, in the Isle Brevelle, parish of Natchitoches." A list of things to be sold follows, and among them we find "Land, slaves, mules, oxen, cows, forge, ferry boat, ploughs," and so on. It is a small place, for there are only four hundred and twenty-two acres in the tract, "a comfortable dwelling house, a first-rate cotton gin and corn mill upon it, and the piney woods are within sight of the house." The slaves listed are as follows: Alfred, a negro man of 24; Cupid, also 24 and suffering from hernia; Joseph, aged 40; Ned, 24; Daniel, 40; Elizabeth, a negro girl of 15; Rachel, Ned's wife, and her two children, Suzette, 6, and Thompson, 4; Sarah, a negro woman, Daniel's wife, aged 29, and her two children, Rosette, 4, and Liza, 2 years old; Daphne, a likely mulatto woman of 28; Selada, a black girl of 18; and Mary-Ann, 70 years old and blind.

Turning over the yellowed pages of the old papers we find, shortly after, an advertisement which must have been read with feverish interest by the belles of the Red River district. It deals with "The New patent duplex, elliptic, or double steel spring hoop-skirts." Here we read that every objection to the hoop-skirt has been overcome by a new device invented by a gentleman called J. W. Bradley. "In all crowded churches, assemblies, carriages, cars, in the home or on promenade, the new double hoop is sure to give satisfaction. When brought in contact with any pressure whatever, it folds to every emergency and exigency as easily as though it were of silk or muslin, yet it is made of steel springs!"

One can imagine what pleasure such an advertisement must have brought to girls in the convent, those "doves, adorable creatures, little loves" that Lestant describes so fondly in his diary. And it must have pleased the good nuns, too, as the skirt is described as a garment which can "never offend the modesty, as the single-hoop skirt sometimes does." I suppose this means that the double-hoop was less likely to tilt up and expose the legs to view—a dreadful thing which sometimes happened even to the most careful young lady; and for this reason the girls wore lace-ruffled pantalets which reached to the ankle.

Nearby is another advertisement which is particularly tantalizing to-day, for it describes the charms of the Pelican Saloon of Campte, a town nearby, in which the proprietor lists the following "Beverages for Thirsty Planters: Whiskey, Brandy, Absinthe, Cherry Brandy, Claret Wine, Port, Madeira, Kirsch, Hostetter Bitters, Curaco, London Cordial Gin, Ale, Dublin Porter, Lager Beer, Daly's Whiskey, Assorted Syrups, Cigars, Lobsters, Oysters, Salmon, and Champagne!" He states that he has just acquired a new and splendid slate-bed table "for the accommodation of those fond of the innocent game of billiards."

In the next column we find an advertisement for Godey's Lady's Book, and the following poetic notice by Mr. I. Souter, jeweler:

> I. Souter hereby sends
> The information to his friends,
> Be they few or be they many,

> And to his enemies, if he has any,
> That he is now in Natchitoches,
> To repair clocks and fine watches.
> Jewelry also, he will repair,
> As well as can be done elsewhere.

The verse is bad, but the rhyming of "watches" and "Natchitoches" is inexcusable; for the town's name is pronounced "Nak'-a-tosh" with the accent on the first syllable. Let us hope that Mr. Souter was a better jeweler than poet.

But this is enough of an uneventful day in 1851. We have more interesting things before us.

Chapter Nineteen

SIMON LEGREE

In the diary, a part of which you have been reading, are perhaps ten entries like this: "Mr. McAlpin slept here last night." There is no description of the man, nor anything more than the fact that he was entertained in passing. This was Robert McAlpin, a bachelor who had come from New England thirty or more years before, and who owned a plantation of 4800 acres, twenty miles away. It was McAlpin's custom to ride on horseback to the town of Natchitoches, eight or ten times a year. On his trips to town he passed the night at the Prudhomme plantation. He would arrive on horseback, take supper with the family and retire early; he left before daybreak. It is probable that Lestant Prudhomme would not have mentioned the visits at all, had he not been so meticulous as to the arrivals and departures of all guests; and sometimes there is a note of regret that these chance callers spoiled his quiet evenings with his family and friends.

The references to McAlpin's visits are in 1850 and in 1851; there are none after this date for the obvious reason that McAlpin died early in 1852. He did not live to answer the accusations which were made against him.

As early as 1850, we find the United States in bitter turmoil on the questions of slavery and States' Rights. Shortly after, Harriet Beecher Stowe published "Uncle Tom's Cabin." The book, as every one knows, was a bitter arraignment of slavery. It met with instant success; edition followed edition; newspapers took up the cry; acrimonious discussions arose. This was what many had been waiting for; here was a picture of slavery in all its horror. Women in New England cringed as they read of the brutality inflicted upon the negro slaves. Men in the South declared furiously that Mrs. Stowe had libeled the slave-owner; they cited instances, gave figures to show that the slaves were well treated and happy. But even in the South there were champions for the book; although banned in many localities, tattered volumes of the story circulated secretly.

Simon Legree became the figure which, in Northern men's minds, typified the Southern slave-owner, just as Uncle Tom became the symbol of all slaves.

The plantation of Simon Legree was described by the author as being in Louisiana, on Red River. Its exact description was given, the hills, the swamps, the distance from the town of Alexandria. Men living in the Red River country made calculations, and found that the description fitted the McAlpin plantation exactly. And there were other things too striking to be coincidences.

McAlpin was a New Englander; so was Simon Legree; McAlpin had a reputation in the neighborhood for being harsh with his slaves; he was a bachelor and a heavy drinker—so was Legree. And, most damning of all, McAlpin's body-servant was called "Uncle Tom."

The story grew as the months passed by. It was said that Harriet Beecher had visited McAlpin in 1840 or thereabouts, and had visited others in the neighborhood. At any event, a strange lady from the North had come to the Red River country and had been seen talking with the negroes in the fields, riding on the cotton wagons, watching the operations of the cotton-gin. A man in the town of Alexandria produced a picture said to be a portrait of Mrs. Stowe, and which bore the stamp of a photographer of Alexandria. A copy of "Uncle Tom's Cabin" autographed by the author and bearing the cryptic statement: "Do you recognize this?" was sent to Dr. S. O. Scruggs of Cloutierville. Dr. Scruggs was a neighbor of McAlpin's.

But McAlpin was dead, his plantation had been sold and his slaves scattered. The story of his cruelties was forgotten in the general debacle which came with the Civil War and Reconstruction.

But stories like this have a way of reappearing when least expected.

In 1892, forty years after McAlpin's death, Judge D. B. Corley of Abilene, Texas, made a pilgrimage to the McAlpin plantation, located the cabin which had once housed the old negro called "Uncle Tom," bought the cabin from its owner, Mr. Lammy Chopin, and transported it bodily to the World's Fair in Chicago!

Judge Corley seems to have been what one usually

calls "a character." He was the author of a book called "The Lives of the Twelve Apostles" which was advertised in a sensational manner by printed questions, such as "What was Mrs. Pilate's given name? What were the names of the Virgin Mary's parents? Who buried Mary Magdalene?" The book was privately printed in Abilene, Texas. It is evident from the advertising that Judge Corley had spent years in searching the Bible; and now he devoted his abundant energies upon "Uncle Tom's Cabin" and Simon Legree, and Robert McAlpin.

In order to prove that the cabin which he intended exhibiting at the World's Fair was the real cabin, he took numerous affidavits from people in the vicinity. In order to prove that Robert McAlpin and Simon Legree were one and the same man, he took more affidavits. He interviewed old slaves who had served McAlpin. And he published the results of his investigations in a book which is now a literary curiosity—"A Visit to Uncle Tom's Cabin." It is probable that he sold this paper-bound volume at the exhibit in Chicago.

Judge Corley begins with a few informal interviews in his spirited style. Here is an extract from the part dealing with Mr. L. Charleville, a merchant of Cloutierville:

He said that he had served in the Mexican War under General Taylor and in the Civil War under General Lee; that he had lived in that section of the country all his life and knew Robert McAlpin well; that he believed that McAlpin was among the cruelest, if not the cruelest slave-holder he ever knew; he had read the book "Uncle Tom's Cabin" and said Mrs. Stowe did not tell of one half of his meanness. That he was notoriously cruel to his slaves; that at times they would despair and kill themselves. He remembered one case in

WOODLAWN" ON BAYOU LAFOURCHE, 1840

particular, where at his grandfather's sale some negroes were being sold and that Robert McAlpin bid upon one of them, whereupon the negro man spoke out and said to McAlpin: "If you buy me I will kill myself before night. I will not try to live with such a man as you are." And that, upon such a positive statement, McAlpin stopped bidding on him.

Judge Corley interviewed another old man who said:

How come that woman up North, that wrote the book, got the man's name wrong? His name was McAlpin, not Legree. I knew him well. He was the worst man in the whole country. That woman didn't tell one half his meanness. He sewed a nigger up in a sack and drowned him in the river.

Judge Corley discounts this statement, but believes that "straws show which way the wind blows." Now he comes down to serious business and takes a few affidavits. The first one is by Mr. Lammy Chopin, the son of J. B. Chopin, who bought the plantation at McAlpin's succession sale. Mr. Lammy Chopin is living on the place now, but has built a new house, because a railroad has bought right-of-way through the plantation and the track passes close to the old McAlpin house.

The affidavit follows:

My name is L. Chopin. I am forty-two years old and was born and raised in Natchitoches Parish, Louisiana. In the year 1852, my father bought at public sale the Robert McAlpin plantation, situated on Red River in the southern portion of the parish, and moved upon the place shortly afterward. The occasion of the plantation being sold was on account of McAlpin's death. He being a bachelor, the estate was wound up and the proceeds distributed among distant relatives.

Outside of a few years spent in Europe at school, I have lived on this plantation all my life, and until the Texas and Pacific Railroad ran through the place I lived in the old McAlpin residence. A portion of the old residence was torn down by the railroad, and the roadbed now runs through it; the balance of the building is used as a section house.

When my father first moved on the place, or at least a few years afterward, he had one of the two rows of China trees cut down because it made too dense a shade. . . .

This mention of China trees is made for good reason according to Judge Corley, for Harriet Beecher Stowe describes the double row of China trees before Legree's house. The affidavit continues:

After I assumed control of the place at my father's death, I continued the work he had begun—tearing down and removing the cabins in the negro quarters—as it smacked too much of slavery. The negroes preferred living in different parts of the plantation, rather than in a group. The only cabin remaining is the cabin known as "Uncle Tom's Cabin." This I have kept intact and have religiously kept it on account of the tradition connected with it, which makes it the cabin that Uncle Tom occupied on the Legree plantation.

Tradition has it that McAlpin was the Legree of Mrs. Stowe's book. From all reports of white and black, he was a very cruel master to his slaves, and when drunk would abuse them dreadfully and is said to have caused the death of several of them. He was a very hard drinker and died from the effects of drink. He was buried on a little hill near the residence, and his grave can still be seen there, although very much dilapidated. His name is the only white man's grave there; the place has always been and is still used as a plantation burial ground, and quite a number of negroes are buried around his grave.

When quite young I knew the place as the Legree plantation and the cabin as Uncle Tom's; and the fact is well known, not only here, but all over the country, as I have received many letters from dif-

ferent states, asking for pieces of boards from the cabin to be kept
as relics.

For years I have kept the cabin for the sake of its association
with Mrs. Stowe's book, without any thought of it ever being of any
money value and without a thought of its ever being moved from the
plantation, but lately I have been approached by parties from Chicago
and New York who have offered to buy the cabin with the view of
bringing it to the World's Fair at Chicago. Those offers I refused, and
refused at first to entertain any idea of its being moved to Chicago.
But repeated representations were made to me that such a cabin,
so closely connected with such a well-known book as "Uncle Tom's
Cabin," was in a manner public property and the opportunity should
be given to everybody to see it.

The document is signed by L. Chopin, and is sworn out
before the district clerk on October 15, 1892.

There follows the statement by Mrs. Valery Gaiennie
who says in part:

I have always lived on the Gaiennie plantation, about two miles
from the McAlpin place. I knew Robert McAlpin well. He was always courteous to us, but I have heard that he was very mean to his
slaves. . . . When I was young, there was a lady from the North that
visited Mr. McAlpin. She did not associate with us; did not care to
know us, it seemed, and being a Yankee we did not care to have anything to do with her either. I have heard that she later wrote "Uncle
Tom's Cabin," but I do not know this for certain. . . .

I remember the old negro called "Uncle Tom" very well. He
used to cross me over the river when we used to go to McAlpin, and
used to wait around the yard and table; he was a respectful and kind
old man. I have always heard that Mr. McAlpin was very cruel to
him, and I have heard my own slaves say that he used to whip "Uncle
Tom" and treat him harshly. "Uncle Tom" used to look very sad,
and I used to feel sorry for him. . . . I have always heard that most
of Mr. McAlpin's cruelty was done when he was under the influence

of liquor. . . . He had the reputation of being a great drunkard, but before ladies he was gentlemanly.

Now we have the affidavit of one John Sylvestie, sworn before H. M. Hyams, Clerk of the Tenth District Court. I do not know whether Sylvestre is a white man or a negro, but it is probable that he was black:

I am eighty-seven years old. I used to live at Monette's Ferry two miles from McAlpin. I used to pick cotton for Mr. McAlpin. He was very cruel to his slaves, and when he was drunk he did not care what he did; he used to beat them. Old Tom used to work about the yard and McAlpin was very cruel to him.

Another affidavit by S. Parson, sworn before the same notary:

His neighbors all knew Robert McAlpin as a man who was excessively cruel to his slaves. I remember that, whilst at work, and when he would pass, the men would all curse him for his cruelty. It was commonly circulated that several of his slaves had died from abusive treatment. He owned an old man called Tom.

And now we have the most interesting document of all, the testimony of one of Robert McAlpin's own slaves. I do not know if this sworn statement would have weight in a Louisiana court, but it gives the most detailed account that we have:

My name is Washington Slidell. I am a colored man and about eighty years old. I knew Mr. Robert McAlpin and remember him well. He bought me in New Orleans when I was eight years old and I was owned by him as a slave up to the time of his death, at which time I was thirty-four years old. Mr. McAlpin died on what is now called the Chopin plantation and is buried on that place.

Mr. McAlpin, when drinking, was mean and very cruel to his slaves. On one occasion I remember we were working in some new ground, which had just been put in cultivation. It was so cold at that time that we had to work with our coats on. The cook, whose name was Mary, didn't cook dinner to suit him, and he whipped her unmercifully, and tied her, entirely naked, to a stake. He broke her jaw with his walking stick. When he had finished whipping her she could not walk, and we had to carry her into the kitchen. She died that night about nine o'clock.

Mr. McAlpin was very mean to Tom and another slave he owned named William.

He was harder on the house servants and yard boys and meaner to them than to the balance of us, because they were around him more when he was drunk.

Mr. McAlpin had two yellow girls (mulattoes) that worked in the house. Their names were Rebecca and Lucinda. He did not allow any of us field hands to talk to these girls. He kept them as his wives.

Once when my brother talked with one of these girls, he whipped my brother nearly to death. He sold Rebecca and kept Lucinda because she would not let us talk to her. He sent Rebecca to New Orleans and sold her after keeping her several years, because he was afraid that she might poison him on account of his cruelty to her. When he was sick she gave him his medicine.

I am so old now that I can't remember much more that happened while I was owned by Mr. McAlpin, but I do know that all of his slaves were mighty glad when he died.

And the old slave signs with a cross, as he cannot write. The document is sworn before John A. Barlow, Clerk of the District Court, on December 8, 1892.

There is more testimony of a similar nature, but this seems sufficient to prove that McAlpin possessed something of the nature of Simon Legree, whether he served as the model for the character or not.

The Natchitoches "Enterprise," commenting editorially

on the removal of the cabin to the World's Fair, prints in part:

Why is this believed to be Uncle Tom's cabin? Because every scene about the old McAlpin plantation fits Mrs. Stowe's description to a nicety. The cabin, the residence, the location, all tally with the picture drawn; and tradition tells us that Robert McAlpin was such a character as Mrs. Stowe's Simon Legree. Her own evidence is given in one of the reviews of her work wherein she states that the character called Simon Legree was suggested *by a letter from her brother* then in New Orleans, who visited a planter on Red River; and the further evidence, which is obtainable from old residents, that *her brother visited Robert McAlpin,* is proof positive so far as circumstantial evidence can make it that McAlpin was the real Legree. . . .

Now we have another difficulty. It was the brother of Harriet Beecher Stowe who visited Robert McAlpin. Yet others say that it was Harriet Beecher herself. Judge Corley, our untiring searcher after truth, writes to the brother and receives the surprising reply from Charles Beecher of Wysox, Pa., that he cannot remember who he visited in Louisiana! "I remember incidents, but not names and dates," he writes. He adds that he did spend some time on a Red River plantation.

The "Times-Democrat" of New Orleans in the issue of December 4, 1892, has a long story of the cabin's removal to the World's Fair, and voices no complaint that the cabin be exhibited as a relic of slavery and of a cruel Louisiana planter. In fact, the newspaper states that the fact is well known that certain planters were cruel to their slaves, and that the possibility of abusive treatment to negroes in isolated communities was one of the greatest evils of slavery. A very sensible and sane view, it seems to me.

But thirty years after this—in 1924 to be exact—a
violent controversy rose in the State concerning Uncle
Tom. McAlpin had been dead for seventy-two years.

Louisiana was building roads through the State; a new
highway was to pass through the old McAlpin plantation,
from Natchitoches to the town of Alexandria. Some one
proposed to call the new highway "The Uncle Tom Trail."
Immediately a storm arose. Men and women wrote letters
to newspapers, saying that to do such a thing was to libel
the fair name of Louisiana. The Alexandria "Town Talk"
printed an editorial called "Will it Pay?" in which the
measure was opposed. The Daughters of the Confederacy
issued a resolution condemning such a name for a Louisiana
highway; and the man who had suggested the name was
denounced as "unsympathetic to Southern Ideals." Still
others rose to say that there was no truth in the story of
McAlpin's cruelty to his slaves; they denied that any
Louisiana planter was ever cruel to any slave, anywhere.
However, a few old residents rallied to the defense of their
beliefs. They did not care whether the road was called
"The Uncle Tom Trail" or another name; but they
brought up the McAlpin story again and repeated its unpleasant details. At last the Louisiana Historical Society
appealed to Mr. Phanor Breazeale of Natchitoches to
settle the matter, once and for all. Mr. Breazeale is a well-
known lawyer, who believes that Mr. McAlpin is the
victim of a tragic mistake, and that a grave wrong has
been done to his memory. He goes further, and removes
the scene of the story from the parish of Natchitoches and
places it in the parish of Pointe Coupée.

In the Quarterly of the Louisiana Historical Society

(Vol. 7, No. 2, page 305) is published the letter from Mr. Breazeale in which he takes issue with the story and "gives the bare facts in such plain array that the record is now made up and the legends put at rest." The letter to the editor of the magazine, dated February 14, 1920, is as follows:

The story has not the remotest foundation in fact. That is to say, the fact that the scene of Mrs. Stowe's great novel is laid in this parish [Natchitoches] is utterly unfounded.

My recollection is distinct that in one of her letters published either in her biography or in one of her books she showed that she had never visited Louisiana and that the scene of her story was laid in the parish of Pointe Coupée and was entirely imaginary in all of its details.

There grew up a legend here that some time in the early 40s she had visited this parish and had been the guest of an old gentleman named Robert McAlpin, who owned a large plantation on Cane River at the site of the present station of Chopin on the Texas and Pacific Railroad, and that Robert McAlpin was the original of her character of Legree and his body servant was Uncle Tom. In the course of time this legend grew until the actual cabin occupied by Uncle Tom was pointed out, being located almost on the right of way of the T. & P. R. R. I have been in the Pullman on the T. & P. and heard people from the West get quite excited in pointing out Uncle Tom's cabin, and telling a whole lot of things about it that were not correct.

When the Chicago Fair was held, several people came down there and bought this old cabin from Mr. Chopin, the then owner of the place, and exhibited it at the Fair as the original Uncle Tom's Cabin. I do not think though that it amounted to very much as an attractive exhibit.

As a matter of fact, the cabin that was so pointed out and so taken to Chicago was a modern cabin, having been built about 40 years ago to the knowledge of people now living on that plantation.

The proof appears to be abundant from old people, one or two

now living, who knew Robert McAlpin, the alleged original of
Legree. All these describe him as a man of very benevolent character-
istics. My father, when a little boy, knew him well as he was in the
habit of visiting this town [Natchitoches] eight or ten times a year.
My father described him as a man with white hair, smooth face, and
ruddy complexion and the idol of all little boys in town. As soon as he
reached town he would get all the little chaps and give them all sorts
of things such as marbles, knives, candy, etc., and he seemed to have
a great fondness for children.

Inquiry among the old people of that neighborhood thirty or
thirty-five years ago shows that no one had ever heard of any cruelty
on the part of McAlpin towards his slaves. The succession records in
this court show that when he died he owned that large plantation
comprising some three or four thousand acres and some seventy or
eighty slaves.

This property finally came into the hands of Dr. J. B. Chopin
about the year 1855 and at his death in 1878 descended to his four
children; his youngest daughter, Marie, is my wife.

The old dwelling house was on top of the hill on the banks of
Cane River; at the foot of this hill was this alleged Uncle Tom's
cabin. In 1883 the T. & P. Railway was constructed through there
and the line ran partly through the dwelling house. It is a very high
hill and quite a deep cut. The railway bought the house and twenty
acres of the land along each side of the railway, paying $8000.00 for
it. Mr. Lammy Chopin, then living on the place, built another dwelling house and remained there until about 1900. He became owner of
that part of the McAlpin property on which these buildings were
erected. On the opposite side of the river my wife acquired as her
share, the plantation there which was sold some few years ago.

So you see when these matters are looked into and investigated
these old legends and stories fade away.

It is interesting to compare Mr. Breazeale's statement,
made in 1920, with that of his brother-in-law, Mr. Lammy
Chopin, made twenty-eight years earlier. Even families
seem to disagree.

So here you have the story of Robert McAlpin who lived and died a bachelor on his remote plantation. It is difficult to make an outsider realize the bitter quarrels which have arisen concerning this man so long dead. But, innocent or guilty, McAlpin never knew that his name and Legree's were linked together. He died as he lived, alone, and was buried among his own slaves.

I visited the plantation a few years ago and wandered about on the hillside where once the house stood. But of the house itself, nothing remains; there are a few gnarled crêpe-myrtle and cedar trees which indicate the old garden; the China trees have all disappeared. The railroad track is close by. In the distance the cotton fields lie green in the sun.

The cemetery is on another hill. Tall pine trees grow there. There are many graves, all without marks of identification. Among them is the ruin of a square brick tomb. I stood beside it, under the pine trees, thinking of the man who had been lying there for more than three quarters of a century. Was he a brute, like Simon Legree? Or was he innocent of the things said against him? There was no answer to my question, and I turned away and wandered among the other graves; those of negroes who, like McAlpin, are lying there forgotten. Perhaps among the graves his body-servant Tom is also lying. At any rate, they are equal now.

Chapter Twenty

HOW TO GET A RICH WIFE

SOCIAL life in Louisiana was enlivened in 1858 by the publication of a remarkable book in New Orleans. It was written by one S. S. Hall and was called "The Bliss of Marriage, Or, How to Get a Rich Wife." It was dedicated to none other than James Buchanan, President of the United States, although the reason for such a dedication is not quite clear. But the book, by nature of its contents, created a sensation and brought about half a dozen duels.

It began, conventionally enough, with a long drawn-out consideration of the various phases of matrimonial bliss—in a nice and discreet manner, of course—and continued for 183 pages with such chapters as this: "The Age at Which Persons Should Marry," "The First Visit," "How to Win Her Love," "Ninth Visit," "Popping the Question," and so on. Turning over the pages, you will find that Mr. Hall is not content with giving advice, but at frequent intervals inserts a warning in the blackest of italics. Such phrases as this jump at you from the printed page: *"Marry no woman who sleeps until breakfast,"* or *"Never compete with a rich man,"* or—and this is a classic line of advice to young ladies—*"Eternal vigilance is the price of a husband."*

In the first chapter we find this astonishing statement: "Most young men begin life with overflowing passions, unchecked by reason, and led on by alluring temptation of corrupt associates they readily conclude that the great object of life is to revel in luxury, and to think there is naught to do but sing a song, take a glass of champagne and pop the question." But Mr. Hall soon assures us that this is a mistake. There is much more to be learned about women—especially those with a "comfortable fortune." So the writer gives advice as to glances, gestures, the language of flowers, and what not, admonishes the young man to let the lady talk at least half of the time as "it is her right, and she expects it."

All of this is typical of the period and serves as mere padding, for the sensational part of the book is reserved for the last chapter. Having delivered his lecture on behavior, Mr. Hall then comes down to business and prints a list of the eligible young ladies and gentlemen of Louisiana, and gives the fortune of each. The usual delicacy of the Victorian era is shown in this: only the initials of the young ladies are given, but the young men's names are given in full. No one with less than forty thousand dollars is included, and in those days forty thousand dollars was a comfortable sum.

The list is interesting because it shows the distribution

of wealth among plantation families. The list of the young
ladies of fortune is imposing enough in the city of New
Orleans, but the daughters of plantation owners put them
quite to shame. In New Orleans we find:

Miss H. Z.	.	.	.	.	$200,000.00
Miss R.	.	.	.	.	$250,000.00
Miss L. C.	.	.	.	.	$100,000.00
Miss M. R.	.	.	.	.	$150,000.00
Miss L. H.	.	.	.	.	$100,000.00 and so on.

Among the gentlemen we find:

D. C. Jenkins	.	.	.	.	$150,000.00
C. D. Dreaux	.	.	.	.	$199,000.00
H. C. Bard	.	.	.	.	$ 55,000.00 and so on.

The Natchez territory was rich indeed, as were
other plantation communities: the Teche country, Bayou
Lafourche, Pointe Coupée, and other sections boasted a
number of eligibles, but Baton Rouge seems to be the
mecca for all ambitious young men. Here we find an imposing list of heiresses, and one strikingly original note.
Miss M. E. D . . . e is listed with a fortune of $300,000.00
and has the word "intellectual" after her name. How she
got that way, I cannot imagine, as she is the only young
lady in Louisiana who is listed with any comment as to
mental equipment. And at this late date it is impossible to
say whether the rating was intended as a compliment or
a warning.

At the end of the book we find this choice paragraph:

Those who cry loudest against the evils of money matches will
sooner than any other class of individuals seize the first opportunity

to better their pecuniary condition. These ranting public censors are generally bankrupts in love, or such persons whose position in society would forever preclude them from the possibility of successfully aspiring to a rich girl's hand. There is more than one instance upon record in which a nice young man has been heard to proclaim most vociferously against fortune hunters, and in less than six weeks unite in the bonds of matrimony with an old lady of forty-five years of age for the pittance of seventy thousand dollars. This idle twaddle about fortune hunters is a ridiculous bugbear, gotten up by designing persons to frighten timid young men.

All of which goes to show that our grandfathers might talk of doves and moonlight, mocking-birds and magnolias, but when it came to marriage they were practical enough.

Chapter Twenty-one

AN OLD LADY'S LETTERS

THE facts of history are but an outline of the picture of the times; the picture is black and white. If one seeks color, he must study the foot-notes.

In collecting the material for this book, I have gone into strange byways, hoping to find—around this corner or behind that tree—something overlooked by others who have covered the ground before me. Old diaries, letters, and account-books have been read with much more interest than the printed histories; and I have talked with many old men and women of their memories.

It was in Natchez, Mississippi, that I met Mrs. Vincent Perrault, a descendant of a long line of plantation people. She had been born on a Louisiana plantation and had lived on one the greater part of her life. An ancestor had been a judge in the trial of Aaron Burr; her father, a planter, was mayor of Natchez during the Civil War and knew General Grant. When I met Mrs. Perrault she was in her late seventies, and she was ill when I called to see her. But she entertained me for an hour with old stories of peculiar vividness.

"If only," I said, "you would write these things down!"

She smiled. "I will write them for you, if you like," she said, "but they will be fragments, nothing more."

But I did not expect that she would write to me. Why should she? I was a stranger, and she was ill; and writing is tedious work. But it was not more than a week later when her first letter came. Only a paragraph, but so amusing that I replied at once, begging for more. A correspondence began. Sometimes she wrote to me of her ancestors; sometimes she wrote bits of her life on a plantation, prior to the Civil War.

By rearranging the letters and placing incidents in their natural order, a real picture of the times has emerged.

My father was born on January 8th, 1815, at Bralston Plantation on the Mississippi. This was the day that Andrew Jackson led the American forces against the British on the plains of Chalmette near New Orleans. At Bralston, the cannonading could be heard, and old "Mammy" Winnie—who came into my grandfather's room to announce the news that a son and heir had been born—thought that the cannon fire was a celebration for my father's birth. There were five girls, you see, but only one boy. . . .

This is from Mrs. Perrault's first letter. Later she wrote of her father's family, and in three short paragraphs told a story which challenges the imagination; surely there is plot for a novel here:

My father's mother was a Miss Glasscock. Her father, my great-grandfather, had come from Virginia to Louisiana. He ran away from

LOADING STEAMBOATS AT THE LEVEE

LUXURY ON BAYOU LAFOURCHE.
"BELLE ALLIANCE," 1845

home and came here to make his fortune—this was about 1770. He made the fortune and went back to his father's house to see him. When the son arrived, the negro butler did not recognize him, as he had changed with the passing years, and told the young man that his master was entertaining a party of gentlemen, and would see him when dinner was over. The son turned on his heel and walked away, saying over his shoulder: "Tell my father that Thomas Glasscock is not accustomed to waiting on anyone." The butler was frightened and ran and whispered the news to the older man. When the father heard the message he rose from the table and shouted orders that his carriage be hitched up at once. He followed his son, but never found him, and never saw him again. . . .

Thomas Glasscock, my great-grandfather, lived on a Louisiana plantation. On the next plantation lived Mr. Dale who had married a beautiful Creole girl from New Orleans. This lady was the toast of the countryside and was admired by all the gentlemen of the neighborhood. One summer evening Mr. Dale sat at his desk writing. The doors and windows were all open to catch the evening breeze. A shot rang out from the dark cluster of oak trees which grew nearby. The shot killed Mr. Dale and killed also a little negro boy who sat on the doorstep eating his supper of bread and milk. The man who murdered Mr. Dale was never discovered. Later the beautiful widow married Thomas Glasscock.

Fifty years later, an old gentleman who remembered the tragedy went to a clairvoyant in New Orleans and asked who had killed Mr. Dale. All of the actors in the drama had died, and the question was asked in idle curiosity. To his surprise, the clairvoyant replied that a man named Glasscock had committed the murder. The story, when repeated, caused more than one man to ponder. It does not matter that I tell you this, for all of the name have gone long since.

Then she writes of her mother's family, and continues with her own recollections. From this point, the letters make a connected narrative, so I shall offer them to you with no further comments of mine.

When my grandfather Watson came to ask for the daughter of Brian O'Bruin he was only 19 years of age and my grandmother was only 14. But our great-grandfather, having lost his wife, thought it best for his young daughter to have a protector in case of anything happening to him, so the consent was given, and a goodly slice of land from Bruinsburg Plantation as well as twelve slaves to start them on their way toward cultivating their bottom lands. Miss Bruin was given her old "mammy" to assist her in the house. Often I have heard my mother tell how they closed the windows and doors of the house when my grandfather Watson had gone out into the fields with the slaves. "Mammy" Winnie did this to keep out intruders, for the country was full of Indians. Bears, wildcats, and other wild animals were numerous and dangerous.

So here the young couple lived, near her father's big plantation at Bruinsburg, while her father, Judge Bruin, carried on his work as one of the first Judges of the Mississippi Territory. One can imagine the feelings of this good man when he had to undertake the preliminary trial of his wife's cousin, Aaron Burr. He was assisted by five other judges, and the crowd was so great at the courthouse at Washington, Mississippi, they were forced to try Burr out under big oak trees that are still standing. . . .

After time had passed and the young family of my grandfather Watson had grown apace, he moved to Panola Plantation, on the Mississippi River in Louisiana, but not far from Natchez, Mississippi. Five of his daughters had married and it would soon be my mother's turn. She had just returned from Nazareth, Kentucky, where she had been for three or four years, finishing her education. She was graduated under able instruction of Sister Columbia Carroll, a niece of John Carroll of Carollton. Many of the Louisiana planters sent their daughters to school at Nazereth. The first time my mother saw my father, he had come to Nazereth to see a cousin of his who was to graduate with my mother. A crowd of girls (unknown to the good nuns) were peeping through the blinds of one of the rooms that overlooked the lawn in front of the school. The big chestnut horse that the young planter from Louisiana was riding, broke away from his master and went racing over the garden with Mr. Dix in full pursuit. Little did the young daughter of Mr. Watson think that before a year rolled away she would meet the rich young planter in Natchez and that he would fall in love with her.

Their meeting took place at his great aunt's country house, "The Vale." He was playing on his violin, accompanied by his cousin, Miss Gailhard. When she (Miss Watson) entered the parlor, he lifted his eyes from the music and saw the girl who was afterwards to become his wife. He did not play any more, but spent the rest of the evening talking to her. When my mother returned to Panola Plantation, the young planter paid frequent visits, while his overseer attended to his interest at home. A happy time the young planter had at Panola, riding horseback with the ladies, fishing at Lake Bruin, and camping out with a party of hunters who once played a good joke on him.

They killed a deer and, while the young lover was in a different part of the wood, the rest of the party stood the buck by the side of a tree, fixing it firmly in position; they tied a string to the deer's tail and, hiding themselves in the underbrush, they waited for the young man's return. Of course, my father thought the buck was alive and fired immediately, but to his astonishment, the deer stood wagging his tail. He fired again. Still the deer wagged his tail. He became suspicious, advanced, and found out the trick. His indignation was so great, he was withheld with difficulty from turning his gun on the men who had played the joke. . . .

It may seem an odd thing to say, but I can almost coax myself to believe that I actually *saw* my own mother's wedding! As a child I heard it described over and over, down to the last detail. Through an unusual series of circumstances, it became rather an unusual event, even in this part of Louisiana where old-time weddings were large gatherings.

Mr. Dix, my father, was well known in the community and had many friends on plantations and in Natchez. My mother's family, the Watsons, were similarly situated. My grandfather Watson was a plantation-owner and had many other interests; his family was large and he had many relatives and friends. Accordingly, invitations were sent out to the whole countryside.

In those days, transportation was so difficult—there were only horses and carriages and steamboats—that one took it for granted that not one third of the invited guests would be able to attend. Arrangements were made for a hundred and fifty guests, or thereabouts, and these arrangements were thought to be ample. All day long the guests were arriving, driving up from distant plantations. By twilight the house was filled, and the ladies had retired to make their toilettes.

But friends of the two families had planned a surprise. A steamboat was chartered in Natchez, and more than a hundred guests arrived aboard the boat shortly after sunset. The boat deposited them at the plantation landing and departed with the promise of taking them back to Natchez in the morning. One can imagine the consternation that more than a hundred extra guests caused by their unexpected arrival. There was food and drink enough for all, but in a remote country house there was no way of providing room for them. Not even dressing rooms were available, and to make matters worse, the ladies had brought their carpet bags and band-boxes and their negro maids; and the gentlemen had brought their bags and their valets.

The old planter did the best that he could. The ladies were assigned to the dining room, the library and the bedrooms, and the gentlemen were left outside.

This part of the story has been told to me, over and over, by my father, who was forced to give up his quarters before the onslaught of young ladies. He retired with the young men to a grove of trees beyond the flower garden, and here the men dressed by flickering candlelight, and by the light of the moon. It must have been a strange sight to see! For here were fifty or more of the young men of Natchez, bathing from buckets, and dressing in the open, assisted by the negro men, who held the candles and did what they could to help. Suffice to say that at the hour appointed for the wedding, a group of spick and span young men emerged from the magnolia grove, and crowded into the house to meet the ladies, and to witness the wedding ceremony.

A band of musicians from New Orleans played for the dancing —the waltz, the polka, the minuet and mazourka. When the orchestra was exhausted the plantation band took up the strain where the city musicians left off, and to the music of guitars and fiddles, the dancing continued.

My grandfather threw open his wine-cellar, and the gentlemen imbibed freely. I remember that my mother told me that the first intoxicated gentleman she had ever seen was at her own wedding. I am afraid that a good many of the gentlemen fell asleep in the garden among the roses!

Supper was served on long tables on the back gallery. A caterer from New Orleans was in charge, and even the additional guests did not put him out of countenance, although the serving continued the whole night long.

The ladies and gentlemen kept at their dancing until sunrise, when the sound of the steamboat's whistle recalled them to the plantation landing. The crowd from Natchez got aboard again and went back home, and the others crowded into their carriages and began the long drive back to their plantations.

My own childhood was spent at Bralston Plantation, where my father was born. The first thing that I remember is a crevasse. One night there was a storm, and the levee broke. The evening before the children had played in the garden; the lawn was smooth and green and the flowers were all in bloom—the rose garden was magnificent, I remember—but the next morning, three feet of water covered the whole plantation. The servants rowed about in skiffs, carrying breakfast and dinner from the kitchen to the big house where we lived. The day following, scaffolds were built to make paths to various parts of the plantation. How well I remember one of our nurses paddling me around in a *piroque*. She was part Indian and an expert rower, but her skill did not serve her very well this time; unfortunately she did not look around in time to prevent our dashing against the trunk of a tree. We were thrown out, and were rescued from drowning by our old English gardener.

Every day my brothers made it a point to fall in the water, getting wet from head to foot. Finally my good mother, finding it such a difficulty to keep them in dry clothes, adopted a scheme to make them more careful. When one fell into the water, he was put to bed until his clothes were perfectly dry.

One morning my eldest brother decided to put out a hook and line and catch fish from an upstairs window. He tied his line to the handle of a handsome majolica pitcher on the washstand. An hour afterwards he heard a great commotion, as the pitcher began dancing around in the bowl. There was a terrible squawking outside. The pitcher flew up in the air and out of the window. We looked out to see an old grey gander swimming with the hook in his bill and uttering distressful cries. Finally one of the negro man-servants caught him and released the poor old fellow from his suffering. But alas for the beautiful pitcher, it was broken into a hundred pieces.

My mother told my father that we must leave Bralston as she could not have the lives of the children imperiled constantly. There were no steamboats available at that time, so three big flat-boats were brought. On one they bestowed the household effects, my mother, father, children and house servants. On the next boat were the slaves, their wives and children and cabin furniture. The third flat-boat contained the mules, horses, cows and calves and chickens. We removed to high ground until the water receded and return was possible. The stock was taken to another plantation, and the slaves went along to take care of it; but the family and house servants removed to our house in the town of Natchez.

I was a very small girl when I paid my first visit to New Orleans. I was dressed in my best bib and tucker and was ready and waiting long before the steamboat stopped at our landing to take aboard the bales of cotton which had been grown and ginned on the plantation. We went along with the cotton to New Orleans, for my father was taking each and every member of the family to the city with him. We went like a royal retinue, or at least I suppose we did. Certainly we were treated with every courtesy, and certainly there were enough of us; for we brought the house servants, too. I remember the steamboat perfectly, but I remember next to nothing about New Orleans. Our return was even more enjoyable to me, for we brought many things with us.

Many boxes of drygoods were opened and the materials assorted.

A dressmaker—an Englishwoman who lived with us on the plantation—was given the task of making dresses for my mother and for all of the children. In the other boxes were materials for clothes for the slaves. My mother sorted it all out in one of the upper rooms of the plantation-house; then she sent for the best sewing-women on the place. My mother supervised all of the cutting, fitting and sewing of the clothes for the negroes; she examined every garment to see that it was adequate and well made.

It always amuses me when I hear people say that the mistress of a plantation did nothing in those days before the Civil War. As a matter of fact, the ladies worked from dawn until dark. They supervised everything pertaining to house management. They trained women to sew and cook, they trained women as nurses for the sick. A knowledge of medicine was essential. My mother studied old medical books far into the night sometimes, for there were times when she must know what to do until the doctor could be summoned. There were numerous servants, but they had to be watched, even the best of them, or things went wrong; some of them would shirk and throw the bulk of the work on others. It was very necessary that the plantation mistress keep a firm hand on the household management.

It was to the planter's advantage to see that each negro had assigned to him the task that he was best fitted to do. Some of the men were trained as carpenters, some as gardeners; most of them, of course, tilled the fields. There was always a plantation band at Bralston, and there had been one there for many years. My father furnished the guitars and fiddles, and those negroes with any talent for music were given the opportunity to learn from a white musician who sometimes visited us. The band played for all of our parties and dances, and their music was much better than some of the orchestras that I hear nowadays.

Our one diversion was entertaining guests. That is, we either visited or had visitors nearly all of the time; and a visit in those days was an event. The plantations were so far apart that when one came to visit, one remained for a week or more. I well remember the arrival of visitors, a neighbor and his family. They arrived in carriages,

master and mistress in one, children and nurses in another, and a
wagon trailing after piled high with trunks and bags.

We never sat down to a meal without ten or twelve people at the
table, for there were always friends or relatives visiting us. For breakfast we had: hot waffles, buttermilk biscuit, broiled chicken, cane
syrup, scrambled eggs and hominy. For supper the same menu was
served, with the possible addition of preserved or ripe fruits. Sometimes there was venison instead of broiled chicken, and sometimes
mutton. Dinner was served in the middle of the day and was our
most elaborate meal; for dinner we had gumbo or soup, baked chicken
or turkey, vegetables from the garden, jellies, fish or shrimp from the
river. There was some such menu every day, with as many variations
as possible. Our cook did nothing but cook, and she had two assistants,
half-grown girls, who helped her.

It seemed a gay life as it was filled with social activities, but it
was not idle. I remember hearing my mother say that for twenty years
she went only twice to Natchez and New Orleans. Her babies came
so frequently, and she was always busy with them, and with
entertaining company.

As I write, many unrelated episodes come to my mind. I shall
relate one, which, for some reason, remains vividly remembered.

It was Hallowe'en. The black cook was taking a supply of food
down to the negro quarters for a special feast; there had been company at the big house and my mother had ordered the cook to prepare
enough so that the negroes could have part of it. The cook, a fat old
woman, went first bearing a dishpan piled high with good things;
she was followed by some eight or ten little negroes who had been
summoned to help. Each little boy or girl was armed with a smaller
pan. I went along with the cook as I wished to see the negroes have
their surprise. It was a chilly night and the stars were very bright.
Suddenly, from behind a clump of bushes, a terrible burning face
appeared. It was a pumpkin, of course, with a candle inside, but it
appeared dreadful to us. With one loud yell, the cook threw the
dishpan into the air, and ran with all her might back to the house;
the little boys and girls shrieked in chorus and threw away their pans
and ran too. I ran with the rest, frightened half out of my wits. The

dinner for the negroes was scattered in the road. My brothers were well punished for their part in the affair, but the little negroes from the quarters were not punished; the loss of their surprise dinner was considered punishment enough.

My dear old aunts lived in exquisite comfort just outside of Natchez; both had little maids who sat on the front seat of the landau and took care of their large silken bags which contained handkerchief, knitting and purses for small purchases. . . . They were charming old ladies, but I hated to go visiting there. The formality was too much, after our freedom on the plantation.

I hated to roll up the long graveled drive leading to "Itania," as their house was called. The house was built more for comfort than beauty; a long gallery ran the whole length of the house in front. A hall led back between rooms to the dining room. In this hall was a beautiful old pier table; above it hung a portrait of a boy and his dog; beneath the pier table a mirror was inserted, and oh, how many times I knelt beneath the table to watch myself in the glass! A tall "Bishop's chair" stood on either side of this table, to give dignity and distinction. Smaller chairs were placed around to accommodate those callers who came to see my aunts on business. The door at the left of the hall as one entered, gave into a parlor, with a velvet carpet and a mirror with carved gilt frame which reached from the mantel to the ceiling. There were carved rosewood chairs—made by Belter. A little table was so lovely that it stood all by itself in a corner. On either end of the white marble mantel stood tall vases of carved alabaster, and between them were bronze lamps with rows of prisms and with crystal globes. There were always vases of fresh flowers in the parlor. Sliding doors opened into a similar room—another parlor furnished in the same rosewood furniture. On the other side of the hall was an enormous room, the library. Carved bookshelves reached from floor to ceiling, covering the walls, except the openings of doors and windows. From this room, a door opened into a wing— where my aunts' bedrooms were situated.

At the end of the hall was the large dining room. Children in those days were served first—a "first table." When my aunt entertained at dinner, we were fed at the same time, but our table was set on the back gallery, outside the dining room windows. Two footmen and a butler, all negroes of course, served. They were excellent servants. First dishes were served to the grownups, then the footmen passed to our table and served us. From our table we could look in and see what the guests were doing at table. I shall never forget the butler. His name was Marshall, and he was a mulatto—a distinguished looking yellow man with a long black beard. I thought at first that he was a Spaniard or Mexican. He always wore evening clothes, had tremendous dignity, and woe betide the child who dared enter his pantry. The apartments of the sons of the house opened from the dining room, and were situated in another wing of the house. There was a bedroom for every member of the family, and the long wing stretched out to a nursery and other rooms. At the very end was a billiard room.

Sallie was a ward of my father's, and everyone called her a beautiful girl. Her father and mother were dead and she lived with us after she left school. In those days, young girls did literally nothing. She sat in the sun and entertained her many beaux, and finally selected the handsomest, or the richest among the crowd that came a-courting. It was necessary—or so they thought—that she must attend all the balls and parties, and must spend part of the season at least in New Orleans, at Mardi Gras balls and at the French Opera. She gave house parties on the plantation and entertained her friends from New Orleans in return.

Cousin Sallie had, among her suitors, a young man that she had met at Green Brier, White Sulphur Springs. He was a rich man's son from the upper part of Mississippi and did very little but enjoy himself. Both my cousin Sallie and he were well mated in this respect. He came down to visit her at Bralston; and as the time approached for the wedding, every steamboat that stopped at Fairview Landing brought boxes of drygoods and beautiful costumes for her trousseau. The wedding dress was of brocaded white satin, with a veil of fine white lace, and the contrast to her brunette type was calculated to produce a beautiful effect. The old Bralston home was a long rambling house, one story high. The front door opened directly into the double parlors. The parlors, on her wedding day, had been made into a bower of roses and formed a lovely setting for the bridal party. The back gallery was laid with the wedding supper. A caterer came up from New Orleans to supervise everything. All was in readiness for the wedding; the guests had arrived and bridegroom, with the minister and best man. They stood in their appointed places, and the bride entered from the library on my father's arm. Truly she appeared a dream of beauty. The bridegroom handed his license to the old minister to glance over before beginning the ceremony and a look of amazement came over the old gentleman's face. He spoke out so everyone in the room could hear:

"Well, Mr. Owen, the license is made out for the wedding to take place in Mississippi, and here we are in Louisiana!"

"Consternation!"

"Of course the wedding will have to be postponed until the mistake is rectified," the minister said.

"But," said the young man, "cannot some way be found out of the difficulty? The wedding must take place this evening. All of our plans will be upset."

The old minister said that he could see no way out of the difficulty. Then my father said something to the bride, who smiled and nodded her head. Then my father spoke up and said: "What is to prevent my calling up several of my men and letting them bring the required number of skiffs to the landing; then let the bridal party with the minister and guests get in the boats, row across the river to the Mississippi side. The young people can be married on the sandbar, then return home for the supper and dancing."

All acceded to this proposal, and the skiffs were brought. The negroes came trouping from the quarters. Dozens of skiffs appeared. The bride and bridegroom and the guests—about twenty-five young girls and forty young men, not to mention the older people, the minister and the children, rowed across the river, and standing on the sandbar beside the Mississippi the ceremony was completed. "How romantic! How beautiful!" everyone said.

When the minister held up his hand in blessing, the plantation bell rang out from across the water, and we could hear the negroes cheering on the opposite bank of the stream.

Our summer home in Natchez was built on top of the highest point on the River road. The whole town lay like a flower garden beneath us. We could stand on our front steps and see the immense river curving in a big bend above. Our house was called "Kenilworth" from the name of the man who built it—not for Sir Walter Scott's novel, as everyone supposed. The house was at the top of four broad green terraces. Tall cedar trees stood at each corner of the building. Oak trees were between them. There was always delightful shade on the topmost terrace. The second terrace was filled also with oak and arbor-vitæ. The third terrace was broadest and a green lawn curved into a crescent, with pear trees at either end. There was a last terrace which went down to the river's edge. The road passed at the extremity of the lowest terrace and there was a summer house with a brick platform where carriages stopped to allow ladies and gentlemen to enter the gate. The carriage then passed on, around the foot of the terraces to the stable, and remained there until called for.

We had at that time an old slave woman named Fanny. Her mind was not exactly right. She would leave her comfortable cabin, go under the bluff on the river bank, build a fire and cook, whenever she felt like it. Father would always know of her whereabouts by the plume of smoke which rose from under the bluff. So he would go out on the river bank and say: "Poor Fanny. I am afraid she has drowned herself! Poor old Fanny!" This always made Fanny furious. She would call back: "No, I ain't drowned myself. Here I is! You just go on back inside de big house and lemme alone!" So away my father would go, with Fanny quarreling at his heels.

It was a time of practical jokes. My father had an old slave named Ike who was watchman over the cotton bales in the gin. Unfortunately the old man would fall asleep and snore so loudly he could be heard—roaring—from far off. My father determined to break the old man of this habit. One beautiful moonlight night as Ike began his usual loud snoring for the benefit of the surrounding countryside, my father took his violin and stole softly down to where the old man lay asleep. He drew his bow across the violin strings with a resonance calculated to arouse the soundest sleeper. The old man snorted like

"MONMOUTH" AT NATCHEZ IS STURDY
AND HONEST — 1846

a bull and stopped snoring. My father waited quietly until the old man started snoring again, then again he drew his bow across the strings and began to play "Turkey in the Straw." The old man sprung up from the gunny-sacks on which he was sleeping and cried out: "Gawd! De devil is after me sho!" With this he leaped up and began racing down the big road like a marathon runner. My father slipped quietly back to the house. No mention was ever made of the episode. But old Ike slept no more—or if he did, he did not snore.

I was a very young girl when the South seceded from the Union. My father was then Mayor of Natchez, and the troops were leaving from the City Hall. They had assembled there waiting for the steamboat which was to carry them away. Everyone was going to see the boys leave, for they were our brothers, our cousins and our friends.

I remember it as though it were yesterday, for I stood on the steps of our house weeping because I was left behind. My sister had gone off with some other young ladies, the others had gone, and now as I stood crying on the steps with my negro nurse, I saw my mother and a cousin driving off in the cousin's coupé. . . . I think that they had forgotten me, for when they saw me standing there in tears, my mother called to me to come quickly and jump into the carriage, just as I was. I scrambled down the terraces, one after another, and got into the coupé with them.

When my tears were under control, I was conscious of a vague picture, strange flags waving, men in uniform hurrying along, women with sunshades walking, women carrying flowers, negroes carrying flowers, old men and old women walking carrying red roses, and somewhere in the distance a band was playing. We drove first to the City Hall.

While the men were waiting there for the arrival of the steamboat, a crowd of little boys congregated to watch them. One young fellow hid behind the wide door, and being something of a ventriloquist, he made a loud noise which resembled the whistle of a steamboat far off. There were immediate cries: "Here comes the boat, boys!" and "Time to march to the river!" The soldiers formed into ranks under the commands of their officers. There were cries of "Attention! Squads right! March!" And off they started.

But a man, who was on the bluff waiting for the steamboat to round the bend, came out and asked where they were going.

"To the river," said the officer curtly. "Did you not hear the steamboat whistle?"

"Well, there's no boat in sight, sir!"

"That's odd. . . . Hey! Wait a minute! It must have been that little rascal that can imitate anything. Find him, men!"

The dignity of the troops was upset, but there was nothing to do but break ranks and go back and wait. An immediate search was made for the bad little boy, but all of the boys had disappeared.

Finally the boat did come. All the roads leading down the bluff were filled with ladies in their elegant carriages. Many slaves were allowed to come along to see their masters go off to war. Many of the negroes carried flowers. There were old men walking, old ladies walking, boys and girls carrying flowers. I can never forget an exquisite pyramid of red roses that Mrs. Minor sent down to the steamboat landing for the soldier boys.

When the steamboat tied up at the wharf, the people crowded aboard and nearly turned it over. Wild shrieks went up from the ladies as the boat listed. The police arrived, shouting out orders. Women clung to men's necks, crying. But many were brave and smiled. Everyone said that the parting was for only a short time. The bell rang for the boat to leave. The whistle blew, and the town people made a dash for the shore. Amid the tears of relatives, amid the waving of handkerchiefs and sunshades, the boat steamed away with the "bonnie blue flag" flying bravely. I could see men crowded on the upper deck of the steamboat; I could see flags and flowers, and the gleam of the sun on the brass musical instruments. As the boat rounded the bend above, I could hear the music faintly, and could even recognize the tune. It was "The Girl I Left Behind Me."

Few of them ever came home again.

On the way home an incident occurred—one of those ridiculous unrelated incidents which remains in the mind when important things are forgotten. I had a beautiful sister who had gone down to the river-landing ahead of us, and as we began our slow ascent of the long drive to the top of the bluff, I saw her again, riding with another young lady in an open carriage just ahead of us. The friend was wearing a new bonnet which was the pride of her life. It had been pointed out to me, earlier in the day. It was said to have cost a hundred dollars, and it had been the talk of Natchez for a few days before. But the grand bonnet was doomed that day. The excitement had frightened the dogs and chickens out of their wits; dogs were barking in the road and behind fences, and chickens were squawking in the road as the crowd passed by. As I sat watching the magnificent bonnet in the carriage ahead of us, an old white rooster spread his wings and flew down from the ridgepole of a house. He landed in the open carriage ahead, and hung upon the new hat. His wings were flapping and he was squawking so that the disconcerted young ladies began to shriek with emotion. Then rooster and hat fell together under the carriage, and as I watched, the wheel passed over the bonnet, ruining it for good and all. Oh how I laughed! And I received a severe reprimand from my dear mother, too. . . .

The day the Yankees took possession of Natchez, we were driving quietly down Main Street to look at the river, never dreaming of what was before us. Just as we came about half-way down toward the bluff, we were met by our friend, Mrs. Wilson, an old, old lady. She was running along the middle of the road, her bonnet strings standing straight out behind her. When she saw us, she screamed:

"Go back, my dears, go back!"

"Why, my dear old friend?" cried my mother.

"The devils have come to town!" she shouted, and on she ran, like the wind.

My mother was puzzled and ordered the coachman to drive down the road to the bluff, so that we could see what was so disturbing to our old friend. A minute later we were staring down at the broad river and at a black plume of smoke arising from a gunboat. From the sides of the vessel, blue-coated men were descending on tarred ladders to the waiting yawls. Now my mother understood that the Federals had come to take possession. She ordered the coachman to turn the carriage about, but he sat there sullenly, as though he did not hear her. Up the hill came the marching men, their guns on their shoulders.

It was then that the foolish Silver Greys—a body of men stationed there to protect Natchez—fired a volley at the gunboat . . . and in return, the town was shelled. My father was a Silver Grey but not an officer. He begged the handful of men not to shoot down on the Yankees coming to the landing for fresh water, but they paid no attention and fired a volley. . . . The rest you know; Natchez was bombarded.

A little girl, my classmate and dearest friend, was killed in the shelling. . . . I do not like to think about it, even now.

The war dragged on; time passed and we saw our doom before us. At last the day came when Grant's army crossed the Mississippi and took possession of Vicksburg. My father, in his position as Mayor of Natchez, found it necessary to confer with General Grant on business, and so he rode away on his chestnut horse. The general received my father with every courtesy, listened to his request and granted it, and then continued to talk on other matters. At last he went outside with my father, and held his stirrup until he had mounted his horse. Then stepping back, he gave the military salute. My father raised his hat, put spur to his horse and rode home again.

That night he told me about it. He held one of my curls, I remember, and said: "You are perhaps the only little Southern girl who can say that General Grant held her father's stirrup." Perhaps it was because of this that I have always thought of General Grant as a very fine gentleman, even if he was our enemy.

The last visit I paid to our plantation, I shall never forget. It was just at the close of the war. "Mammy" dressed me in a gay silk dress and told me to walk down the middle of the wide road leading from the house, through the negro quarters, to the gate which opened into the cotton field. She told me to count the negroes who would come out of their houses to welcome me, as they had done before the war. Why she did this, I do not know, for surely she must have known that the negroes were all gone.

I went down the road, singing gaily to attract the negroes' attention, but only one cabin door opened and the old house-keeper came out to see me. She was the only negro left in the quarters; all the other cabins were empty. When I got to the big gate which led to the fields, I looked through, expecting to see the fields white with cotton, and the cotton pickers with their baskets. But there were no negroes, and there were no cotton fields lying snowy in the sunshine. Not a soul was in sight, and the fields were bare and brown. I turned and walked back to the house, blinded by tears of disappointment and sorrow. At the gate of the flower garden I met "Mammy." Her head was bent down and she was crying.

Part IV

SPLENDOR AND RUST

Chapter Twenty-two

A PLANTATION TOUR

WELL then, let us start on our tour of Louisiana. It is a long trip. We shall have to travel more than a thousand miles together. Here is the battered automobile. Get your bags together and let us go. I want you to see all that remains of Louisiana plantation life to-day.

We leave New Orleans when the sun is not yet high, and perhaps we can spend the night in Baton Rouge, more than a hundred miles away. Our speed depends upon you. For there are many plantations along the Mississippi between here and our destination, and I want you to have a glimpse, at least, of all of them.

The city lies behind us now and we have reached the fields of cotton and sugar-cane. One can breathe out here. There, standing against the sky, is a sugar-house, towering above the fields. It appears flat, as though cut from

cardboard. Six tall smoke-stacks tower higher still. In
winter, at grinding time, smoke will rise from those chimneys; but now the mill is deserted and empty. Grinding lasts
scarcely longer than six weeks, and for the rest of the year
the machinery stands idle.

We are driving near the Mississippi, beside the levee.
We shall follow the river all day.

D'ESTREHAN

One of the first houses of importance on the highway,
after we leave New Orleans, is the D'Estrehan plantation-
house. It lies just there, ahead of us, in that grove of trees.
I shall stop the car before the gate and you can look your
fill.

The name D'Estrehan is famous in Louisiana, for the
family came with Bienville. The house is now the property
of an oil company and one of the officials lives in it. It has
been restored almost beyond recognition. It appears to
be almost new. The house dates from the beginning of the
nineteenth century and is a development of the simpler
plantation-house. The dwelling is flush with the ground,
and the arrangement is like the earlier type, rather than
like those houses built twenty years later. The columns are
imposing and the high pitched roof is amusingly cut with
small dormer windows. On a house as large as this one they
appear diminutive. The two-storied wings add dignity and
grace. It is said that the wings were added twenty years
after the house was built, but if so, the architect knew what
he was about. I wish I could tell you the architect's name,
but no one remembers. Odd, isn't it, that those bygone
builders have vanished so completely? No one knows any-

thing about them. Yet see what monuments they have left behind. . . . You have seen enough? Let us drive on.

The road is growing more interesting now, and the oil tanks are left behind. Just ahead of us—perhaps twelve miles from New Orleans and two miles beyond D'Estrehan —we come to:

ORMOND

Do not ask me who built this old house, for I have never been able to find out. Look at it instead. How solidly it stands there, all warm reds and yellows and framed in gnarled oak trees. The colors must have been gay once, but now they are subtle in their fading glory. It seems luminous, don't you think, as you look upon it from the road? And how deceptively simple it is. Many tourists pass by with hardly a glance, but "Ormond" is worth visiting. We may go inside, if you like. . . .

See, as we approach it, how it towers above us. It is so broad that it does not seem high when one looks at it from the road. I want you to look carefully at this house, for it is characteristic of the late eighteenth-century dwellings in Louisiana. Note how pleasingly irregular it is. The central portion is of the usual type—a wide house of two stories, set flush with the ground, and with galleries encircling it. The piers which support the second floor are square and are made of brick; the tapering colonnettes which rise above them to the roof are of hand-hewn cypress. There is a simple wooden railing on the upper porch, but the lower porch has no railing. The openings are wide and the house can be thrown open almost like a pavilion, or it can be closed as tightly as a fort.

Look particularly at the wings which rise at either end of the house. Do you see that they are really separate buildings? They stand fifteen feet away from the house proper, but they are connected with open galleries. Both wings are higher than the house, and the left wing is higher than the right one. And yet how happy the combination is. The lower floors of the wings are of brick, the upper floors are of wood. Mr. Suydam, who illustrated this book, has made an excellent sketch of it. I suggest that you look at it now, for his drawing can tell you more in a moment than I can with a whole book of words. But a black-and-white drawing can give no idea of the color of the house. And in its color lies one of its greatest charms. . . . You'll have to take my word for it.

I have never been able to find out why the house was called "Ormond" nor have I been able to learn the date of the building, but from the interior woodwork it is safe to say that it dates well back in the eighteenth century. The mantels in the upper rooms of the wings are identical with eighteenth-century houses in the Vieux Carré of New Orleans.

The history of the house? This is all that I know: At the beginning of the Civil War it passed into the hands of the Citizens Bank of New Orleans. It was occupied for many years by the McCutcheon family, who were related in some way to the D'Estrehans. It is said that a murder took place on the levee, just in front of the house. A man called Bazile La Place—La Place is a good old Louisiana name, too—was murdered by the Ku Klux. But that was a long time ago.

When you pass "Ormond," you should go in, for the

house is as interesting within as it is outside. It is occupied now by the overseer of the plantation which surrounds it, and visitors are permitted to go through the building, only a small part of which is occupied. From the upper gallery one can see the old red-brick cabins of the negro quarters stretching away through fields of sugar-cane. . . .

TREPAGNIER

A mile or more beyond "Ormond," we come upon the old Trepagnier house, which is abandoned now, and which stands, ready to fall to pieces, quite near the road. Not even a fence separates it from the highway, and the building is so dilapidated that one would pass by with no more than a glance, were it not for the excellent proportion of the house. It is quite small, but beautiful in line. Brick below and wood above. Its construction is primitive; it is put together without nails, wooden pegs being used throughout. The walls are thick and the chimneys wide. The house has been abandoned for a long time. Negroes are living there, and doors hang crazily from their hinges and a multicolored group of drying clothes dangles from clothes-lines stretched from pillar to pillar. Let us be driving on. There is little left to admire here.

WELHAM

The houses that we have passed are all near the highway and are easily pointed out, but you must look closely, or you will pass "Welham" by. And that would be a pity, for it is a fine house and has many unusual features. It can be seen, far back from the road, near the town of La Place.

It appears to be a large house of red brick. Beyond it many white-washed outbuildings can be seen. It is surrounded by a grove of fine oak trees.

As one approaches "Welham" from the roadway, it changes color in a most surprising way. The house, which was red only a moment ago, is now white. On closer inspection the mystery is explained. The house is of brick, but the front has been covered with plain white plaster. Six large columns support the roof, rising two full stories; there is a fan-light transom above the wide front door. The roof is surmounted by a square cupola with a white balustrade. The batten shutters are of faded green. The place is dignified, yet somehow gay. A place of definite personality. Unfortunately, we have no picture of it. It dates from 1835.

ANGELINA

We are driving now along "the German Coast"—called so, because German pioneers settled here, shortly after New Orleans was founded in 1718. They were a thrifty lot, those Germans, and they prospered. They intermarried with the French-speaking people around them, and many of the German names have been lost, or changed beyond recognition. For example there is the name "Troxler," a good German name, you will admit, but it is now "Trosclair." The old Trosclair house "Angelina" is just ahead of us.

The whole place has an air of desolation and decay. It might well be a haunted house. It stands full two stories high, and the building is of brick, plastered over outside. There is a wide veranda upstairs and down, with Ionic columns on the lower floor, and fluted Corinthian columns above. Every column is askew. The roof sags crazily down. Window blinds hang from broken hinges. The house might serve as a symbol of the plantation system.

Beyond the main dwelling are several smaller outhouses, all in a sad state of decay, and rising above a mass of shrubbery two hexagonal dove-cotes may be seen. They are of warm red-brick and are surmounted by high hexagonal roofs. Each roof is topped by a fine wrought-iron weather vane; one vane shows the conventional crowing cock, and the other a trotting horse. The horse leans forward at a dizzy angle.

Descendants of the original owners are living at Angelina. Oddly enough, none of the Trosclairs speaks English, and the old gentleman shrugged his shoulders when I spoke of the house: "Why should I repair it?" he said in French. "Soon the river will take it." He pointed to two stakes driven into the ground at each end of the porch, and I understood what he meant. The Mississippi is eating into the land, and the levee must be moved further back from the river's edge. In another year "Angelina" will be gone, as so many fine houses have gone before. Despite its decay, the house is not extremely old. It dates from 1852.

JEFFERSON COLLEGE

Some seven miles beyond the town of Lutcher we find Jefferson College, a fine group of buildings which were constructed in 1830. This college for the young men of Louisiana was given by Valcour Aimé, a rich planter, to the Marist Fathers in that year, and from 1830 until 1928 it was used as a boys' school. But now the buildings are for sale, and their ultimate fate is uncertain. The main building is a

square structure with white columns on all four sides. Wide
verandas encircle the house. It is enormous. It is balanced
by two formal buildings also with white columns and set
slightly behind it—one on each side. Each of these buildings
is as large as the usual plantation-house. A small white
chapel stands under the oak trees on the south side of the
group of buildings, and two long barracks-like structures
of whitewashed brick form the sides of the quadrangle. A
high brick wall separates the college grounds from the public road, and the buildings appear suddenly, seen through a
gate of wrought-iron. Just inside the gate are two well proportioned lodges. These have verandas with small fluted
columns. There are many fine oak trees within the quadrangle, and the play of light and shadow on the forest of
columns is pleasant indeed.

Just beyond the college and outside the brick wall, one
finds the priest's house, a two-storied red-brick building with
fluted columns and green batten window blinds. It is the
usual type of Louisiana country-house, standing in a grove
of oak trees.

CONVENT OF THE SACRED HEART

A few miles beyond Jefferson College one finds the old
Convent. Its gray façade faces the river. The front of the
building is broken by many windows with closed green shutters. The central part of the structure rises higher than the
ends. There is a high battlemented roof. A large flower garden surrounds it. Religious statues are set in groves of trees.
The Mississippi will soon take the Convent garden. The
building will be spared, but the levee will pass before its
door. This is a famous school, for here the daughters of

planters were educated. The town of Convent takes its name from the Academy of the Sacred Heart.

UNCLE SAM

Seven miles or more beyond Lutcher, we find the "Uncle Sam" plantation. Once it was as fine a group of buildings as could be found in the State. Six outbuildings constitute a pleasing architectural group about a central house. The house is square and its apparent size is increased by a wide gallery which surrounds it. The roof is supported by twenty-eight Doric columns with large plain capitals. The entablature is plain and very wide. The roof is broken by dormer windows. There is a gallery upstairs and down. The house has window blinds of faded green. It was once yellow, but now the color has faded to a rich cream. The outbuildings are diminutive copies of the central structure. They are also yellow, but are only one story high. They, too, have columns which are of the plain Doric type. The two largest ones are the *garçonnières*, or boys' houses, designed to accommodate the sons of the old planter. Between the *garçonnières* and the main building, but set far back, are two smaller houses. These are like the large house and the *garçonnières*, but they are no more than cottages. They, too, have columns and a veranda. At either end of the group of buildings are the *pigeonnieres*, octagonal towers of brick painted yellow, each surmounted by a high octagonal roof. On the south side, an avenue stretches away to the negro quarters. There are perhaps forty cabins set in two long lines, and at the end of the "street" is the sugar-house towering against the sky. Behind the house, and beyond the quarters, the sugar-cane fields stretch out green in the sun. This was once the home of one

of the richest planters in the State. It dates from 1836. The
river bank is caving here and it is likely that the group of
buildings will go into the river in a year or two. The grove
of oak trees has gone that way already. The levee passes
quite near the house.

COLOMB

Half-way between Convent and Burnside one finds the
old Colomb house, built by that eccentric gentleman, Chris-
tophe Colomb, who claimed Christopher Columbus as an
ancestor. It is still occupied by the Colomb family. Once it
was set in a grove of oak trees, but now the levee passes
before the door, and the highway grazes the columns which
support the roof. The house is unusual in construction.
There are eight white columns across the front, set in twos.
There are three front doors, all exactly alike, each with an
ornate transom above. The roof is surmounted by a square
belvedere. From the roadway, this belvedere appears small,
but it is in reality a large bedroom reached by a narrow,
steep stairway. Within the house one finds surprising spaciousness. There is a wide central hallway with two large
rooms on each side. At the rear of the house one descends
four steps into a long sitting-room which is the entire width
of the house. Beyond this sitting-room is a wing. This wing
was the original house, built in the latter part of the
eighteenth century. The house that one sees nowadays was
built between 1835 and 1840.

VILLAGE OF UNION

Tourists whizzing along the highway frequently pass
through the village of Union with hardly a glance. It is a

small town straggling along the road beside the levee. Here one finds French spoken almost exclusively. There are quaint shops where sunbonnets are for sale, and where the old Frenchwoman behind the counter will give you a cake for *lagniappe,* a custom which has almost entirely disappeared in Louisiana. There is an interesting plantation-house here, but it stands surrounded by a mass of cabins and cottages. The river has eaten away the land and the village has been cut in two, but the part which remains is well worth stopping for.

BURNSIDE

Built in 1840 by Colonel Preston of Charleston, South Carolina, Burnside Plantation is reminiscent of some of the fine old Carolina or Virginia houses. But it has the Louisiana quality of spaciousness, and it is amply proportioned. It is now owned by Dr. and Mrs. Miles of New Orleans, who come only occasionally to stay here. It is a house of two stories with columns on three sides. It is surmounted by a square cupola. Behind the house is a second structure, connected at the second floor with the main house, but on the ground floor a driveway passes between the buildings. The house is gleaming white and is set in a fine grove of live-oak trees. A few years ago one could see only two columns of the house at the end of a long avenue. But now the river has cut through the grove, taking more than half, and the house may be plainly seen from the road. It is, however, not on the main highway. At the town of Burnside the highway turns and goes direct to Baton Rouge, eliminating perhaps fifteen miles, but if one wishes to see the old houses he must proceed beside the river. Burnside Plantation is the first house you will see after leaving the highway. Look at the octagonal *garçonnières*, they are unusually fine.

BELLE HELENE

A few miles nearer Baton Rouge is Belle Helene, an imposing plantation-house built in the grand manner. It has the usual white columns across the façade. It is now in a sad state of dilapidation. This was originally Ashland plantation, and the house was built by Duncan Kenner in 1841.

CHATSWORTH

Chatsworth plantation is perhaps fifteen miles from Baton Rouge on the river road. It is an enormous house which was never completed. In 1859, when Louisiana prosperity was at its height, construction was begun, but the advent of the Civil War freed the slaves and left this mansion incomplete. There are large Corinthian columns across the central portion, and the two wings are ornamented with fluted pilasters. Wide steps lead up to the veranda. Inside, the house is ornate. The woodwork is very fine, and typical of the Greek revival. There are silver knobs and locks on the doors. The house contains fifty rooms, some forty feet square. But for all its grandeur, it is uninteresting. This is due partly to the fact that it was never completed, and partly because it was built as a show place, rather than as a dwelling. There is a feeling of artificiality about it, as though it were a stage-set which had been left out in the rain. I do not know the name of the original owner.

"THE COTTAGE"

We are now within ten miles of the town of Baton

THE PAYNE HOUSE NEAR WASHINGTON,
BUILT PRIOR TO 1849

L'EXQUISE — CHASE HOUSE, CLINTON

Rouge. This is my own country, familiar since childhood, when I used to ride about from one plantation-house to another on a one-eyed white pony. Frequently I rode these ten long miles in the summer sun; it seemed nearer a hundred miles to me then, but now one can drive out from town in half an hour. This old house, half hidden behind the live-oak trees, is "The Cottage," the home of the Conrad family. It is unpretentious and charming—a two-storied structure, square, with a veranda on three sides, and with large Doric columns reaching from the ground to the roof. The columns have plain, square bases, and plain capitals. The entablature is unornamented. There are tall narrow wings on each side, at the back of the house; they are ornamented with square pilasters. The blue slate roof is broken by dormer windows. The wide doorway is well proportioned, with a fanlight above and small fluted pillars on each side. Inside there is a central hall and four large rooms upstairs and down. The house still belongs to the descendants of the family which built it in 1830. It is now the property of Mrs. Fanny Conrad Buffington-Bailey.

An old gentleman whom I knew was fond of telling a story of his childhood which centered about "The Cottage." As a small boy, in the year 1850 or thereabouts, he had stood on the levee waiting for the arrival of *The Princess,* one of the finest steamboats afloat on the Mississippi at that time. He was expecting his mother and father to return from New Orleans. He saw the boat pass in midstream and turn toward the bank, but as he watched he heard a dull explosion and saw the cotton-laden boat burst into flames. Mr. Conrad sent all his slaves out in skiffs to rescue the men and women who were struggling in the water. Many of them were frightfully scalded by steam from the broken boilers. Sheets were spread on the ground under the oak trees on the lawn, and barrels of flour were broken open and the contents poured on the sheets. As the scalded people were pulled from the river, they were stripped and rolled in the flour, where they writhed and shrieked in agony. The little boy went from one sufferer to another seeking his father and mother. They were not there. They returned from New Orleans on a later boat, but he never forgot the anguish of his search.

BATON ROUGE

Ten miles from the Conrad plantation, we find the city of Baton Rouge, where we may spend the night. Once there were many fine examples of Spanish and early American architecture here, but time and "progress" have done for nearly all of them. The old Laycock house remains. Once remote, it now stands in the suburbs of the city. It is the usual type of country-house, austere and imposing, with six Doric columns, and with wide verandas upstairs and down. The Daugherty-Prescott house on North Street was built in 1840 and is typical of the fine houses of its day; there are verandas on three sides and square brick pillars supporting the roof. The railings of iron work are very fine. It is still in possession of the original family, and is furnished throughout with antique furniture. Among the prized possessions is a dinner set painted by Audubon.

There is a group of interesting buildings at the old campus of the Louisiana State University. They are in the true Louisiana tradition—dignified and imposing, with wide verandas and enormous white columns. These were once barracks for soldiers. There were five buildings originally, arranged in a pentagon, but one slid down the hill into the Mississippi. The four which remain are well worth going to see. Sherman, of Civil War fame, was the president of this University in 1861, at the time of the secession of Louisiana. He left the college, joined the Union Army and led his march to the sea.

The State Capitol stands on the bluff above the Mississippi. It is a "castle" built in the style known as "Flamboyant Tudor." Mark Twain in his "Life on the Mississippi" remarks somewhat unkindly that he would like to add one thing to it—a charge of dynamite.

There are adequate hotels in Baton Rouge and we may rest here to-night. To-morrow I shall take you to the plantations in East and West Feliciana.

Some forty miles northeast from Baton Rouge, and accessible by highway, we find the town of Clinton. It remains unspoiled, old-fashioned, and sedate. There is an imposing courthouse, pillared on four sides, and one of the streets fronting the square has a row of lawyers' offices, built in the classic tradition. I shall say no more than this, for Mr. Suydam's drawing at the beginning of this chapter is enough with further word of mine.

In the town there are many beautiful houses, notable among them the Chase house, near the public square. A full page drawing of it will be found in this book.

Outside of town one finds the "Stone House"—not built of stone, but occupied by the well-known Louisiana family of that name. There is also the Bennett house and the group of fine buildings which constitute Silliman College. Clinton

was very prosperous in those thirty years just before the
Civil War; it was the center of a rich plantation country.
The classic tradition may be observed in a score of houses,
and—amusingly enough—a three-storied warehouse with
Doric columns is perhaps the largest building in town. All
in all, it is a pleasant place. Look at the illustrations and
you will see for yourself.

Seven or more miles west of Clinton, and connected with
a straight highway, is the town of Jackson. Here one finds
the old buildings of Centenary College, which, after standing abandoned for twenty years, are used now as a tuberculosis hospital. Centenary is typical of its time—1840. There
is a large, square central building, with a magnificent auditorium inside, an auditorium typical of the Greek revival—
all delicate white woodwork and a forest of fluted Corinthian columns. This building is in ruins, and cows wander in
and out. No glass is left in the windows, but the walls and
roof stand as sturdily as they did fifty years ago. A pair of
long, two-storied dormitories are used now for the hospital.
These are of warm red-brick, and each has a veranda with
many cream-colored columns across its façade. Jefferson
Davis, president of the Southern Confederacy, attended college here for a time. At the outbreak of the War between
the states, the entire graduating class enlisted, and every
man was killed before the war was over.

ASPHODEL

A mile from Jackson, and on a hill overlooking Carr's
Creek, is Asphodel Plantation. It stands hidden from the
road behind a dense growth of trees and vines, and one must
have explicit directions in order to find it. I believe it to be

one of the most beautifully proportioned houses in Louisiana. The illustration which you will find in this book will tell you more than any description of mine.

It was built in 1833 by Benjamin Kendrick, who died the year the house was completed, and the plantation passed into the hands of the Fluker family. It is still owned by the Fluker estate, and is occupied by relatives of the family, Miss Kate and Miss Sarah Smith. They are gentlewomen of the old school and seem so much a part of Asphodel that I cannot think of the house existing without them, or think of them existing without the house. Which, after all, is not an exaggerated statement when one learns that, in the last twenty-six years, Miss Kate has left the plantation once, and Miss Sarah has never left it. Neither has ever ridden in an automobile, nor do they intend to. Only once have they seen moving-pictures, and that was when a friend brought a motion-picture machine to the plantation, connected it with the batteries of an automobile and projected the picture on the white-plastered wall of the parlor: "And we enjoyed the novelty very much," says Miss Kate. "But I shouldn't care to repeat the experience," says Miss Sarah.

So here they remain. But they are not lonely. They look after the farm; they have a flower garden, and scarcely a day passes without a visitor. I had told Mr. Suydam about them before we went there, but he shrugged his shoulders and said flatly that he did not believe me. When we were leaving, his completed sketch in his portfolio, I said, "Well, did I, or did I not tell the truth about Asphodel?" He looked at me over the cigarette that he was lighting: "Yes, you told the truth," he said. "But I can't believe it, even though I have seen it myself. It's incredible."

This was early in our tour of the plantations. He found many incredible things before we had finished.

HICKORY HILL

"Hickory Hill," illustrated earlier in this volume, is two miles from the town of Wilson, and two miles off the highway. It was built in 1810 by Captain David McCants of Charleston, South Carolina. Mrs. Freeman, the elderly chatelaine, was, before her marriage, Miss Blanche McCants. She was born at "Hickory Hill." The dwelling is unusual among Louisiana houses in both proportion and construction. It is a house of two stories and an attic, and is raised high from the ground. Its apparent height is increased by its situation on a hilltop. In looking at the illustration, note that the pillars at the ends of the dwelling are square, and the two central pillars are cylindrical. The most unusual feature is the porch, which is open only on one side. The ends of the porch are bricked in. Each end of the porch has a window—complete with sashes and green slat-shutters. Approached from either side, the house appears to be without galleries and is as austere as a child's toy Noah's Ark. The red-brick walls are covered with ivy which has been growing there for a century. The Freemans and their cousins the Scotts, who live on the adjoining plantation, are the oldest families in the neighborhood.

THE SHADES

Seven miles from Jackson, and three miles from Wilson, is the 3500-acre Scott plantation, "The Shades." It is remote, three miles from a highway. No drawing in black-and-white can do justice to this ivy-covered house of red brick,

set on a hilltop in a grove of trees. It was built in 1808 and
has been occupied since that year by the Scott family. Miss
Kate and Miss Eva Scott are the last of the line. It is my
favorite of all plantations. Not that it is the finest house
that I know, nor is it the most beautiful. But it has a quality
which I can only suggest by telling you what it is like to
spend Christmas there.

Chapter Twenty-three

CHRISTMAS: THE MISTLETOE TRAIL

You arrive just at twilight on Christmas Eve—for you have come to spend the holidays with the folks on the plantation.

The little railway station is buzzing with activity; teams are tied to stakes driven in the ground; mules are standing with lowered heads, their warm breath visible in the frosty air, their rough coats caked with splashed mud. One or two motor-cars are beside the platform—not city automobiles with their shining paint and metal, but good old country cars, with muddy wheels and splattered curtains, and with bundles and baskets piled up on the back seats.

A line of milk cans along the platform's edge; packages thrown off the baggage-car fall helter-skelter. Negroes run about, shouting to each other.

A fat woman leans out of a buggy and calls "Merry Christmas!" and you reply gaily as you go toward her. Then, as you come close, she says in surprise, "Oh, I beg

your pardon, I thought you were one of the McNeely boys!"
And you grin as you reply, thinking that she looks like a
heathen goddess as she sits enthroned in her small carriage,
wrapped in numerous scarfs, and surrounded by a jumble of
packages and hampers, her fat cheeks red with the cold, her
small black eyes shining. A little negro girl comes running
up, bearing more bundles, and you turn away, looking up
and down the platform for "your folks."

"Chrismas gif'!"

A burst of soft African laughter followed by a loud
guffaw, and a black, wizened face peers into yours in the
fading light. It is old "Uncle" Billy, now very feeble, a relic
of slavery days, still occupying his cabin on the plantation.

You clap him on the shoulder. "Go 'long, Uncle Billy,"
you say, "you know that the 'Christmas gift' game doesn't
begin until to-morrow!"

But Uncle Billy is not convinced. "S'posin' I don't see
yo' to-morrow?"

Other plantation negroes come trooping up. Here is
Mac Mitchell, another old friend, who directs the dairy;
there is Willie, the "white nigger," so called because he is
an albino with pink eyes, pale yellow hair, and gray skin,
despite his African features and manners. Together you
stand on the sodden platform, your breath rising in streaks
of vapor before you as you speak. How good it is to get
back!

There is a grinding of brakes, a whistle, more cries, and
the train gets under way again, puffing off into the darkness.
One of the negroes has taken your handbag, and you follow
him along the platform, past the wagons, past the steaming
mules.

Over there, by the baggage-room, a member of the plantation family is waiting for you in the car. Greetings are warm, if hands are cold. You are tucked in beside the driver. A smothered "Howdy" comes out of the darkness of the rear seat, and you turn with a shout of greeting. It is Queen, the housemaid, whose black face peers out, her eyes and teeth shining. You have known Queen since she was a little girl, long before she became such an important factor in the life on the plantation. Usually she is dignified, somewhat disdainful, but to-night you have startled her out of her calm by your shout of recognition, and, feeling that she is in the limelight, she giggles, clasping numerous packages in her arms.

The car goes slowly through the village, climbs a hill, and is off into the country, down a long road between pine trees. The air is cold, and the scent of pine trees comes to you sharply. On and on goes the car; down through a "bottom" where oak trees grow, and where the water splashes about the wheels; up another hill, and there upon its crest you see the full moon, hanging low in the sky. From somewhere comes the long drawn-out hoot of an owl. Mile after mile unrolls before you, the lights of the car shining on the trunks of trees, and along the fences as the road curves sharply.

A huge house is outlined for a moment against the sky, standing dark upon a hilltop, its white columns blue in the moonlight, and a yellow gleam marking the open door. The trees blot out the picture suddenly.

Another depression, and the car goes through a creek, climbs the bank and emerges on the plantation road, between clumps of Spanish daggers, black and jagged against the far-off stars. Then an open gate upon which a diminutive negro swings, wide-eyed, open-mouthed, expectant. Some one in the car throws out a stick of red-and-white striped candy to him, and a voice is heard piping "Thanky ma'am!" as the car passes by. There is a sharp turn, and the car stops.

Before you the plantation-house rises, a great house of red-brick, half-covered with vines. Ivy hangs in wreaths on the white columns, as though they were decorated for Christmas. Beyond the porch, soft lamplight streams through an open door. Firelight flickers on the window panes. How good it is to come back to this familiar place, all the lovelier for its familiarity.

A dozen dogs come running out, "huntin' dawgs," four fine pointers, a white setter, then two Airedales with their bristling coats. You are surrounded, yelped over, pawed over, welcomed.

You mount the steps, cross the gallery and enter the drawing-room. The dogs follow you in, and six white cats rise languidly from before the fire, mildly disturbed by your entry. Then dogs, cats, hosts, and you settle down in a group near the chimney.

Queen is with us again, this time bearing a tray with diminutive coffee-cups, steaming, and giving out a delicious aroma. And you sip the hot drink saying over and over to yourself—"I am at home again. This is where I belong."

There are questions and answers. News of absent friends, messages to be repeated.

The family is never more typically itself than to-night. There is a feeling of mystery in the air. The excitement has communicated itself to the servants, and Queen giggles aloud as she removes the tray and empty cups. As soon as the door has closed behind her, you ask about the plans for Christmas, for, on a plantation, Christmas is the most important day in the year.

As it was rainy to-day, and may be rainy to-morrow, they tell you the celebration for the negroes will be held on the front gallery of the house. It will be over before breakfast time. Already thirty-six stockings have been filled. The celebration only includes those negro families living in the quarters. In the old days the celebration was larger, mammoth in fact, but now there are fewer negroes living on the place, and with the continued failures of the cotton crop, the care-free days of plantation life are over. Times are harder now.

But we do not linger on doleful subjects, for to-night the talk is all of holiday plans. The negroes themselves have decided that they want to "hunt down" Santa Claus. This means that Santa Claus must be chased, as though he were a 'possum or a coon. The trail has been laid. Just before dark Miss Eva has gone secretly from the side door of the house, holding in her hand a bag of mistletoe sprigs. She dropped one by the dining-room door, another a few yards beyond in the path which leads toward the barn, another farther down the path, another beside the fence between barnyard and vegetable garden; several more sprigs are dropped along the cabbage rows, and beyond in the pasture. Quite a long distance is left between the sprigs, but far down the pasture several more bits of mistletoe are lying. The trail leads on, down past Uncle Billy's cabin on the edge of the hill, down through the creek, and beyond through a strip of woods. In Miss Eva's walk of a mile or more, she has dropped the mistletoe in a hundred places; finally the trail leads back to the house again, ending just under the drawing-room window.

"But will the negroes find it?" you ask.

There is a burst of laughter: "Wait until to-morrow!" they tell you.

With the first faint streak of dawn you are awakened by the ringing of the plantation bell, and by a wailing chorus of dogs. The dogs howl every time the bell sounds. For years it has been the custom among them; every new dog brought to the plantation learns to join the song.

Blang! Blang!

"*Ow-oo—Ow-oo!*"

The dogs seem trying to outdo all previous efforts this morning, and you abandon sleep with something between a smile and a sigh—and step forth from your warm feather bed upon the cold floor. Matches are upon the mantel, and the wide fireplace in your room is piled high with fat-pine. Three minutes after you have applied the match, you are basking in the warmth of leaping flames. Outside there is a babble of soft African voices, punctuated now and then by a shrill scream of laughter.

Half-dressed you turn your head from the fire long enough to cry "Come in," in answer to a knock. Bap enters, carrying your morning coffee.

"Morning, Bap!" you say.

Bap scrapes one foot against the other in bashful recognition of your greeting, and after some trouble manages to stammer "M-m-m-morning!" And then adds, in a breath, "Christmas gif'!"

As you have been "kotched" fairly this time, you pro-

duce the "gif' " and present it to him. For it is our immemo-
rial custom in the South that any negro who says "Christmas
gif'!" to a white person is entitled to a present. If the
white person, however, cries "Christmas gift" first, he is ex-
empt—although he usually gives the present anyway. . . .
Such is our custom on the plantation, and Bap had caught
me fairly, because I was off-guard. And so he departs,
chuckling.

Dressed, I open the window in order to look upon the
front gallery. A score of negroes are gathered there in the
gray light of early morning; they are chattering like jay-
birds; but my appearance is greeted by a wild chorus of
"Christmas gif'!"

I retire before the storm, closing the blinds, and seek
the plantation folks in the drawing-room across the hall.
The family has gathered and are sorting out the stockings
on a large table, behind tight shut windows. Soon everything is in readiness, and Miss Kate saunters forth to the
front gallery and says casually, "I saw Santa Claus over
there by the fig tree just now."

She has not finished speaking before the negroes, old and
young, have jumped up and are rushing about the yard. A
minute later there is a shout—"*Yeee-!*"

Some one has found a sprig of mistletoe, and instantly
the crowd is wild with excitement. They scatter searching for
the second sprig. Zula, the cook, spies it over by the fence
and utters a piercing shriek. Immediately the whole flock is
in pursuit. They pretend to be hunting-dogs on the scent;
some of them run on all fours, noses to the ground. Others
give loud yelps. They are off!

Over fences and down the lane they go, yelping like

hounds in full cry. Their voices become fainter as they disappear over the fence and behind the barn. Old Uncle Billy, despite his eighty years, is running with the rest. Zula, usually the dignified matron of the kitchen, is giving her two daughters, Lula and Beulah, a run for their money. They are gone.

We remain, laughing, on the gallery.

When the cries have grown faint in the distance, Miss Kate calls, "You can come out now," and Santa Claus emerges from the front door. It is Miss Eva, who now wears a red costume trimmed in white fur; she is padded with pillows beyond all recognition; a Santa Claus mask hides her face and a long white beard hangs down; she carries a pack on her shoulder. The change is so startling that you find yourself weak with laughter as you go to offer assistance in carrying the sack of presents. A moment later Santa Claus is hidden in the smoke-house, just outside the kitchen windows. And it is not too soon, for the cries are becoming louder now; the mistletoe trail has turned homeward.

There they are now, just topping a hill. They are running in a pack. Zula is leading and Uncle Billy is a close second. There are forty negroes, men, women, and children, in the chase. They come nearer, find a sprig of mistletoe which directs them toward the back door, and they come yelping in with increased speed.

But just as they reach the smoke-house, Santa Claus emerges from the dark doorway and stands directly in their path.

Immediately there are screams of terror. The negroes fall back; some of them run and hide behind trees. Santa

Claus has scared them half out of their wits by appearing before they expected him. Some of the negroes are only shamming fear, but some are really terrified. They must be cajoled into approaching the masked saint, who stands immobile by the smoke-house door.

Finally Zula comes up and receives her stocking. Then the others come, one by one. There are bursts of laughter as the presents come tumbling out; oranges and apples, firecrackers, cheap jewelry, one real gift; and, down in the toe of the stocking, along with the candy and nuts, a jew's-harp or mouth organ for every one of them.

They circle the house, carrying their spoils, and range themselves on the front gallery. Queen and Zula are called into service for the time being, and a breakfast is served. . . . Waffles, syrup, hot coffee, scrambled eggs. Eyes flash and lips smack as the negroes eat, with many outbursts of humor.

"Better watch that ole gal! She'll bust herself wide open wid all dem cakes!"

Whereupon the girl retorts: "Ah sho' Gawd will!" and returns to her waffles with renewed gusto.

After breakfast comes the concert. Jew's-harps whine and negroes sing. Not the "blues," but their own plantation songs: "Run, Old Rachael, Run!" and "The Flu" and other ballads originated among themselves. And they sing while the rain patters down.

The plantation folks, those white men and women who have planned all this, and who have not breakfasted themselves as yet, stand looking on, laughing and joking with the negroes.

When the concert is over the negroes trudge homeward

to their cabins, to sing and dance at their own celebrations, and the white folks come indoors.

Breakfast is in the old dining-room, before a fire of blazing pine knots which throws its light upon the dark ceiling and heavy beams, and makes bright reflections in the goblets on the table.

And as you sit breakfasting there, on Christmas, you think of other Christmases which this old room has seen, the merrymakings of a century. For this plantation has been kept in the same family since 1808, when that great-grandfather of the present owners came over the Kentucky hills to build a house for himself in the wilderness of Louisiana.

Chapter Twenty-four

ON TO NATCHEZ

THE town of St. Francisville is situated on a hill overlooking the Mississippi, some thirty miles north of Baton Rouge. In the flush times before the Civil War, this section was as rich as any in the State. It was settled almost exclusively by English, Scotch, and German settlers; there were also French and Spanish. Some were English Royalists, loyal to the King and unsympathetic with the American Revolution. They emigrated to West Feliciana—as the parish is called— shortly after the middle of the eighteenth century. Others came later, at the time of the "Louisiana Purchase." Many of the emigrants were people of wealth and culture; many brought their slaves with them. St. Francisville is not far from Natchez, Mississippi. There are many fine plantation-houses in the vicinity of both towns.

OAKLEY

Oakley plantation, illustrated in this volume, is one of the earliest of these houses; it is situated four miles from the main highway, and from St. Francisville. It was built in 1808–1810 by James Pirrie, a wealthy Scotchman. Slave labor was used; the timber was hewn and the bricks burned on the spot. There are many stories told in connection with this house.

The plantation-owner had one daughter, the beautiful Eliza Pirrie. John J. Audubon, afterward renowned as the author and artist of "Birds of America," was her tutor. Both Audubon and his wife lived in the house for several years. Audubon taught Eliza to draw and paint. He also taught the young ladies of the neighborhood to swim in the large spring-house at Weyanoke plantation, nearby. The water in the spring-house "could be deepened at pleasure." Mrs. Audubon taught the girls to dance, using an abandoned cotton-gin in lieu of a ball-room. Audubon had other pupils besides Miss Pirrie, and in his diary we find some of their names: Jane and Margaret Towles, Margaret Butler, the Misses Randolph, Miss Harbour, and "the Swazie girls."

Miss Pirrie tired of her lessons and eloped with a young aristocrat of the neighborhood; it was raining and the creeks were out of their banks. In true romantic style, her lover carried her through the streams in his arms, wading breast deep. He caught pneumonia and died three weeks later. Eliza married twice after that. Her descendants, the Misses Bowman of "Rosedown" plantation, have a fine portrait of her hanging in the hall. Audubon, it is said, painted the picture.

Oakley is still the home of other descendants of the original owners, Miss Lucy and Miss Ida Matthews.

ROSEDOWN

The Bowman plantation, "Rosedown," is considered by many to be the finest plantation-house in Louisiana. Built and furnished in 1835, it stands intact to-day; the granddaughters of the original owner live there. The Misses Bowman inherited it from their mother, who before her marriage was Miss Eliza Turnbull, the wealthiest and most sought after young lady in the community. A hundred pretty stories are told of her. In the summer she would set out in her carriage for Saratoga Springs, accompanied by members of her family and several slaves. She would leave home in early June, taking a month to drive to Saratoga, remain in that "watering place" for a month, and take another month to drive home, returning in early September. A portrait of her, by Sully, which hangs in the dining-room at "Rosedown," is one of the finest examples of that artist's work that I have seen. The house is magnificently appointed, rosewood and mahogany furniture being used throughout. The porcelain and crystal ornaments are particularly interesting; the mirrors, chandeliers and candelabra were imported from France. The library contains many fine things, among them the elephant edition of "Birds of America" by Audubon, and many portfolios of excellent engravings. Among the prized possessions is a cross-stitch fire-screen embroidered by Martha Washington, inherited from an ancestress who was of the Custis family.

Mr. Bowman died only a few years ago. He was the most distinguished-looking old gentleman that I have ever

AN OLD HOUSE ON WALL STREET, NATCHEZ

"ARLINGTON" AT NATCHEZ IS GRACEFUL
IN DETAIL

seen, and I cannot visit Rosedown nowadays that I do not remember him vividly, a white-bearded patriarch in a white linen suit, coming slowly down the broad steps in the afternoon sunshine, a gold-colored collie at his heels. At the time that I knew him, he was the oldest living alumnus of Yale.

The garden at "Rosedown" was his pride, and rightly so, for it is one of the loveliest in America. It was laid out by a French landscape architect when the house was built, a century ago; and it has been carefully tended ever since. There is an avenue of live-oak trees—an avenue which broadens out as it approaches the house and forms a semicircular drive before the door. The azaleas have grown from shrubs into large trees, and in the spring are ablaze with color. Many classic statues stand at intervals under the trees. The seasons—spring, summer, autumn, and winter—are on one side, and the Continents are on the other. The principal Greek gods and goddesses are there, half hidden in shrubbery. The statue representing America is a delightful conceit—an Indian girl with stone feathers in her hair.

THE COTTAGE PLANTATION

Seven miles from the town of St. Francisville, and situated a mile back from the Woodville road, is "The Cottage," the home of the Butler family. The house is long and low and austere. It has none of the grand manner of "Rosedown," but it is charming in its simplicity. It stands on a high bluff, and one must cross a creek to get there. It is rich in historic interest, and it is the home of Mr. and Mrs. Edward Butler, and of Miss Louise Butler, the Louisiana historian.

AFTON VILLA

The old David Barrow house, "Afton Villa," is typical of the flush times just before the Civil War. Strictly speaking, it is not a plantation-house at all, but an elaborate "show-place," built without regard for expense. It is a castle, with battlements and towers, built in the "flamboyant Tudor" style. There are wide halls, winding stairs, stained-glass windows. There is an observatory on the roof, and terraces before the front door. A formal flower-garden leads down a hill on the east side of the house. It passed out of the hands of the Barrow family many years ago and served at one time as a "Female Seminary." It was falling into dilapidation a few years ago, when it was purchased by Dr. and Mrs. Lewis of Peoria, Illinois, who occupy it now. They have restored it intelligently and well, and have brought it back to its original state. It is more widely admired by tourists than any other house in the vicinity.

ELLERSLIE

"Ellerslie," illustrated in this volume, has been the home of the Percy family for nearly a century. The Percys bought it from its original owner, Judge W. C. Webb, who built it in 1835. It is a house in the true classic tradition, large and square, with large white Doric columns on all four sides. It is beautifully situated on a high bluff, ten miles or more from St. Francisville. It is far off the highway. Mr. and Mrs. Edward Percy, who now occupy the house, have restored and repaired it. It is in perfect condition, yet has the charm of age. After the elopement of Eliza Pirrie, Audubon became tutor for the Percy children and lived at Ellerslie for several years.

GREENWOOD

In "Greenwood," the Frank Percy plantation, we have the best example of the classic revival to be found in Louisiana. You must look at the full-page drawing which you will find midway this book. It will show the impressive dignity better than I can explain it in words. But no drawing can give an idea of the monumental size of this old house. It is so perfectly proportioned that one is hardly aware of its size until one stands beside a pillar, looking upward.

The house stands on a high hill, three miles from the Mississippi. It was built by Ruffin Barrow in 1830, and at that time the plantation consisted of 12,000 acres, nearly equally divided between cotton and sugar. The Barrow family built many fine houses in Louisiana, some in the neighborhood of St. Francisville, others in the Grosse Tête country west of the Mississippi.

There are many other plantation-houses in the vicinity, and all are worthy of study. Among the notable ones are: "Fairview," the Folkes house; "Wakefield," the Stirling place; "Faithorn," the Hereford place; "The Myrtles," another Stirling place; "Live Oak" and "Rosebank." The last named was an old inn, dating from the middle of the eighteenth century.

In driving from St. Francisville to Natchez, one passes through the town of Woodville, Mississippi. There are many old houses in the vicinity, and one of the most interesting is "Richland." It stands on a hill, far from the highway, some fifteen miles west of Woodville. In 1795 this house was given, with a land grant by the Baron de

Carondelet, to "Don Juan Wall," a native of the Barbadoes, and an alcalde under the Spanish government. The house had been built before Mr. Wall acquired it, probably as early as 1775, but no existing record shows the exact date. It is now the home of Evans Wall, the novelist.

NATCHEZ

In those flush years before the Civil War, Natchez was one of the richest cities in the country. Consequently many fine houses were built there. And the fact that Natchez has not been as "progressive" as her neighbor Baton Rouge, has proved the salvation of these old residences. Many of them were the homes of planters whose plantations lay west of the Mississippi in Louisiana. To-day, Natchez possesses more of historic interest than any other community in the South, with the exception of New Orleans. There are so many plantation-houses, and such fine examples, that I cannot list them all here. A few must suffice:

ROSALIE

The ante-bellum home of the Rumble family, "Rosalie," is built on the site of the old fort where the Indian massacre took place in the early eighteenth century. The house dates from 1810. It was the headquarters of General Grant during the War between the States. The drawing-room furniture is good.

MELROSE

"Melrose," the ancestral home of the Kelly family, is still occupied by George M. D. Kelly, a descendant of the

original owner. The house is an imposing red-brick structure, with a portico before the door. Four tapering columns rise two full stories to the gable. The building is
set in an extensive park. The house has its original furniture. The drawing of a plantation dining-room in this volume was made at "Melrose."

AUBURN

The estate of the Duncan family, "Auburn," has been
donated to the city of Natchez and now serves as a park.
The old residence is of red-brick with columns front and
back. The interior woodwork is very fine, and the spiral
staircase rises, unsupported, in the center of the north
hall. This house, being city property, may be visited at
any time.

MONMOUTH and ARLINGTON

The simple dignity of "Monmouth" makes it one of
the most satisfactory of Natchez houses. It is illustrated
in this volume. It was the home of the hero of Buena Vista
and Molino del Ray, General John B. Quitman. This house
was built by General Quitman soon after his return from
Mexico, where, as a comrade of Jefferson Davis, he had
assisted General Zachary Taylor in conducting his cam-
paign. "Monmouth" is owned by Mr. and Mrs. Barnum
of Natchez, who live nearby at "Arlington." The drawing
of a bedroom in this book was made at "Arlington," a
house which has been well preserved and which has a good
collection of antique furniture.

Other houses of unusual interest in the vicinity of

Natchez are: "Richmond," the home of the Marshall family; "The Briars," where Jefferson Davis was married; "Gloucester," home of Winthrop Sargent, first Territorial Governor of Mississippi, built in 1803, and better known as the home of Sargent Prentiss, the "silver tongued orator" of Natchez, whose speeches are still read by every young man studying law; "Springfield," on the Natchez Trace, is famous for the fact that Andrew Jackson married Rachael Robard there. There are many more: "Elmscourt," "Magnolia Vale," "Ravenna," and the old Minor house, to mention only a few.

WINDY HILL

But of all the interesting old houses in the vicinity, "Windy Hill Manor" is among the first. Aaron Burr lived there while in Natchez, hatching his plots for dividing the United States, and for creating an empire in the Southwest. It was here that he listened to the tales of Blennerhasset, of the fabulous wealth to be taken in Mexico, and it was here that he collected his army of adventurers. It is here that he was arrested by United States troops. On February 2, 1807, he was tried for treason under the oak trees on what is now the campus of Jefferson Military College. "Windy Hill" is the home of the Misses Stanton.

Chapter Twenty-five

THAT ETERNAL INDIAN GIRL

ANY traveler in Louisiana is sure to hear, sooner or later, the story of the beautiful Indian girl who jumped from a cliff and killed herself. There is no escape from that story; it follows you from southwest Louisiana—where the "cliff" is perhaps ten feet high—to the northern portion of the State, where such a leap would have been rather magnificent . . . like a high-dive in a circus. I shall tell you the story now and be done with it, for as sure as I leave it out, some one will say: "Oh, have you never heard that touching story of the beautiful Indian girl. . . .?" And I shall commit murder and be hanged for it.

Bear with me, then.

Once upon a time, when Louisiana was young, there lived a beautiful Indian girl. Do not forget that she was beautiful. You may forget anything else you please, but not that. It is the one point on which every one agrees.

In some parts of the State, the Indian girl is said to have been of the Natchez Indians, in others of the Choctaw nation, or of the Houmas. She is sometimes described as one of the Colapissa girls, and once I heard of her as a member of the tribe of Illinois. And she loved a white man.

Now with the man, a difficulty arises. Some say that he was a Frenchman, others a Spaniard, and it is said in the country near Baton Rouge that he was a handsome young American. Be that as it may, he was a man and she was a beautiful Indian girl. And they loved each other.

Her tribe objected to such an affair, for she was a princess, no less. So the lovers met secretly. Some say they were married, some say that they were not married. But, having no interest in the young couple's morals, I shall leave it to you. At any event, the young man was stationed at a fort, near the banks of a stream. The spot where the fort stood has been pointed out to me in forty widely separated points. But in every instance, it stood near a cliff which overhangs a river, bayou, creek, or brook. Water is necessary, for the girl jumped into it and drowned herself. I am a little ahead of my story, but it does not matter, as you will see.

At any rate, the Indians rose in revolt against the whites. In some localities, the whites are said to have oppressed the Indians and the Indians were justified in rising; in other localities, the whites were said to be bold, kind, and full of chivalry, and the Indians were merely unkind wretches.

Anyhow, the Indians rose and crept up to surprise the fort and massacre the brave Frenchmen, Spaniards, or

STAIRWAY AT "ARLINGTON"

Americans, as they slept. But the Indian girl, knowing that her lover would be among the scalped, took to her fiery mustang, Arab steed, or mule, (depending upon the locality again), and riding by a shorter route, went to warn her lover.

Now comes the hard part. Some say that she roused the fort, saved her lover, and that the furious Indians turned on her and drove her over the cliff; some declare that she jumped to death because she had betrayed her tribe and brought death upon her kindred. Others scoff at both versions and give a sterner one: she failed to arrive in time, and when she reached the fort, she found it in flames and her lover dead. Then, with a wild cry, she bounded along until she came to the cliff and threw herself over to death in the placid (or stormy) waters below.

This, roughly, is the story, and Minnehaha will laugh no more. But the ghost of the Indian maiden pursues the traveler from section to section and from town to town. She jumped from a cliff near the Gulf of Mexico; she jumped in the Teche country; she jumped near Opelousas; and she jumped at Baton Rouge. These are widely scattered points, but the end is not yet. She jumped at St. Francisville—where she had plenty of room for a nice dive, and she jumped again at Natchez, Mississippi. She also jumped into Red River, near Alexandria, and she jumped into Cane River, at the outskirts of the town of Natchitoches.

My theory is that she jumped in all of those places and in many others. I think she did it for a living, and that the rest of the story was publicity, spread by some primitive advertising man.

I tell this story for what it is worth—which is not much; and I tell it merely to get rid of it so that those kind persons in different parts of Louisiana who have told, written, or telegraphed this story to me shall not be disappointed. I believe the story implicitly. Perhaps she did jump in all those places, but if so, what of it?

Chapter Twenty-six

WEST OF THE MISSISSIPPI

JUST opposite the town of St. Francisville, on the west bank of the Mississippi, is Pointe Coupée, known since the beginnings of Louisiana as the home of wealthy plantation-owners. Sometime in the past the Mississippi River, in its meanderings, cut a new channel for itself and left its old bed a long inland lake. Hence the names "Pointe Coupée" and "False River." Near the town of New Roads are some fine old plantation-houses.

PARLANGE

Travelers along False River always stop to admire "Parlange," which stands buried in a mass of trees and shrubbery. It is of the authentic Louisiana type—a house as fine as any in the State. It was built by the Marquis Ternant about the middle of the eighteenth century and is the home of a descendant of the original owner. A pair of fine *pigeonnières* are placed at either end of the house, and some distance before it. The *pigeonnières* are of brick, painted white; they are hexagonal and surmounted with high hexagonal roofs. A drawing of one of the Parlange dove-cotes will be found on the title-page of this book, and a sketch of the house is a few pages beyond.

Walter Parlange, the owner, tells a score of romantic stories concerning the house; and I hereby resist the temptation to tell of the bride who went mad on her wedding night, and shall tell instead a story of which there are legal records in proof.

The Parlange tomb, which bears the date 1757, is the oldest in the cemetery at New Roads. Once it figured in one of the strangest law-suits on record. Within this tomb lie the remains of Madame Claude Vincent Ternant. She had been buried in her jewels, as was often done in those days. Her son, a gay young blood of the period, pressed by debts, raised money by selling all his rights, titles, and interests in the succession of Madame Ternant to a certain John Boudreaux. In the course of time, thieves robbed the tomb of its jewels, but the robbers were apprehended in New Orleans, arrested, and convicted. The jewels— including a pearl necklace worth many thousands of dollars —were deposited with the Registry of the Court to be claimed by the rightful heirs. All the heirs came forward to claim property, among them the wild young man who had sold his birthright. Boudreaux, too, came forward, and claimed that portion of one heir whose interest he had bought. The heir contended that when he sold his interest in the succession he did not contemplate the transfer of his interest in the jewels that were buried

A BEDROOM AT "ARLINGTON"

in the tomb of his mother, as that property was "hors de commerce." The Court, however, held that when he transferred that interest, it included all things that might eventually come into the succession, and Boudreaux was given an interest in the jewels. The young son is now lying beside his mother in the tomb.

LABATUT

The grove of oak trees which stood before the old Labatut house has been swallowed by the river, and the dwelling stands close beside the highway nowadays. This house is reminiscent of the houses in the Vieux Carré of New Orelans, in that there is a courtyard behind it, from which the stairs rise to the second story. It is said to be about a hundred and fifty years old. It was built by a Spanish nobleman, Evariste Barra, and his descendants—the Labatut and Puig families—are still living there.

LAKESIDE

Notable among houses in this vicinity is "Lakeside," the home of the Batchelor family, an imposing house of brick, with delicate cast-iron railings. "Lakeside" is a later development of the "Louisiana type," and it is unusual in its lavish use of iron. Even the treads of the wide central stairway are of filigree iron work.

RIVER-LAKE

"River-Lake" plantation, the home of the Rougeon family, is a pleasing place, an old house of the simple Louisiana type, but more interesting than many because of the unusual placing of large, square *pigeonnières* on each side of the front gate. Like the house, the dove-cotes are two stories high, the lower floor being of brick and the upper portion of wood.

Following the Mississippi south again, the highway skirts a rich sugar-cane country. This was all familiar ground to me in my childhood, and time was when I knew twenty families in the neighborhood. But fire and flood have taken the houses, and the families have moved away. The road passes "Camp" Plantation, the old home of my cousins, the Chamberlin family. It stands empty and deserted now. A mile beyond is the Devall sugar-house where every year at grinding time. . . . But why speak of those times now? They are gone and the people have gone with them.

The plantations of the Hill and the Carruth families are still cultivated by the original owners. But the old houses have been replaced by new ones.

If one leaves the river road at Port Allen, just opposite the town of Baton Rouge, and drives west for twenty miles or so, he will reach Bayou Grosse Tête and Bayou Maringouin. At Rosedale the road passes the old Dickinson house—a pleasing, simple structure set in a grove of oak trees; it is occupied by the Mays family. There is also "The Mounds," the Woolfolk house, empty now.

SHADY GROVE

Between the village of Rosedale and the town of Maringouin stands the old Erwin house, "Shady Grove." It faces Bayou Grosse Tête and was built by Isaac Erwin in 1858. It is unlike the earlier types of houses, but it is in no sense a "show place." It was designed for comfort and for stability; only the finest materials were used in its construction. It has passed from the Erwin family long since, and is now used as a school.

BELMONT

The Wiley Barrow house, "Belmont," stands hidden among trees on the bank of Bayou Maringouin, a mile west of the town of the same name ("Maringouin," by the way, means "mosquito"). It has columns on all four sides, an unusual feature in a house of a single story. It was occupied for many years by the Sparks family, well-known planters of Iberville Parish. "Belmont" is so crude in its construction and so irregular that it appears to be one of the older houses. However, upon investigation, I found that it was built only a few years before the Civil War— which goes to show how dangerous surmises may be. The illustration shows the front of the house, but the house presents an identical façade, north, east, west, and south. . . . There are other interesting houses in the neighborhood, but the traveler must face about and return to the Mississippi again, to continue toward New Orleans along the west bank.

NOTTAWAY

In 1858, John Hampton Randolph of Virginia built a mansion in Louisiana. It was called "Nottaway," and was designed by an architect who had built many mansions in Virginia. It is principally notable for its size; it contains forty rooms, and the house is encircled with galleries. It has square pillars and the railings are of cast-ironwork. The structure is all white. . . . And imposing enough it appears, set in a wide green lawn with an irregular grove of oak trees around it. The finest room in the house is the white ball-room gleamingly white, with crystal chandeliers, mirrors, and even a white tiled floor. "Nottaway" is now the home of Dr. W. G. Owen. Inasmuch as it is more characteristic of Virginia than of Louisiana architecture, we have not included an illustration of it.

BELLE GROVE

"Belle Grove," one of the finest plantation-houses in Louisiana, has been allowed to fall into ruin. The enormous structure is ornate but exquisite in detail, and although it was built in 1857 and a fortune was expended in its construction, it is designed with impeccable taste. It is florid, but magnificent. It was owned originally by John Andrews, but was purchased by a well-known Louisiana sportsman of other days, with the odd name of Stone Ware. The Ware family occupied it until fifteen years ago; it has remained empty since that time. The name "Belle Grove" and gaiety, were synonymous in Louisiana. The Wares maintained a private race-track and bred fine horses; their balls were lavish and their house-parties are still remembered when "the good old times" are discussed. The house is in the spirit of the Greek revival, with fine fluted pillars surmounted with carved wooden Corinthian capitals. Its color is most unusual, a rose-color, now faded yet luminous. It glows rosily through dark trees as one approaches. The illustration gives an idea of the appearance of the house, but no drawing can show its mammoth proportions. The house contains seventy-five rooms; some of them are forty feet square. The central hall is exquisite in detail; its length is broken by fluted columns. The stair-case rises in a fine curve to the second floor. There are handsome marble mantels throughout the house. And behind the main dwelling are wings which seem endless. The illustration of a plantation drawing-room was also made at Belle Grove.

BAYOU LAFOURCHE

If you will leave the river road at the town of Donald-sonville and follow Bayou Lafourche, you will see a section where once the richest of the planters lived. There are fine houses there still. Turn your back to the Missis-sippi and take the road on the left side of the bayou.

Between the towns of Donaldsonville and Napoleon-ville, you will find "Belle Alliance" (illustrated), once the home of the Kock family, but now occupied by the Church-ills; another plantation family who lived formerly in the False River section. Beyond Napoleonville you will find "Madewood," a splendid house in a fine state of preservation; it was once the home of Thomas Pugh and his family, and it was built in 1846, when Louisiana was its richest. It was built somewhat in the manner of "Woodlawn," also a plantation belonging to the Pugh family. "Made-wood" is owned by Mr. and Mrs. Robert L. Baker who live there. "Woodlawn" stands empty.

There was an old Louisiana conundrum: "Why is Ba-you Lafourche like the aisle of a church?" and the answer was: "Because there are Pughs on both sides of it." One would have to find another answer to-day, for the Pugh plantations have passed out of the family. But the houses remain, as impressive as any in the State.

If you like, you can continue to the town of Thibadoux, where, just across the bayou, you will find "Reinzi" an early type of plantation-house, chiefly notable for its double, curved stairway which leads up to the front door. Still further—miles beyond—you will find "Ducros," the old Winder place, now occupied by the Palmer family; and again still further you will find "Southdown," the plantation of the Minor family.

But if we return along Bayou Lafourche to the Mississippi, there are other things in store for us.

OAK ALLEY

"Oak Alley," the erstwhile home of Alexandre Roman, Creole governor of Louisiana, stood empty for many years before being purchased by Mr. and Mrs. Andrew Stewart of New Orleans. With the aid of Armstrong and Koch, New Orleans architects, they have restored the building to its original magnificence. It is a successful restoration, and the house is beautiful, as it is seen at the end of a long avenue of live-oak trees. This alley of oaks, from which the plantation takes its name, is two centuries old. The spread of each tree is about one hundred and sixty feet. There are twenty-eight of these oak trees—fourteen on each side of the alley—and the branches interlock for half a mile. One sees the house first through a long tunnel of greenery.

Governor Roman built this house in 1836, replacing an earlier house which had occupied the same site. The twenty-eight columns which surround the dwelling correspond with the twenty-eight oak trees in the alley. The Stewarts have furnished the house throughout with antique furniture.

In the old days the plantation of Governor Roman's cousin, Valcour Aimé, adjoined Oak Alley, but the Valcour Aimé house burned many years ago. Only a few deserted brick cabins remain, buried in underbrush and vines. Both of these plantations are on the west bank of the Mississippi, about fifty miles northwest of New Orleans.

There are more old houses before one reaches New Orleans. At Westwego, surrounded by the tanks of an oil company, you will find the old LeBreton house, standing grimly under its oaks. But oil tanks make a poor background. We will not linger here.

"Belle Chase," the bachelor hall of Judah P. Benjamin, is five miles back of the town of Gretna, opposite New Orleans; a separate trip must be made in order to reach it.

We can return to New Orleans and make a tour of some of the plantation-houses, which are now within the city limits or which are quite close enough to visit in an afternoon if you wish. To name only a few—"Three Oaks," near the American Sugar Refinery, a house which is said to have housed the wounded from the Battle of New Orleans in 1815; the Beauregard house, "Bueno Retiro," a mile further along in St. Bernard Parish; the Estopinol house on the road to Pointe-à-la-Hache, said to be one hundred and seventy-five years old; the Mereaux house at Jackson Barracks; the Stauffer house in Metairie; the Delord Sarpy house, which is buried among warehouses on Howard Avenue, just off Camp Street, in the heart of

New Orleans; the Westfeldt house, at Prytania and First Streets, in the "old American section," or garden district; the Soniat house, on the river road, but off the highway, near the town of Kenner; the old house called "Madame John's Legacy" on Dumaine Street in the Vieux Carré. There are a dozen more, but the guide books will designate them. It is my wish to show you places which are not so well known. . . . And, most of all, I should like to show you the Teche country, and the country north to the town of Natchitoches on Cane River.

Chapter Twenty-seven

SUPERSTITIONS

THE plantation negro is ever alert for omens. He reads meanings into things which the white man ignores or fails to see. The negro has superstitions concerning the sun, the wind, the moon, and the stars; superstitions pertaining to weddings and funerals, eating and drinking; superstitions regarding the men and animals around him, the rats and mice, cats and dogs. He lives in a world apart from the white man's world, and in a world infinitely more interesting and terrible; for every breeze brings an omen for good or bad luck and the sunlight itself must be watched for shadows of passing birds.

In my life on a Louisiana plantation I have written down a few of these taboos; perhaps a hundred or more have found their way into my note-book; but these constitute scarcely one tenth of the superstitions which the negroes know and observe. It is not easy to collect them, for the negro fears ridicule and becomes self-conscious when questioned. Fearful of your laughter, he may reply that he does not believe in signs; yet a moment later, the same negro may reprove you for turning a shoe upside down, or for killing a spider.

Many of the superstitions listed here are, I believe, general. How many of them are purely local, I cannot say. You may draw your own conclusion from them. Here, take my note-book. It may amuse you as we travel on to-gether.

It is bad luck to fall down on Monday.

It is bad luck to have three lights in one room.

Don't spin a chair on one leg; it causes quarrels in the house; the one who spins the chair gets the beating.

If you walk past a place in the road where a horse has wallowed, spit in it—it saves you a whipping.

It is bad luck to leave a chair rocking. You will die within a year.

It is bad luck to dream of muddy water, it betokens trouble.

It is good luck, though, to dream of clear water, as it foretells prosperity.

To break a mirror foretells seven years' bad luck, unless you throw all the pieces in a running stream.

If your nose itches, company is coming.

It is bad luck to put a hat on the bed; it drives the lovers out of the house.

It is bad luck to open an umbrella in the house.

Cross two nails in the nest of a goose and thunder can not spoil the eggs.

In setting a hen, if you want all of the eggs to hatch, you must carry them to the nest in a soup plate during the first quarter of the moon.

If little children put their arms over their heads when sleeping, you should put them down, for they are calling down misfortunes on their heads.

Never kneel on the threshold; bad luck.

If your right ear burns, someone is talking pleasantly of you; if the left ear, you are being criticised.

To pass a child through a window makes a thief of him.

You must always burn and not throw away your hair; for the birds will take it for their nests, and you will become insane.

If you strike your "crazy-bone" you will be disappointed.

If a fly bothers you, name it after a person you know; if you have chosen the person who is thinking of you, the fly will go away.

When a snake is cut to pieces his friends come and put the pieces together.

When in saying goodbye, four persons cross hands in shaking them, it is a sign of marriage.

When you cut a banana, you cut the cross of Christ—so do not cut one.

If you have a sore on the tip of the tongue, it is a sign you have lied.

If you forget what you were going to say, it is a sign that you were about to lie.

If you sweep the feet of a child with a broom, it is a sign that he will walk early.

If you walk by accident on the tail of a cat you will marry within the year.

It is a sign of good news if you see a white butterfly.

Of course, it is bad luck for a black cat to cross your path at night, but it is good luck to pull a black cat's tail.

An owl brings bad luck. If you are walking in the woods and hear one hoot, the only thing to do is to change your course or go back the way you came.

It is bad luck to begin any undertaking on Friday.

If a man cannot make a fire burn it means that he shall have a drunken wife.

It is bad luck to spit in the fire, as it "dries up your lungs" and then you die of tuberculosis.

A mosquito hawk [dragon fly] in the house is good luck; should one get under your mosquito bar, you will be spared a spell of sickness.

To have a spider's web fall across your face is bad luck; it means that your enemies are working against you.

It is very good luck to adopt a child; things will prosper with you.

In visiting a strange house it is unlucky to leave by another door than that by which you entered.

It is bad luck to walk under a ladder.

It is bad luck to fall upstairs, or to trip when going upstairs.

It is good luck to begin an undertaking when the sun shines in at your back door.

It is bad luck to turn things upside down; especially chairs.

If you throw salt after a stranger leaving your house he will never return.

It is bad luck to see the new moon through the trees.

If you plow on Good Friday the lightning will strike your field, and the ground will bleed.

It is bad luck to tell a dream before breakfast unless you want it to come true.

It is bad luck to turn back without making a cross on the ground and spitting in it.

If you see a cross-eyed person you must cross your fingers to ward off the evil eye.

It is unlucky to move a cat from one house to another; or a broom.

If a rabbit crosses your path at night, you must walk backward across the spot to avoid trouble.

Never let a woman into the house first thing on New Year's morning; bad luck.

If you stub your left toe when you are going to make a call it shows that you are not welcome.

Never let anyone eat peanuts in your house and drop the shells on the floor or in the yard; it causes quarrels.

A man and his wife must not wash in the same water; "they'll fight sho'."

It's bad luck to put eggs on your bed; it causes trouble; if a hen lays them there, that's all right.

If you kill the first snake you meet in the New Year, you have got rid of an enemy.

"SHADY GROVE," THE ERWIN HOUSE ON
BAYOU GROSSE TÊTE — 1857

"BELLE GROVE" — 1857 — IS DESERTED NOW

If a married person, rising, turns a chair over, he or she shall never get another spouse.

If a baby is allowed to see itself in a mirror before it is three months old, it will die.

It is bad luck to add fire to fire, or to put a burning coal upon a grate; to avoid bad luck, spit on the flames.

It is bad luck to carry a spade, hoe or axe through the house.

A picture falling from the wall tells of death; if it is the picture of a person, that person is in danger of death or serious injury or illness.

To sing before breakfast means that one will cry before dinner—or, as the negroes say, "Little bird sing too soon in de mawnin' big hawk catch him befo' night."

If rats or mice gnaw your clothes it means that you are going to leave that place. It is bad luck to let a relative mend the hole; some one not related to you in any way should do the mending.

If you move on Sunday to a new abode, you will never leave it.

To step over your fishing-pole means that you'll catch no more fish that day.

To step over a child lying on the floor retards its growth.

If a person or object comes between two persons walking together, they will quarrel.

If you see a pin pointing toward you, pick it up, as it means good fortune; if its head is toward you, let it alone, for bad luck goes with it.

Never give a knife for a present; it causes quarrels.

Never give a fan as a present; it will fan away friendship.

If you lie on a table, it means that you will die and be laid out on one before long.

It is unlucky to sit on a table.

To keep a dog at home, cut a small piece from the end of his tail and bury it under the front steps.

To keep a cat at home rub its two front paws in the soot of the chimney.

To sit on a trunk means disappointment.

If a woodpecker knocks on the house it is a sign of death.

If a hen crows it is a sign of death.

If a mud-dauber's nest falls from the roof of the house it is a sign of death.

Never sweep out the house after sundown, for you sweep some one's soul out of the house with the sweepings.

If a woman puts on her dress wrong side out some one will tell a lie about her; to avoid this, she must wear it wrong side out until noon. The same thing applies to men's garments.

If your right shoe comes untied, some one is speaking well of you; if the left, the conversation is bad.

If a fly follows your nose some one wants to see you.

If a spider drops down on a web from the ceiling before you, it is a sign of good luck.

If you sneeze while eating, you must spit out the mouthful; bad luck otherwise.

It is unlucky to burn bread.

In order to have good luck during the New Year, you must eat boiled green cabbage that day.

It's good luck to dream of a very black negro.

If a baby is allowed to look into a mirror, it will have trouble teething.

If you call a person's name by accident, he or she is thinking about you.

If a baby has thrash there is one sure cure: A little boy who has never seen his own father must blow into the child's mouth.

When you drop your comb, if you will put your foot on it your wish will come true.

To kill a spider makes it rain.

To hang a dead snake up in a tree makes it rain.

To kill a frog and not turn it on its back makes it rain.

If the rain falls while the sun is shining it is a sign that the devil is whipping his wife; also, rain to-morrow.

Blue jay-birds are evil spirits; on Friday they go to hell to report the bad things that happen in the world. Each carries a grain of sand to the devil.

A black cat is a witch and must be treated with proper respect or it will bring bad luck upon you. To have a sleek black cat signifies that you have warded off bad luck.

A yellow cat means money and gold, and it is good luck to keep one.

To kill a buzzard is bad luck, as it is akin to the devil and he takes care of his own.

A red-haired negro is a witch. If he gives you a rabbit's foot, you have an all powerful talisman against evil, and for good luck.

Snakes, frogs, snails, buzzards, blue jays are in league with the spirits of darkness.

It is the worst possible luck to cross a funeral procession, or to meet one; although to see one pass by is lucky.

It is bad luck to count the mourners at a funeral, or the carts or wagons in the procession to the grave. To do so betokens your own death.

If a dog howls in the night it means that some one in the house will die.

If a rooster crows on the back steps, a neighbor will die; if it crows on the front steps it is a sign of company.

If a buzzard sits upon your chimney it means that some one will die within the next few months.

For a bird to fly into the house tells of the death of some member of the family. If it lights on some one his death is certain. If it lights upon a pregnant woman her child will die.

It is bad luck to keep a cripple's crutch after his death. It should be placed upon his grave.

If your enemy dies, you must place white chicken feathers in a bottle on his grave to keep him from haunting you. To slip a few into his coffin makes him powerless against you; but, failing this, bury some in a bottle in the new-made grave. As long as the feathers remain, you are safe, but woe betide you if they decay, and you do not arrange a new supply.

When some one dies his eyes should be kept closed for a time by putting coins on the eyelids. The coins should be buried with him; to spend them afterward is great bad luck.

It is bad luck to have a mirror so tilted that it reflects a corpse; as ever afterward the shadow of the dead will lurk behind the shoulders of the living reflected in it.

At a wake, if one of the horses neighs outside, it is a sign of the death of one of the mourners.

It is bad luck to mix salt and pepper.

It is bad luck to spill salt, it betokens a quarrel unless a pinch is thrown over the left shoulder.

To take a piece of bread when you have one already means that somebody is coming hungry to your house.

To cure warts, rub with a green pea; then wrap it in a piece of paper and throw it away; the person who picks it up will get your warts.

Or, you must count the warts carefully, and then tie as many knots in a string as there are warts, and bury the string; as the string rots the warts will disappear. This is a sure cure.

Another method of curing warts: go where a dead horse is lying, and pick up a short rib; rub it on your warts three times and then throw the bone over your left shoulder and walk away without looking back; the warts will disappear.

To rid yourself of rheumatism, steal an Irish potato and carry it in your pocket; one honestly come by will not do the work.

To cure rheumatism: heat an iron pot red-hot; into this throw three live frogs; the grease which cooks out of them should be saved and used to rub the part of the body that pains. This is a sure cure.

A nutmeg on a string around the neck will ward off neuralgia; a nutmeg on a knotted string around the ankle will cure pains in the leg. A silver dime worn on the ankle will help.

Many old people have the gift of healing. They can cure pain by rubbing with their hands. The way they achieve this power is as follows: catch a live mole and rub him to death between your hands; if the mole bites you, it is certain that you will never be a healer; but if you succeed in crushing it to death before it harms you, you will have the power of healing.

Chapter Twenty-eight

SOME NEGRO PROVERBS

HERE are proverbs and bits of homely wit. They are characteristic of the Louisiana plantation negro, and give an insight into his nature. These proverbs and figures of speech have been taken down at various times and places, and I have gathered them together here because they show something of the negro's kindliness, his humor, and his keen observation. In order to make the meaning clear, I have added a word of explanation to some which seemed obscure.

"Big talk won't boil de pot." (Actions speak louder than words.)
"It wuz swellin' dat bus' de poutin' pigeon." (Pride goeth before a fall.)
"'Cause you like roses ain't no reason to 'spise de sun-flower."
"Lots of big cows got little horns."
"Sitting in de big man's chair." (An expression of reproof for bragging.)
"De foot ain't no good widdout de laig to hang it to."

"De man who plays wid nastiness smells nasty."

"Truth-teller, he little dove; long-tongued liar, he big hawk."

"Countin' the stumps won't clear de field."

"It takes a lot of mud-puddles to make a lake."

"Cat mighty dignified till de dog come by."

"White hen mighty pretty, but de black chicken is de luckiest when de hawk come sailin' ovah de chicken yard."

"Like givin' de fish a drink of water." (Expression for uselessness of effort.)

"Ef yo' keep de lid on de pot, de flies won't fall in." (Don't listen to gossip.)

"Chile, don't try to teach your grandmammy how to pat ashes!" (Don't give advice to old folks.)

"How you know how de jelly tastes till yo' open de jar?" (We only learn by experience.)

"There's a funny smell in a bachelor's house."

"Snake, he ain't got no friend; neither de long-tongue liar."

"When the mare dies you don't give her colt to de cow to raise." (Each to his own kind.)

"De big aig busses!" ("The big eggs break," meaning the anticipation deludes us.)

"Larows to catch meddlers." (Meaning "Do not meddle; something will catch you." The meaning of "Larows" or "Lay-roes" is uncertain. This is a very old expression among negroes, and they have lost the meaning themselves. Some think that "Larows" means "Lay-overs" or "Lay-lows"—in other words, something "laying low" in order to catch meddling children.)

"Death ain't nothing but a robber; but he come to de big house jus' as often as he come to de cabin."

"Ef yo' take a cat to chu'ch, de folks gwine to laugh." (If we do absurd things we must be prepared for the consequences.)

"Like eggs, honey? Den yo' better keep watch on de hen!"

"What yo' spose de bullfrog knows about a looking-glass?" (Every man is blind to his own defects.)

"De nigger is luckier dan de white man at night." (Because you can't see what he is doing in the dark.)

"Yo' can't break de hoe two times." (When the worst happens, there
is nothing left to fear.)

"De dog dat bites off his own tail sets a bad example fo' de puppy."

"Don't give yo' aigs to a fool to carry."

"Ef dey fight yo' in de big road, yo' can run home; but what yo' goin'
to do when de fightin's in yo' own cabin?"

"A quiet wife is mighty pretty."

"Jaybird must have done lots of favors fo' de devil, befo' de devil
teach him to crack acorns dat way." (Said in derision of an over-
clever person.)

"It's a funny thing, but de jaws is de only part of de body dat likes
to work!"

"Drown de cat and make de kittens cry!" (A motherless child is
unfortunate.)

"De cat say: 'De barn is full of rats. Kitten, go git some and quit
a-pesterin' me!'" (Make your children work, or they will abuse
your kindness.)

"It ain't no use sayin': 'Please give me a glass of milk!' to de cow."

"Call a dog a dog; he won' bite yo' for it!" (The guilty dare not
resent the accusations of the righteous.)

"You've got to tie your handkerchief to fit yo' haid." (Circumstances
alter cases.)

"Old *Used-To* don't wuk no mo'!" (Other times, other manners.)

"Ef yo' sit on de bucket all day, yo' won't draw no water from de
well."

"Horse don't care what de rat say." (Big natures can afford to ignore
small thrusts.)

"Axers got to be waiters." (Beggars cannot be choosers.)

"Ef yo' wife can cook, send yo' bucket to de spring!" (In other
words, get her a job cooking in the white man's kitchen, so she
may provide food for you.)

"'Gimme' an' 'Much obliged' got to be twins in dis world."

"De wagon rattles de loudest when it's coming away from de sugar-
house." (Empty heads are coupled with loud talk.)

"When de preacher comes in, de chickens cry." (Because they know
they will be fried chicken for dinner.)

"Lazy man don't wear no shoes."

"Ef yo' say to de white man: 'Ain' yo' forget yo' hat?' he say: 'Nigger, go git it!' " (So don't give superfluous information.)

"Ef yo' pulls de dawg's tail, yo' mus' expect what yo' gets!"

" 'I don't sail the air just for fun!' says Carencro." (The buzzard, like man, must work for his food.)

"De dawg and de cat both wag dey tails—but, oh my!" (Each one has a different way of expressing himself.)

"Yo' can't expect to see de cow a-sitting on de chimbley!" (Don't expect the impossible.)

"Persimmon in de tree-top ain't no good to me." (What is out of reach is of no use.)

"Rabbit ain't skeered of gittin' stuck in de briar patch." (Every man is at ease in familiar surroundings.)

"Lightning strike de big house befo' it hit de cabin." (Those in high places are in greater danger than those in lowly ones.)

"Neighbor's chile is ugly and bad, not good like ours." (We are blind to the faults of our own children.)

"*Don't-Care* slept outdoors all night." (Almost invariably used as an answer to the child who says "don't care," when admonished by an elder. This personification is characteristic of the plantation negro.)

"White man's watermelon smile and say: 'Nigger, who I for?' "

"Servants got to see and don't see, hear and don't hear."

"'Tain't no use singin' psalms to a dead horse."

ALL PLANTATION NEGROES GO TO CHURCH

THE DRAWING-ROOM AT "BELLE GROVE"
—AS IT WAS

Chapter Twenty-nine

BAYOU TECHE AND CANE RIVER

THERE is a last trip which we should make together—the long ride out through the Teche country, then north through the Attakapas region, to end our journey on Cane River near Natchitoches, the oldest town in the State.

You are tired, perhaps, from our rambles together, so we will drive swiftly through the flat, fertile country west of New Orleans. This was called "The Sugar Bowl" in the old days, for these fields furnished nearly enough sugar to sweeten the world. Nearly enough. We shall leave the Mississippi two hundred miles behind us this time, for I want you to see the Acadian country—the loveliest and most fertile land I know. We will go without stopping to Franklin—one of the prettiest of Louisiana towns, all cool and green and white, with old houses standing back on smooth green lawns, amid clumps of banana trees and oleanders.

"OAKLAWN"

Near Franklin we will find "Oaklawn" on Bayou Teche. It is now one of the show places of the section, although the house of Judge Alexander Porter which once stood there was destroyed by fire. Claude Barber, a Texas millionaire, admired "Oaklawn" so much he bought it a few years ago, and was busy restoring it when it caught on fire and burned. Undaunted, he had architects reconstruct it as nearly like the old house as possible. His garden is extraordinarily fine, but as the house is not the original, it is not illustrated.

In the vicinity of Franklin there are other places of interest: The Don Caffrey house; "Dixie," the plantation home of Murphy J. Foster, former governor of Louisiana; there are other houses worth studying within the town of Franklin. And beyond lies New Iberia, in the heart of the Teche country.

"THE SHADOWS"

Gigantic oak trees, draped in trailing gray moss, hang over the still bayous; the moonlight falls on these dark festoons and casts swaying shadows upon the motionless water. Mocking birds sing their liquid songs in the fields. Plantation-houses, white pillared and stately, stand in groves of dark trees. From the negro cabins one can still hear the sound of singing and the twang of the banjo in the evening when the work is done.

The old Weeks house at New Iberia is called "The Shadows." I saw it first by moonlight. Pale light lay along the roof in a silver stream, and shone upon the eight large columns framed by tangled trees. All the colors seemed faded by the moonlight. There were patches of black shadows. Somewhere I could hear the trickle of a fountain.

My hand was lifted to knock upon the door, but I paused, there in the deep shadows of the porch, and turned my head. Framed between the columns at one end of the arcade, I saw an old formal garden, with its rectangular lawn and graveled walks, and pagan gods of stone glistening with the heavy dew of summer. Groups of century-plants raised their sharp polished leaves higher than my head; roses were pale in the moonlight, and in the center of an open space, camelia trees surrounded a classic bust of marble. Magnolias were spilling their fragrance in the night air, and mingled scent came from the flowers which lay invisible in the heavier shadows. From somewhere came the flutter of birds' wings, and the soft rustle of stirring leaves.

And then, as I stepped to the edge of the porch, looking out between the columns, almost at my feet lay a rectangular pool, with the full moon reflected in its quiet depths, and its fountain standing a luminous silver flame.

By day, the four acres which constitute the garden seem a riot of tropical foliage, a perfect setting for the house which David Weeks built back in 1830 and which has been the home of the Weeks family since that time. It is now the home of Weeks Hall, of the fourth generation, one of Louisiana's most important younger artists. Mr. Hall inherited the house some years ago, and has spent several years in supervising its restoration. Armstrong & Koch, New Orleans architects, have had charge of the work.

Nothing has been changed, but all has been restored to

its original form. Now the house appears just as it did when it was built—only it is lovelier, for time has brought out new colors in the warm red-brick walls, and the garden has had a century to grow in.

Like so many of the Louisiana plantation-houses of the Greek revival period, the dwelling is flush with the ground, the lower floor paved with brick and marble.

The staircase is outside the house, rising from one end of the front porch. Downstairs there are sitting-rooms, a dining-room, kitchen, and rooms for bachelor guests. On the floor above are the drawing-rooms, now used as a studio by Mr. Hall, the master's bedroom and the guest room. There is also a large back hall with the windows overlooking Bayou Teche.

This is a house beautiful in all its finely wrought detail. The roof is in dull-blue slate, and the walls of the house are of dull red-brick. The woodwork is light cream color, the wooden blinds dull green. The spaces between the last two columns at each end of the house are enclosed in green blinds, affording an outside living-room with perfect privacy.

Within, the detail of woodwork and plaster work is exquisite. The acanthus leaf pattern is used in the plaster cornices, and the pilasters beside the doors are like fluted columns. The rooms are approximately thirty feet square, and in the back of the house, on the ground floor, there is a square back hall into which every room on that floor opens. In this room there are three double wooden doors, which may be thrown open thus transforming this room into a loggia overlooking the bayou. From this room a steep and narrow flight of stairs rises to the second floor, stairs ending in a square hall similar to the one below. And from this upper hall or sitting-room, entrance to all bed-rooms can be made.

The fact that a screen of trees surrounds the four acres of garden gives the impression that one is in a deep wood, and from the bedroom windows one looks out across the garden to the quiet Teche, shimmering in the sun, and to a rolling country beyond dotted with old live-oak trees with their swaying moss. Beyond this, one catches a glimpse of the fields of sugar-cane, billowing in the breeze.

Throughout the house the walls are covered with smooth plaster, something between gray and green in col-or. The interior woodwork is all white and the floors are of dark wide boards. The house is furnished throughout in true plantation style. There are enormous four-post beds of dark shining mahogany, beautifully grained. Brilliant color is brought in—also in true plantation style—in the use of window curtains of turkey red, without which the house would have a tendency toward somberness.

Old portraits of little girls with hoop-skirts and ring-lets, smile wistfully down from the walls. In dark corners mirrors gleam. In the bedrooms, the beds are covered with hand-woven cloths made by the Acadian weavers, beautiful in design and rich in color, with red predominating.

I can hardly describe the warm comforts of these bed-rooms on a frosty day, when log fires are lighted on the hearth and when one is wakened by a man-servant bearing the coffee tray. One lies there, propped up in bed, sipping coffee, while the curtains are thrown back to admit the sun-light. I have never been able to decide whether this old house is more charming in winter by firelight and candlelight, or in summer, when the breeze from the bayou billows the curtains and causes the candles to flicker beneath their glass cylinders.

Leaving New Iberia one may drive to the quaint town of St. Martinsville, once called "Little Paris" by French aristocrats exiled by revolution in France. An old inn (illustrated) is reminiscent of another age than ours. It stands solidly beside the road, still serving as a haven for travelers. Behind it, Bayou Teche lies blue in the sunshine, and the moss-draped oak trees lean over like old men dipping their beards into the water. It is lazy and good in St. Martinsville, but the road stretches out before us. We will drive north, this time, up through the center of the state, through the town of Opelousas, and beyond to the old village of Washington. Here, if one asks the way, he can find the Splane house, three miles from the highway—a house filled with the peace of another age than ours.

PAYNE

Five miles or more north of Washington, one can see the squat, white columns of the Payne house, standing in the middle of a bare field. Only caretakers live there now, and one may drive in and examine the dwelling at leisure. It is owned by the Thistlethwaite family.

It has several features which are unusual. The central outside staircase is pleasing, and the open driveway under the house and under the stairs is repeated in only one other plantation-house that I know. The house has a "homemade" air, as though a planter designed it according to his caprice.

Its proportion is satisfying. One regrets the barren outlook.

The story goes that an eccentric bachelor lived there for forty years alone. He was fond of animals and had the house full of dogs and cats. In his later years he allowed even chickens to have the run of the house, and hens roosted on the footboard of his bed. As he grew older he developed delusions of persecution and imagined that his neighbors plotted to kill him. He thought that enemies were hiding in the shrubbery and behind near-by trees. Accordingly he ordered his servants to clear away every bush that was large enough to conceal a man. It was done. He died soon after. No one has cared enough for the place since that time to plant trees again. And it is a pity, for the house is as charming as any that I know. Look at the picture of it and see if you do not agree. I have been told that it was built in 1849, but it appears older. However, one must not speculate in these matters, so I give you the date that was given me—1849.

This is our last stop until we reach Natchitoches—a hundred miles away. I told you that this journey was a long one. By leaving the road we could go to "Chretien Point"—a very fine old house somewhat like "The Shadows" in New Iberia—or we could stop at "Lloyd Hall" between Cheneyville and Lecompte; but I have given my word that our trip will end to-day, and end it shall.

NATCHITOCHES

Natchitoches is the oldest town in the State, but there are few of the old houses remaining. At Natchitoches we take the Cane River Road and drive south again toward the town of Cloutierville . . . any one will direct us.

BERMUDA

Ten miles or thereabouts from Natchitoches, we find "Bermuda," the Prudhomme plantation, built in 1821. Those of you who have read the diary of the young Creole gentleman of fashion will recognize this house as "Phanor's." Mr. Suydam's illustration gives an excellent idea of the house. This is the oldest Louisiana type—a "raised cottage."

MELROSE

Melrose plantation—do not confuse this Melrose with the other plantation of the same name at Natchez, Mississippi—is the home of the Henry family. The house is now the property of Mrs. Cammie Garrett Henry. She has lived here for thirty years. Until a few years ago, this plantation-house was many miles from a highway, but now the graveled road passes its door. The illustration gives an idea of the house, but the garden is beyond the black-and-white of pencil drawing. It is the finest garden that I know—a place of riotous blooms and glowing colors. There are more than three acres in flowers. "Melrose" dates from 1833.

Somewhere behind the house—and quite invisible from the highway—is an old cabin built of cypress timbers, mud, and moss. It stands buried in greenery, out of sight and out of mind. . . . I live in it half of the year. It is my workshop. For four years, now, I have done my writing here. I shall tell you something more of "Melrose" tonight, for I hope that you will come and stay awhile with me. I want to tell you about the negroes on New Year's

Eve. But first I must take you further and show you "Magnolia" and "Marco," far down Cane River.

MAGNOLIA

"Magnolia" is the home of the Hertzog family, a brick house, painted gray, and set at the end of an avenue of fine oak trees. The magnolia grove gives it its name. The original house was burned during the Civil War. This house was built afterward, on the site.

MARCO

Miles down Cane River and miles off the highway—ask directions as you go along—you will find the old Marco house. It belonged to an Austrian (or Italian or Slav, I have never been able to get it straight) called Marco Maranovitch. He made a great fortune, and although a bachelor he raised a family of quadroon children. His money has made them rich. To-day his descendants own much land along Cane River. But the old house stands empty. It dates from 1820, it is said. It is the usual Louisiana type, but it is on a larger scale than most of the houses of its day. The open brick-paved driveway through the center of the lower floor is unusual. The front doors are very wide. The living quarters are all on the second floor. Even in its dilapidation the house has an arresting quality. It is a house I like to return to again and again. I've done it, too. Why, I have no idea, and it is not easy to reach by automobile. The road is dangerous—running as it does beside the river—and in wet weather it is impassable.

Nearby was the plantation of Robert McAlpin, who has been accused of serving as the model for Simon Le-

gree. Marco and McAlpin had business dealings. McAlpin often visited this house. It may be that the two men
had tastes in common. Who can say now, three quarters of
a century later?

We have reached the end of our journey. Our tour has
been rapid, and we have passed many places by, but you
have seen enough of old Louisiana to understand something of plantation life.

And if you will come with me, back to the cabin at
Melrose, I will tell you of the negroes' festivities on New
Year's Eve, and then we shall say good-by, if you like.

Here's my hand. Are we still friends?

Chapter Thirty

NEW YEAR'S EVE

IT is a winter night on the plantation. The negroes are having a "chicken fry." You can feel festivity in the frosty air, as along the road beside the river dim shadows flit by in the dusk. Silhouetted against the fading sky men and women on horseback are riding noiselessly across the fallow fields. A glow along the eastern horizon gives promise of a full moon; already the sky is beginning to lighten behind the black trees. From mud chimneys of cabins blue wood smoke rises straight up in the twilight air, carrying with it the faint tang of sizzling bacon.

Snatches of songs are heard, and quite near some unseen singer is twanging upon a guitar:

"Chicken in de bread tray, pickin' up de dough!
Granny, will yo' dawg bite? No, chile, no!"

The singing negro passes on, followed by a chorus of laughter, deep-throated and melodious, languid and sweet.

From far off you can hear another verse, fainter, fainter,
dying away:

"White folks in de parlor, eatin' cake an' cream. . . .
Nigger in de kitchen, eatin' pork an' beans!"

It is Messy-Lena who is giving the party to-night. Perhaps some ambitious mother named her "Messalina" when
she was a baby; or perhaps some waggish white person has
had a hand in the naming; but "Messy-Lena" she is, all
the three hundred pounds of her. By day she is a cook
for the white folks at the Big House on the plantation,
but by night—and to-night particularly—she is the queen
of colored society, and all roads lead to her door.

You sit in darkness in your cabin, for the husband of
this social leader has borrowed every oil-lamp you possess
in order to light the cabin he shares with his fashionable
spouse, down by the cotton gin. Only one guttering candle
remains, stuck in the old tin candlestick on the mantel.

Although you can see little enough in the gathering
darkness outside the cabin door, the night is quick with
voices, some near, some far, calling in the lanes.

To-night is different from other nights—just as Saturday night is always different from those of the week
days. For to-morrow is a holiday for every one—white
and black—on the plantation. Even the mules know the
difference, for a short time ago you heard them braying
and kicking as they were unharnessed from the plows.
This seems incredible, but you have noticed the phenome-
non often enough before, and you have asked the negro
field-hands about it.

"Yass suh! De mule sure know when Sadday night

come! Yass suh! De mule lots smarter dan de hoss. He know he ain't got to wu'k to-morrow!"

You sit thinking, there in the dimness of your cabin, that it is this enjoyment of Saturday night, perhaps, that links the mule and the plantation negro so closely together. For surely there is a deep understanding between them, a well-known affinity. Mules work for negroes as they never work for white men. And now the mules are cavorting about, there behind the barn. They kick, they bray, they fight, they squeal. You can hear the thud of their heels against the walls of the stable, and the vast empty building reëchoes like a giant drum.

From the darkness of the fields comes the shrill voice of a woman, light with laughter:

"Lissen at dem mules! They acts like they wuz goin' to a party too!"

There is the sound of a scuffle in the gloom, as some dusky swain attempts a liberty with his dark-skinned belle, and the woman's voice is raised in anger:

"Keep dem black hands off'n my clean dress, nigger! Keep 'em off, or I'll strike yo' down!"

And the deeper voice, in expostulation: "Honey, don't be flashin' dat razor on me! Ah ain't doin' yo' nothin'!"

After a time it is quiet again, and the moon comes slowly above the tree-tops and hangs over the river, round and red.

And then, through the still night air, tinged with the kiss of frost, comes the soft *zoom! zoom!* of the double-bass, and the high and irresponsible whining of an accordion. The dancing is beginning, down at Messy-Lena's cabin.

What a night for a party! What a night! What a
night! Blood is tingling in your body, stirred by the music
coming out of the dark. It seems, as you sit there in your
lonely cabin, that witches and devils are abroad. The air
is charged with electricity; festivity is infectious.

You pull on your boots and coat and stroll slowly down
the river road, watching the reflection of the round red
moon floating on the river's quiet surface. From afar off
comes the moan of a dove, echoed, a moment later, by the
sharp chittering of a screech-owl in a china tree. How glad
you are that the owl is near your cabin, rather than near
the scene of festivity—for the unholy laughter of one of
these flitting creatures is sufficient to throw a pall of gloom
over even the gayest gathering of negroes.

"It's dat squinch owl!" they say, rolling their eyes.
"Somebody's goin' to die!"

But to-night no evil omens disturb the *soirée* at the
cabin by the gin; for even here, a quarter of a mile away,
you can hear the shrill shrieks of laughter and the shouts
of the men. The party is well underway when you reach
the edge of the circle of torchlight.

The house shared by Jack and Messy-Lena is ablaze
with light. Ropes are tied from tree to tree, and upon
these ropes, at six-foot intervals, are *flambeaux*—torches
made by the simple expedient of stuffing short lengths
of rope into pop bottles which have been filled with coal
oil. The flames burn straight up in the still air and show
a large group of black men and women in the yard before the white-washed cabin.

The hum of laughter and talk is plainly audible above
the whining of fiddle and accordion. Half a dozen wide

planks have been thrown upon the ground, side by side, and upon this uneven and splintery surface a score of couples are gyrating to a slow dance. The music moans and wails, and the dancers squirm and twist. Slow. Slow. With half-shut eyes the men hold the women tight against their bodies; and the women, seeming half-asleep, loll against their partners.

What strange movement is this? A couple stops short in the shuffling glide and begins to jerk forward and back, the woman's foot advances an inch at a time, with a sharp quick movement, while the man withdraws his foot before her. With feet wide apart, and with knees bent, they pause and then regain the upright position with a quick slide; then they are off again with shuffling step as before.

One couple is unusually good at this, and those on the side lines are fascinated. "Look at dat ole big-footed boy inchin' up!" they cry.

A young mulatto with a great mop of kinky hair is dancing with a skinny black girl, their flying feet flop in wild abandon. It is "de pony lope." But the fast-dancing couple is the exception. Most of the dancers are taking the tempo at half-time, allowing two full beats for every step.

Many good church members are here, and as they recognize you in the flickering light, they profess to be shocked by what they see. But you notice that even the old men and women are watching the whirling couples with absorbed interest. All the world may not love a sinner, but it likes to watch him.

The air is filled with the rich scent of frying chicken,

and when the music stops you can hear it sizzling in the pan. You peep in the kitchen window of the cabin, and there, before a roaring fire in the mud fireplace, two old mammies are attending the chicken frying. Pans are set upon the glowing embers of the log fire. Through the window you can feel the heat of that blaze, and you see that both old women's faces are dripping with sweat— but they are smiling and happy, gossiping together as the chicken sizzles.

They are quite alone in the kitchen, as every one else is outside at the dancing platform—that is, every one but Messy-Lena, who is holding court through the window of her bedroom; for the cabin consists of two rooms only, bedroom and kitchen. Messy-Lena's enormous bulk is encased in baby blue, a whale of a dress, trimmed in yards and yards of cheap white lace. She hangs out of the window, conversing with friends outside, and making a fascinating picture, doubtless; for Messy-Lena is a woman of charm—or at least so you surmise from the number of her admirers. Now and then she laughs her high, melodious laugh, which causes others to laugh too, whether or not they have heard the humorous remark which causes it. Just now she is quoting a favorite proverb, as she reproves some dusky braggart:

"It wuz swellin' dat bus' de poutin' pigeon!" says she, trilling her high laugh against the chorus of deeper guffaws which follow this sally.

You leave Messy-Lena to her admirers and go to the front of the cabin again. On the edge of the gallery several old crones are seated, black and wrinkled, dressed in their best, and wearing gold hoops in their ears. You saunter close, standing in the shadows, to see what the discussion is about. From their gestures and expressions of disgust, it is evident that they are talking about a young black girl who is seated near them. The girl, for the moment, is alone, for her swain has gone for a plate of fried chicken for her. You listen shamelessly:

"Mighty funny, jus' de same, dat Creola done got two wrist-watches!" one old woman is saying in a loud tone, and another nods and says, "Wouldn't surprise me none to heah she done done wrong!" And then, in chorus, they say "Uh hum!" and stare at Creola.

She overhears the conversation and turns to them with a loud snort of indignation.

Creola's costume is a marvel. Her hair has been straightened and stands out from under the brim of her small hat, a hat which is pulled rakishly over one eye. Her white dress is elaborate, more suitable for midsummer than for a frosty night; but she has remedied this by wearing a man's red-flannel undershirt which shows plainly at the neck and elbows. Her large feet are encased in white slippers. She looks like a walking advertisement for a jewelry store, for she is ablaze with imitation pearls, diamonds, and rubies. She has earrings, bar pins, necklaces, bracelets—and sure enough, a wrist-watch shines on either wrist.

But just now her usually placid face wears an evil expression. She rises and confronts those aged gossipers. But just as she is about to release the venom that she has in store, Jack, Messy-Lena's husband, appears and leads her off to dance. A diplomat is Jack, often you have noticed it.

The old women, however, are not intimidated in the least, but continue their conversation in even louder tones:

"Ef I wuz Messy-Lena," says one, "I'd sure keep a watch on dat sporty nigger man of mine!"

But Jack, far from being disconcerted, swaggers more than ever as he leads Creola toward the dancers. He is even coy, for just as he arrives at the edge of the splintery platform, he hits Creola a resounding smack upon her shoulder—and she, with a burst of ribald laughter, falls into his arms and they are off. Slowly they twirl, and Creola's "inchin' up" is something to see!

And you hear from a delighted onlooker that Jack once invented a dance called "The Seven-Years' Itch"—a dance now famous on the plantation.

In the shadows back of the cabin a flask is being passed from hand to hand. This is "shinny," a home-made drink, corn liquor that tastes like concentrated lye and suffices to make one very drunk even if taken in small doses—provided, of course, that your throat is tough enough to swallow the burning fluid.

Messy-Lena, it appears, has had shinny, too. For her movements are a little unsteady, and she utters a high, nasal shriek as she comes out of the cabin door and down the steps, in order that she may dance with a tall, thin, very black negro man who hums *"Zoom! Zoom!"* along with the fiddles.

The dancers are sweating now, despite the chilly night. Some one has given shinny to the members of the orchestra. The music is growing faster. There is a bawdy swing to the melody. There are significant pauses, followed by yells from the fiddlers and a renewed scraping of bows. The dancers are singing with the music. The man who is imitating the double-bass is heard above the others: *"Zoom!*

Zoom! Zoom!" he cries in a clear baritone voice. And
Messy-Lena takes a high note with the ease of a black
Galli-Curci. Feet are stamping, fingers are popping; the
party is getting wild.

Now comes a surprise number. A thin black girl moves
forward into the light of the flaring torches, and a hum
goes over the crowd:

"Dat's dat Lizzie!" black boys say to one another. "Lizzie's goin' to sing de blues." And they nudge each other.

And sure enough, Lizzie does. Above the whine of the
fiddles and the accordion, her voice rises in a melancholy
wail, a song written—or rather invented (for it has never
been written down until now)—by a local musician:

> "I sweats and I washes all day at de tub,
>   I wuks till I'm ready to fall . . .
>   An' how come dat brown gal dat lives in de lane
>   Done got her a red parasol?"

And there comes a moan from the listeners: "Uh hum!"
and the chorus rises, mournful and clear:

> "Papa, sweet papa, won't you let dat brown girl be?
>   (I say, Oh let her be!)
> Papa, sweet papa, come home every night to me . . .
>   (Oh come home to me!)
> An' if you don't come home, my razor's
> Goin' to set yo' po' soul free!"

Then comes the second verse, even slower and more
plaintive:

> "Miz Pig she runs on little high heels,
>   Miz Cow she bounces 'long!

> Dat brown gal's got some high-heel shoes,
> An' I know she's done done wrong!"

"Uh-hum!" wails the chorus.

> "Papa, sweet papa, better let that brown gal be!
> (I say, Oh let her be!)
> Papa, sweet papa, come home every night to see.
> (I say you better see!)
> 'Cause if yo' don't come home, sweet papa,
> You'll find another man with me!"

This is a very daring song on the plantation, and the church members are openly scandalized. There is a murmur in the crowd against these "scan'lous" doings.

But Lizzie has started another song. This one is called "Goodnight Corrino, Goodnight," and with the opening bars several members of the crowd make audible remarks about Lizzie's "wuthlessness." Even Messy-Lena appears worried, a frown creasing her black and shining forehead.

You listen with all your ears, expecting sensational developments, but you are disappointed. The song seems endless, and is merely a girl's plaint relative to the faithlessness of one "Corrino"—who turns out to be a man, unexpectedly enough—who has deceived her. The dusky maid tells how she intends to "walk de worl'" till she finds the black despoiler of hearts, so she may kill him. At the end of the sixth verse, the hostess calls out suddenly, "Dat's enuff, black gal!" and the song ceases abruptly.

The audience is indignant, and the women all turn away from Lizzie as she takes her place in the crowd. The psychology is a little difficult to understand until you ask Jack for an explanation, when he relates, in a whisper, that

Lizzie—who is also known as "Miss Cooter"—has just wrecked a wedding in the vicinity by luring the bridegroom away, and Messy-Lena is outraged that such an abandoned woman has come to her "chicken fry"—and made herself conspicuous, to boot.

The next number is an interminable recitation by a thin, lanky, coal-black girl of fourteen, who speaks in a high sing-song voice almost unintelligible. It is not until she is half-way through that you are able to understand that the recitation is none other than Longfellow's "The Wreck of the Hesperus." Hester who is reciting, has learned the piece "by ear"—being unable to read—and in many instances has substituted phrases of her own for those she does not understand. For example, for the line "She shuddered and paused like a frightened steed"—where Longfellow refers to the ship in the storm—Hester recites, "She shuddery pause like a froggy skin!"

Loud bursts of applause greet the conclusion of this refined number. Then the dancing is renewed with vigor, and in the shadows the shinny bottle passes again from hand to hand.

Jack now takes his place in the orchestra, beating on a large pan in place of a drum, sometimes butting it with his head in moments of excitement. And now, above the tramping and the banging, and the shrieking of the musical instruments, there are frequent shrill shouts. The shinny is taking its toll. Arguments begin in various quarters, and a fight is narrowly averted by Messy-Lena's diplomacy in dancing off with one of the combatants.

Something brutal and cruel has come into this happy gathering, some savage thing. Soon there will be a fight.

You can feel tension in the air. The negroes, like tinder, are ready to be set ablaze at a touch.

Time for innocent onlookers to go home.

Back in your cabin, you can still hear the *zoom! zoom!* of the double-bass and the banging of the tin pan. A dog is howling at the moon. Owls call in the trees. The moon, white and silvery now, hangs high in the heavens, dragging a train of stars behind her.

The cabin is chilly, and you kindle a blaze with fat pine-splinters to have light enough to undress and creep into bed. Lying there with the patchwork quilt tucked under your chin, you listen sleepily to that irregular *zoom! zoom!* of the distant music.

The westering moon is throwing a shaft of light across the bed when you are wakened by a frenzied screaming—a woman's voice in deadly fear. You spring up and look out of the open door. The cabin yard is in shadow and you can see nothing.

"What is it?" you call. "What's the matter?"

And then seemingly close at hand, comes the wail: "Oh Lawdy, Lawdy! He done kilt me!" And then another scream of dire anguish.

The white folks over at the Big House have heard the disturbance and are coming out with lanterns; you can see them flickering through the trees. Catching up a bath-robe you go, barefoot, through the dewy grass, over the stile, into the stable-yard, and toward the sounds of distress.

Near the kitchen door of the Big House a dark form lies on the ground; a black woman, who moans feebly. It is Messy-Lena. The white folks are leaning over her. The mistress of the plantation holds the lantern high, and pushes back two long plaits of white hair that have fallen about her own shoulders. Her two sons and the plantation overseer are with her.

"We'll have to carry her into the house," says the mistress, taking charge of the situation. "I'm afraid she is badly hurt."

Messy-Lena is a heavy load for even four able-bodied men. We carry her to the kitchen and put her upon a long bench by the wall. Blood is streaming from a wound on her forehead; her eyes are closed; her three hundred pounds are dead weight. She moans feebly.

"Who hurt you, Messy-Lena?" you ask, as you wipe her face with a handkerchief.

"Dat man of mine been drinkin'," she whispers.

"You mean that Jack did this?"

"Yas sah! Dat's what I mean," says she, beginning to moan afresh. "He's done kilt me dis time, sho!"

But the mistress is smiling now. "Why, Messy-Lena, it's hardly more than a scratch. . . . Let me see. . . . The knife just grazed your cheek. It's only a trifle; but an inch more and he would have killed you. . . . Wait! Hand me that bottle of arnica. Now, Messy-Lena, you can sit up. I'll bandage it for you."

Still moaning that she is "kilt," Messy-Lena sits up and wipes her eyes. Inch by inch she goes over her fat body, feeling this part and that. Finally she is assured that the cut on her face is the only wound, and then she begins to talk to us.

"I jus' declare but dat nigger of mine is de mos' jealous man I ever see!" she announces with pride in her voice.

The mistress turns away to hide a smile.

"New Year's Eve parties often end like this!" she remarks.

"Now ain't dat de truth!" says Messy-Lena, smiling in her turn. "Yass'm, it sure is!"

And barefoot, you go back to your cabin, sneezing as you go.

Bibliography

BIBLIOGRAPHY

"History of Louisiana," by Le Page du Pratz (London, 1774).

Martin's History of Louisiana.

Gayarré's History of Louisiana.

Fortier's History of Louisiana.

"Creole of Louisiana," by George W. Cable.

"Strange True Stories of Louisiana," by George W. Cable.

"Creole Families of New Orleans," by Grace King.

"Social Life in Old New Orleans," by Eliza Ripley.

"The Memories of Fifty Years," by W. H. Sparks.

"Old Plantation Houses in Louisiana," by Natalie Scott and W. P. Spratling.

"Stories from Louisiana History," by Grace King and John R. Ficklen.

"New Orleans, As It Was," by Henry C. Castellanos.

"Historical Sketch Book and Guide to New Orleans," New Orleans Press (1885).

"In Acadia," compiled by F. F. Hansell & Bro., New Orleans.

"The Louisiana Book," compiled by Henry Rightor.

"Uncle Tom's Cabin," by Harriet Beecher Stowe.

"A Visit to Uncle Tom's Cabin," by D. B. Corley.

"James Colles, His Life and Letters," edited by Emily Johnson de Forest.

Publications of the Louisiana Historical Society.

Publications of the Mississippi Historical Society.

Diaries and scrap-books lent by Miss Laura Baker, of Natchez, Miss.

Letters lent by Mrs. Emily J. de Forest, of New York City.

Letters, diaries, and manuscripts lent by Mrs. Cammie Garrett Henry, of Melrose Plantation.

Manuscripts and documents lent by Miss Louise Butler, of "The Cottage" Plantation, St. Francisville.

Letters lent by Mr. Weeks Hall, of New Iberia, Louisiana.

Various papers collected and lent by Mrs. Charles C. Pitcher, of Alma Plantation.

Papers pertaining to the Nicholls family, lent by Thomas C. Nicholls, of New Orleans.

"Life and Labor in the Old South," by Ulrich B. Phillips.

Letters of Mrs. Vincent Perrault, of Natchez, Mississippi.

Files of The New Orleans "Times-Picayune."

Files of the "Courier de la Louisiane."

An article, "New Orleans Amusements a Hundred Years Ago," by Noel Straus.

Files of The New Orleans "Item."

Files of The New Orleans States.

"Life on the Mississippi," by Mark Twain.

Pamphlets and papers lent by Miss Mercedes and Miss Louise Garig, of Baton Rouge.

Family papers belonging to Mr. and Mrs. Walter Parlange, of Parlange Plantation.

Papers pertaining to the Prudhomme family lent by Irma Sompayrac Willard.

"Father Mississippi," by Lyle Saxon.

"Fabulous New Orleans," by Lyle Saxon.

And many other documents, letters, and diaries acknowledged in the text.

INDEX

Acadians, arrive in Louisiana, 96; on the Teche, 98
Acadian ball, 115
Afton Villa, 326
Aimé, Valcour, 343
Alexandria, 55
Allain, 100
Alligator, as food, 58
Almonester, 100
Almonester, Andres, 94
American planters in Louisiana, 132
American Theater in New Orleans, 128
Angelina Plantation, 298
Animal baiting, 129
Archinard family, 173
Arlington Plantation, 329
Asphodel Plantation, 308
Attakapas, Indian tribe, 96
Auburn Plantation, 329
Audubon, John J., 323

Baby, dancing master, 79; killed by Indians, 83
Bachelor dinner in 1851, 249
Ball, in 1805, description of, 108
Barrow family, 327
Baton Rouge, 55; early description of, 63; plantations near, 306
Bayou, defined, 52
Bayou Goula, early description of, 63
Bayou Lafourche, 341; Acadians settle on, 96
Bayou St. John, called Tchoupic, 58
Bayou Teche, 357; in 1805, 111
Beauregard, 100
Beauregard Plantation, 343
Belle Alliance Plantation, 341
Belle Chase Plantation, 343
Belle Grove Plantation, 340
Belle Helene Plantation, 304
Belmont Plantation, 339
Bermuda Plantation, 364
Bienville, 51; his Indian wars, 77
Biloxi, 51
Blake family, 31
Bouligny, 100

Bralston Plantation, 272
Breazeale, Phanor, refutes Mc Alpin's story, 264
Brignier, 100
Bruinsburg Plantation, 274
Burnside Plantation, 303
Butler, Miss Louise, historian, 147

Caffrey family, 358
Campbell family, 186
Camp Plantation, 338
Canary Islanders, settlers in New Orleans, 96
Canonge, 100
Canonge, Judge, 154
Carroll, John, of Carollton, 274
Chalmette, 100
Chase House, at Clinton, 307
Chatsworth Plantation, 304
Chopin family, 255
Chretien Point Plantation, 363
Christmas customs, 312; on the plantation, 312
Circus in 1851, 238
Civil War, effects of, 54; troops leaving Natchez, 285
Claiborne, governor of New Orleans, 104
Clinton, town of, description, 307
Cloutier, family, 167
Colomb Plantation, 302
Company of the West, collapse of, 57
Convent etiquette, in 1850, 175
Convent life, in 1851, 239
Convent of the Sacred Heart, 300
Cottage Plantation, 304; home of Butler family, 325
Cotton Exposition, of 1885, 54
Creole, families, list of, 99
Creole family affection, 236
Creole family life, 171
Creole hospitality, in 1805, 112
Creoles, prosperity, 53; their fine houses, 98
Crevasse, destroys plantation, 277
Criminal trial, in 1846, 157
Cruzat, 100

Dangerfield Family, 7
D'Arensbourg, 99
Davis, Jefferson, 308, 330
Deblieux family, 180
de Boré, 100; Etienne, his experiment, 98
De Buys, 100
de Clouet, Alexandro, 86
de Flaugeac, Garrigues, 100
de Kernion, Huchet, 99
De la Chaise, 99
De la Ronde, 100
de Launay, Luis, 87
de Lauzon, Charest, 100
De la Vergne, 100
De Livaudais, 99
de Mandeville, Marigny, 99
de Meuse, his grant at Pointe Coupée, 64
de Mézières, Marquis, his land grant, 64
Devall Plantation, 338
De Pontalba, 99
de Roaldes, 100
De Soto, 51
D'Estrehan Plantation, 294
de Vaudreuil, governor of Louisiana, 79; his lavish entertainments, 79
de Villemont, Madame, 94
de Villeray, Rouer, 99
de Villiers, Jumonville, 100
Dogs, 12
Doswell, steamboat on Red River, 186
Dreaux, 99
du Fossat, Soniat, 99
Du Pratz, Le Page, early Louisiana planter, 57
du Vernai, M. Paris, his land grant, 64

Eisenach, Duke of Saxe-Weimar, 127
Ellerslie Plantation, home of Percy family, 326
Elocution, 35
Entertainments, curious diversions, 125
Erwin family, 338
Etienne de Boré, granulates sugar, 53
Evangeline, story of, 97
Execution of murderers, 93

Fireworks in New Orleans, 130
Flat-boatmen, 141
Flea remedies, 16
Fluker family, 309
Forstall, 100
Fortier, 100
Fortier, Alcee, Louisiana historian, 95

Fort Rosalie, Natchez, destroyed, 66
Foster family, 358
Franklin, town of, 357
Freeman family, 310
French explorers, 51
French Theater in New Orleans, 126
Fur-trapping, near New Orleans, 96

Game, plentiful on Mississippi, 60
Garconnières, 33, 301, 303
Gayarré, 100
German Coast, of Mississippi River, 298
Germans, 57
Glasscock family, 272
Going to pieces, 20
Greenwood Plantation, 327
Grima, 100
Grimmer, J., 231
Gris-gris, negroes' attachment to, 68

Hall, Weeks, 358
Hecla, steamboat on Red River, 183
Hertzog family, 197
Hickory Hill, 310
Hunting expedition in 1850, 175

Iberville, 51
Indian conjurers, remedies for illness, 62
"Indian Father," first play produced in Louisiana, 79
Indian legend, 331
Indians, despoil plantations, 77; indifference to Christianity, 61
Indigo, early Louisiana staple, 98

Jackson Square, in 1815, 123
Jackson, town of, 308
Jefferson College, 299
Jewels buried with corpses, 336
"The Joyous Coast," 230

Kenner, Duncan, 302
Kentuckians, flat-boatmen, 121
King, Grace, describes Creole banquet, 99

Labatut Plantation, 337
Labedoyere, 99
Labiche, Emmeline, real name of Evangeline, 97
Labillebeuvre, 100
Lafreniere, 99
Lakeside Plantation, 337
Lambre family, 167

Index

La Tourette, John, surveyor of plantations, 149
Law, John, "Mississippi Bubble," 52
Laycock Plantation, 306
Lebreton, Juan Baptist Cezaire, his murder, 85; plantation, 343
Le Grand, Colonel Claudius F., 133
Le Grand, Julia, her journal, 138
Liquor lists, in 1851, 251
Louisiana, census of, in 1846, 149
Louisiana Historical Society, 85
Louisiana, in 1836, 136; prosperity before Civil War, 140
Louisiana Purchase, significance of, 100
Louisiana State University, 306
Louisiana, under Spanish rule, 95

McAlpin, Robert, 248, 365; as model for Simon Legree, 253
Macarty, 100
Madame John's Legacy, 344
Madewood Plantation, 341
Magnolia Plantation, 365
Manon Lescaut, Louisiana romance, 97
Marco Plantation, 365
Marigny, Bernard, 53
Marigny, Philippe, entertains Louis Philippe, 99
Marron, runaway slave, 68
Massacre Island, name changed, 58
Matthews family, 324
Meadows family, 20
Melrose Plantation, home of Henry family, 364
Melrose Plantation, near Natchez, 328
Metoyer family, 167
Mexican War, territory added by, 101
Mississippi River, an early overflow, 59; description of plantations, 142; fortification of, 51; in 1830, 132
Monmouth Plantation, 329

Natchez, bombardment of, 287; country of, 59; plantations near, 328–330
Natchez Trace, early description of, 61
Natchez-Under-The-Hill, 140
Natchitoches, founded in 1715, 64; in 1850, 193; town of, 363
Negroes, a blues singer, 375; and mules, 369; celebrate Christmas, 312; description of early slave farm, 67; methods of curing sickness, 67; New Year's Eve celebration, 367; proverbs of, 353; smell of various tribes, 72;

superstitions of, 345; their dances, 371
New Iberia, 362
New Orleans, destroyed by fire, 98; early description of, 63; founded, 51; in 1805, 107; the battle of, 122; "The City of Sin," 121; vice, 122
Newspapers, in 1851, 245
Nicholls family, 102
Nottaway Plantation, 339

Oak Alley Plantation, 342
Oaklawn Plantation, 358
Oakley Plantation, 323
Old families, 5
Old music books, 231
Opelousas, wild times in, 119
Opera in New Orleans, in 1823, 127
O'Reilly, Spanish commander, 96
Orleans Theater, 126
Orleans, Duke of, visits Louisiana, 98
Ormond Plantation, 295

Panola Plantation, 274
Parlange Plantation, 335
Pascagoulas, an Indian tribe, 58
Pauline, execution of, 160; negro slave, 151
Payne Plantation, 362
Pellerin family, 113
Perier, governor of Louisiana, 78; his Indian wars, 78
Perrault, Mrs. Vincent, her letters, 271
Pirrie, Eliza, 323
Pitot, 100
Pigeonnières, 336, 338
Plantation, ante-bellum, described, 143; ball, described, 148; breaking up, 2; era, duration of, 53; gardens, described, 146; house, of 1840, described, 145; kitchens, described, 147; life, in 1836, 133; life, in 1850, 278, 279; life near Natchez, in 1850, 281; prosperity on, 54; superstitions, 346; wedding, 282; wedding, in 1830, 276
Plantations, falling into ruin, 55; prices of, in 1830, 134; tour of, 293; west of the Mississippi, 335
Plantation-houses, American, 54; early types, 143; near Baton Rouge, 145; on Bayou Lafourche, 145; the Louisiana type, 144
Planters, entertainments in New Orleans, 122
Porter family, 358
Prudhomme, Lestant, 166

Prudhomme, Phanor, 171, 173, 174
Prudhomme Plantation, 364; Plantation-house, 232
Pugh family, 341

Quadroon Balls, 109, 126

Rabbeneck, owner of Pauline, 153
Rack, used to procure confession, in 1771, 91
Red River, overflow feared, in 1850, 170
Reinzi Plantation, 342
Richland Plantation, home of Wall family, 327
Richmond Plantation, 330
River-Lake Plantation, 337
Robieu, François, 155
Rocques, Leonce, 178
Roffignac, 100
Roman, Alexandre, governor of Louisiana, 342
Rosalie Plantation, 328
Rosedown Plantation, 324
Runaway slaves, advertisement of, 246

Sarpy, Delord, plantation-house, 343
Scott family, Christmas celebration, 312
Senegals, intelligence of, 73
Shades Plantation, home of Scott family, 310
Shady Grove Plantation, 338
Shreveport, 55
Slave insurrection, Louisiana's first, 64; punishment, a mild case, 177; quarters, on plantations, 143
Slaves, cruelty to, 259, 260, 261; Indians, sold in Santo Domingo, 78; negroes, how procured, 78; number in Louisiana, in 1846, 149; sale of, 250
Smith family, 309
Social life, in 1858, 267
Southdown Plantation, 342
State Capitol, at Baton Rouge, 307
Statues, in gardens, 325

Stauffer house, 343
Steamboat explosion, in 1850, 305
Steamboating, in 1850, 176
Steamboats, 140
St. Francisville, plantations in vicinity, 327; town of, 322
St. Geme, 100
St. Martinsville, 362
Stone house, at Clinton, 307
Stowe, Harriet Beecher, 255
Sugar-cane, introduced into Louisiana, 53
Sunday, as a feast day, 122; breakfast, in 1850, 172
Superstitions, of negroes, 346, 347, 348, 349, 350, 351, 352

Taffia, intoxicating drink, 74
Temba, the hunter, 85; torture of, 91
Ternant family, 336
Theatrical entertainments, in 1823, 127
The Shadows Plantation, 358
Torture, of slaves, 65
Travel, by ox-wagon, 111; difficulty of, 106
Trepagnier Plantation, 297
Tureaud, 100
Turnbull, Miss Eliza, 324
Twain, Mark, comments on plantation life, 307

Uncle Sam Plantation, 301
Uncle Tom's Cabin, controversy, 255
Union, village of, 302
Unzaga, governor of Louisiana, 86
Ursuline nuns, fight with pirates, 79

Vicksburg, Mississippi, in 1836, 136

Ware family, 340
Washington, Martha, 324
Welham Plantation, 297
Wiltz, Lorenzo, 87
Windy Hill Plantation, 330
Woodville, Mississippi, town of, 327